"Having churned out ice cream at home and in professional kitchens
for a quarter century, Lebovitz can guide even a beginner to a great frozen
experience . . . Truly the Good Humor man of home ice cream."
—*San Francisco Chronicle*

"*The Perfect Scoop* digs right into what you need to know for successful
ice creams, sherbets, gelatos, sorbets, frozen yogurts, and granitas."
—*New York Times*

"All in all, I'd be surprised to learn that there's a better
ice cream book out there."
—Michael Ruhlman

THE
PERFECT
SCOOP

revised and updated

THE PERFECT SCOOP

revised and updated

200 Recipes for Ice Creams, Sorbets, Gelatos, Granitas, and Sweet Accompaniments

David Lebovitz

PHOTOGRAPHS BY
Ed Anderson

TEN SPEED PRESS
California | New York

CONTENTS

INTRODUCTION

The idea to write a book devoted to frozen desserts came to me when I was teaching cooking classes. People were constantly surprising me with questions about making ice cream. I had worked as a professional baker and pastry chef, and was used to making ice cream in restaurants, but I found it interesting that so many people had questions about churning their own up at home. Standing in front of a group of fifty people one day, after a few hands shot up with more questions about making ice cream, I asked for a show of hands to find out how many people made their own ice cream. Almost half of them enthusiastically did. After a little unscientific market research showed strong sales of ice cream makers, I had my next book idea.

I spent the next couple of years churning up frozen dessert recipes, going through gallons of milk and cream, cracking dozens of eggs, chopping up blocks of dark chocolate, toasting nuts, caramelizing sugar, whipping up marshmallows, and hitting the markets to find the ripest fruits and berries to come up with a well-rounded book of recipes for ice creams and sorbets, as well as all my favorite things to accompany them.

Writing and testing recipes for a cookbook is quite a bit of work, especially for someone who's as committed—and obsessive—as I am. Should my Vanilla Frozen Yogurt (page 55) call for sugar, or would it be better with half sugar, half honey? Is ½ teaspoon of lemon juice right, or would ¼ teaspoon be better? I originally envisioned a recipe with Greek yogurt, but maybe I should also test regular yogurt to compare. You see what I mean . . . and that was just one recipe. Thankfully, I love tinkering in the kitchen to find just the right combination of ingredients that work (and taste) best for each recipe, and everything that came out of my ice cream machine was dutifully sampled and evaluated. I often enlisted friends, neighbors, and even the occasional deliveryman,

to get their opinions. (When I told my regular UPS guy that I was moving to France, he was understandably upset.)

My freezer was filling up at such a rapid clip, though, so to make room for the next batches that were ready to be churned, I started handing off containers to everyone I knew—from the guys at the market in Paris who sold me strawberries and peaches to the owners of my local pharmacy when I learned they had a freezer in the back for storing drugs. Which I saw as an opportunity: "Why not use it to store ice cream, too?" I asked. And they, too, became the recipient of countless tubs of ice cream.

***

Right from the start, *The Perfect Scoop* was to be a compendium of techniques and my favorite recipes for making ice creams, sorbets, and granitas at home, with lots of variations and suggestions for taking them in your own direction. Especially close to my heart are the mix-ins because I love stirring and layering things into ice cream: pralined almonds, homemade marshmallows, peppermint patties, and a shiny-dark fudge ripple that stays soft enough when scooped up are meant to dial up the fun.

It was incredibly gratifying that when the book was released, the positive feedback was immediate. I got messages from people who'd never made ice cream but who declared that the book became their ice cream bible, and from experienced ice cream makers and pastry chefs letting me know that many of the recipes had become part of their permanent repertoires. It was surprising how the world of small-batch ice cream took off shortly after, and soon, a variety of manufacturers began offering more machines and devices (at various price points) for churning ice cream at home.

There was also a notable boom in the number of ice cream shops that opened in cities and neighborhoods around the world. I'm not taking responsibility for that, or the increase in sales of ice cream machines (although if a company wanted to name a machine after me, I'd be delighted to accept the honor), but I was happy to be part of the burgeoning interest in artisan ice cream shops. My dream had always been to open my own place, and although that never came to fruition, I've had thrilling experiences when visiting the shops of others.

When I walked into Ice & Vice, an edgy ice cream shop in New York, the young owner, a blue-haired Ken Lo, came bounding out of the kitchen to give me a big hug. I've exchanged virtual messages (that only an ice cream geek could love) with Jeni Bauer of Jeni's Splendid Ice Creams in Ohio about the size of ice crystals, and with gelato legend Meredith Kurtzman about which ingredients make the best Italian-style ice cream. I've agreed to disagree with Nathan Myhrvold, the mastermind of *Modernist Cuisine*, over what exactly ice cream is. And I've sampled the rock 'n' roll flavors of Henri Guittet, the owner of Glazed, who quit his office job to churn up dazzling ice creams at his shop in Paris, at the foot of Montmartre. Henri confessed that *The Perfect Scoop* was the inspiration for his becoming a *glacier*, but he used the recipes as groundwork for inventing a whole new palate that would have startled Carême back in the days of yore, but is delighting Parisians today.

When the opportunity came to revise and update *The Perfect Scoop* (first published in 2007), I jumped at the chance to get back in the kitchen and add some new recipes. I've included nearly a dozen, and this edition also sports a fresh look and all new photographs. I used a pretty heavy hand with the mix-ins in some of these new versions, such as Caramel "Crack" Ice Cream (page 52) and S'mores Ice Cream (page 56)—which I'm not apologizing for! A few are for adults only, such as the Negroni Slush (page 171), which was so good that I made it twice more the same week I came up with it because I couldn't keep my spoon out of the tub. (I also

needed a nap after each bowlful.) Others, like the Labneh Ice Cream with Pistachio-Sesame Brittle (page 60), reflect a renewed interest in the flavors of the Middle East. There's Hot Honey (page 202), for those who want to spice up their scoops, and Candied Bacon and Bourbon Ice Cream (page 48) that takes bacon off the breakfast table and pairs it with boozy, butterscotch-flavored scoops.

***

I began the first edition of *The Perfect Scoop* with what I called "a nostalgic tale" about my first job scooping ice cream back in my twenties. I described it as "my first and craziest, most insane summer job" because the shop was incredibly busy and each shift had me up to my elbows in ice cream. But the look on people's faces when I handed over their scoop made the job worth it. I'm a few years older now, but I'm still scooping ice cream. In fact, my love of ice cream has only grown.

When you've written several cookbooks, at some point you're inevitably asked, "Which one is your favorite?" Each book I've written is special; it's like asking parents which of their children they like best. Although it's difficult—and not fair—for me to name the favorite of my cookbooks, I'll let you in on a little secret: *The Perfect Scoop* was the most fun for me to write. And I got to do it twice! Everything I've created for this book was a joy to churn up the first time around, and creating the updated version was just as exciting. I hope you have as much fun enjoying the ice creams and other frozen treats as I did creating, and re-creating, them for you.

CHAPTER 1

Basics

If you've never made your own ice cream before and you're used to the store-bought stuff, prepare to be impressed. Nothing beats the taste of freshly made ice cream spooned directly from the machine. Thankfully, it's easy to make the freshest, most unbelievably tasty ice creams, sorbets, sherbets, and granitas in your own kitchen.

In this chapter, you'll find all the information you need to do it. Starting with step-by-step instructions and photos for making the perfect ice cream custard, I'll take you through the process, dicuss pitfalls to avoid, and guide you through steps to take in case you manage to fall into one of them. Good ingredients, the right equipment, and an understanding of the basic techniques are the keys to making perfect ice creams and sorbets. I'll also give you information about the various types of ice cream makers and advice to help you choose the right machine to buy.

MAKING PERFECT ICE CREAM CUSTARD

Many of the ice cream recipes in this book are French-style ice creams, which means they are custard based. Others are Philadelphia style, which refers to ice creams made by simply mixing milk or cream with sugar and other ingredients. French-style ice creams tend to be richer and smoother, due to the emulsifying properties of egg yolks. My fruit-based ice creams are usually Philadelphia style, because I prefer to let the flavor of the fruits come forward without the additional richness. But in some cases I offer a flavor in both styles, so you can decide which you prefer.

If you've never made an ice cream custard before, follow these step-by-step instructions to ensure success (in some recipes, note that the procedure may vary slightly). Although I make my custards in a saucepan over moderate heat, you may wish to cook your first few custards in a double boiler, or use a flame tamer to diffuse the heat, until you get the hang of it. They will take longer to cook, but you'll appreciate the extra time to watch and make sure they cook to just the right consistency. After you've made a custard a couple of times, it'll become second nature.

1. If you're using an ice cream maker that requires prefreezing, make sure the canister spends the required amount of time in the freezer— whatever's recommended by the manufacturer. Although the canister may feel frozen to the touch before the recommended time, if you use the machine prematurely you might end up watching the custard go round and round without ever freezing—a big disappointment. So don't cheat! Most canisters require 24 hours of prefreezing. Machines with built-in compressors usually can be used right away, but check the manufacturer's instructions that came with your model.

2. Before getting started, prepare an ice bath to expedite the chilling of the custard. To make one, put some ice into a large bowl and then add a cup or two of cold water so the ice cubes are barely floating. You could also partially fill an empty sink with ice and some water. Most custard-based ice cream recipes call for straining the hot, just-cooked custard right into the cream, which helps stop the cooking and expedites cooling. Set the bowl of cream into the ice bath, put a strainer over the top, and be sure to keep the setup nearby (as in, not on the other side of the kitchen); after you've cooked the custard, you'll need to strain it into the bowl right away.

3. Heat the milk or the liquid called for in the recipe with the sugar in a saucepan on the stove. Always use nonreactive cookware, such as stainless steel or anodized aluminum, because other types of cookware can react unfavorably with fruit and other acidic ingredients.

4. In a separate bowl set on a damp kitchen towel or a silicone baking mat to keep it steady, whisk together the egg yolks.

5. The next step is to temper the yolks with the hot milk. Here's where you need to be careful. Once the milk is hot and steamy, slowly and gradually pour the milk into the egg yolks (see top-left and-right photos on the facing page), whisking constantly, which keeps the yolks moving and avoids the risk of cooking them into little eggy bits. I pour the milk into the eggs directly from the saucepan, but you might find it easier to remove the saucepan from the heat and use a ladle to add the hot liquid while whisking. If you add the hot liquid too fast or don't whisk the egg yolks briskly, they'll cook and you'll end up with bits of scrambled eggs.

CONTINUED

6. Scrape the tempered egg yolks back into the saucepan. Then stir the custard over moderate heat, using a heatproof utensil with a flat edge. I like to use a flexible silicone spatula, although a straight-edged wooden spatula works well, too. Cook, stirring nonstop, until the mixture thickens and coats the spatula. While cooking the custard, be sure to scrape the bottom of the saucepan while stirring. Don't be timid; keep the custard mixture moving constantly while it's cooking, and do not let the custard bubble or boil!

CUSTARD RESCUE

If your custard does boil or curdle, rescue it by blending it—while it's warm—with an immersion or in a standing blender on the lowest setting. If using a standing blender, leave the cap of the lid ajar (if your blender lid has one) to let the steam escape, but drape a kitchen towel over the blender to avoid getting splattered with hot liquid. Never fill a blender container more than half full with hot liquid because the steam can force off the lid when the machine is turned on. Ouch.

You'll know your custard's done when steam rises off it and, as you scrape the spatula across the bottom of the pan, you feel it starting to thicken. (You'll notice some of it sticking to the bottom of the spatula as well.) Test it by running your finger across the spatula coated with custard: it's done when your finger leaves a definite trail that doesn't flow back together (see bottom-left photo, page 7). You can check for doneness with an instant-read thermometer, too; it should read between 160°F (71°C) and 176°F (76°C) when the custard is done. The higher end of the temperature range will make a creamier custard, but be careful not to overcook your custard—you don't want scrambled eggs.

7. It's ready! Without delay, take the custard off the heat and immediately pour the hot mixture through the strainer into the bowl of cream in the ice bath (see bottom-right photo, page 7) and stir. This will lower the temperature of the custard right away to stop the cooking. Stir frequently to help the custard cool down. Once it's cool, refrigerate the custard and cover with the lid slightly ajar. It should be very cold before churning. I recommend chilling most mixtures for 8 hours or overnight, and always churn in an ice cream maker according to the manufacturer's instructions.

8. Although some experts say that most ice cream benefits from being allowed to "ripen" in the freezer (whatever that means . . .) for a few hours before serving, I'm happy to enjoy the soft, fresh custard right from the machine. Ice cream with mix-ins and swirls, however, will hold up better in the bowl if stored in the freezer for a few hours after chruning. If your ice cream has been in the freezer for a longer period of time and is very firm, it will most likely benefit from being taken out 5 to 10 minutes prior to serving to allow it to soften to the best texture. For tips on keeping homemade ice cream soft in the freezer, see "How Can I Make Softer Ice Cream and Sorbets?" on the facing page.

KEEP IT CLEAN AND PLAY IT SAFE

Ice cream is a dairy product, so it's important to keep things as hygienic as possible. Make sure all equipment is extremely clean. Wash your hands after handling raw eggs, and clean the washable parts of your ice cream maker in very hot water (or as indicated by the manufacturer) after each use. Chill custards with eggs and dairy products promptly and store them in the refrigerator.

All of the ice cream recipes in this book that require egg yolks are cooked as custards on the stove top. If you have concerns about egg safety, use an instant-read thermometer to check the temperature. Most harmful bacteria don't survive at temperatures higher than 160°F (71°C). Pasteurized eggs in their shells are available in some areas and can be used if you wish.

INGREDIENTS

Alcohol

When added to ice cream and sorbets, alcohol does two things: it prevents them from freezing too hard (alcohol doesn't freeze) and it provides flavor. In some recipes, you can omit it if you'll be serving kids or anyone who is avoiding alcohol. In other cases, it's a vital flavor component, as in the Prune-Armagnac Ice Cream (page 88).

I frequently use kirsch, a distillation of cherries, to heighten the flavors of many fruit- or berry-based frozen desserts because it doesn't interfere with the fresh fruit flavors. Just a few drops can transform a ho-hum fruit puree into something vibrant. Similar options are Poire Williams, or another eau-de-vie.

I give suggestions in some cases for certain brands of liquor, but when I don't, feel free to use whatever tastes good to you, and what fits your budget. My rule for buying liquor for cooking is to get a brand that you wouldn't mind drinking on its own.

HOW CAN I MAKE SOFTER ICE CREAM AND SORBETS?

This is my most frequently asked question about homemade ice cream. Home freezers are colder than freezers in ice cream shops, and homemade ice cream (at least my homemade ice cream) doesn't have processed stabilizers or anything other than pure, natural ingredients in it. (Although I occasionally "cheat" in recipes and use sour cream, which is lower in fat than heavy cream and often has natural gums.) Most frozen desserts, especially sorbets, will get quite firm if left in the freezer because fruit is about 90 percent water and water freezes very hard. The best strategy in my book (which this book is) is to take the ice cream or sorbet out of the freezer 5 to 10 minutes before scooping it. But here are a few others strategies:

Alcohol

Adding a splash of alcohol will give your ice creams and sorbets a better texture because alcohol inhibits freezing. For fruit-based sorbets and sherbets or frozen cocktails, spirits like kirsch, vodka, gin, and eau-de-vie will enhance the flavor and produce a softer texture by preventing ice crystals from forming. Use caution, though: if you add too much, the mixture might not freeze at all and you'll be left with a runny mess. In general, you can add up to 3 tablespoons (45ml) of 40-percent (80-proof) liquor, such as rum or whiskey, to 1 quart (1l) of custard or sorbet mixture without any problems. If you want to add wine or champagne to a sorbet mixture, you can add up to ½ cup (125ml) per 1 quart (1l), unless the recipe says to use another amount, such as in Spritz Sorbet (page 146).

Sugar

Many liquid sweeteners, such as honey, golden syrup, molasses, rice syrup, glucose, and corn syrup, are roughly 25 percent sweeter than granulated sugar. Corn syrup is sometimes added to sorbets that are especially prone to getting icy. (Note that the corn syrup you buy in the supermarket is not the same thing as high-fructose corn syrup. See page 11.) Some liquid sweeteners have a more pronounced flavor and may, or may not, be compatible with the flavor of the ice cream or sorbet. For those wanting to use a liquid sweetener in their frozen dessert base for a smoother final result, substitute up to 25 percent of the granulated sugar in the recipe with one of the liquid sweeteners mentioned above.

Gelatin

Gelatin can be added to sorbets to make them smoother. It binds water and reduces the size of ice crystals. Sprinkle 1 teaspoon of unflavored powdered gelatin over ½ cup (125ml) of the cold sorbet mixture (before it's frozen) in a small saucepan. Let stand for 5 minutes, then gently warm the gelatin until it dissolves. Add the gelatin to the sorbet mixture. Note that gelatin is an animal product and isn't suitable for vegetarians or people on certain diets.

Berries

Nothing is better than fresh berries in season, when they're at their peak. I've never tasted a "fresh" strawberry or raspberry flown in from across the world that was as good as one from nearby, so I avoid them. I do use frozen berries, which can be quite tasty if you find a good brand, and they're generally less expensive than fresh berries. If buying frozen, choose berries that are unsweetened and individually quick frozen (IQF). When measuring frozen berries for recipes by volume, be sure to measure them while they're frozen, because they decrease substantially in size after defrosting.

Fresh berries should be plump and juicy when you buy them. Strawberries should be very fragrant and uniformly red, with no green "shoulders" or darkening bruises. Peek under berry baskets before buying to see if there's dampness, which often indicates unseen spoilage.

I don't wash blackberries and raspberries because they're fragile and will lose their delicacy, but fresh strawberries should always be rinsed and drained well before they're used, to remove any grit. Fresh blueberries and cherries should be rinsed and drained as well.

Butter

For the recipes in this book that call for butter, use either unsalted or salted butter, as noted.

Chocolate

Buying chocolate in bulk is more economical than purchasing little bars, and dark chocolate will keep perfectly well in a cool, dark place (not the refrigerator) for several years. See Resources (page 259) for some recommended brands and sources.

BITTERSWEET AND SEMISWEET CHOCOLATE *Bittersweet* and *semisweet* are interchangeable terms for dark chocolate, and chocolates labeled as such in the United States must contain a minimum of 35 percent cocoa solids (ground cocoa beans). Premium brands have proliferated, including bean-to-bar chocolates, which often boast a higher percentage of cocoa solids, so I advise you to taste as many chocolates as you can (a delicious task) to find brands you like in your price range. I usually use dark chocolates in the range of 55 to 70 percent cocoa solids; you'll find the percentage marked on the packaging. In a couple of recipes, I advise using chocolate with a certain percentage of cocoa solids for best results. Unsweetened chocolate, often called bitter chocolate, contains no sugar. Do not use bittersweet chocolate in place of bitter chocolate.

CHOCOLATE CHIPS Most chocolate chips are formulated with less cocoa butter so they'll retain their shape when heated. I use them in baked goods like meringues and cookies (and for snacking), but not for melting. Most supermarket chocolate chips are fine to use, although I usually treat myself to premium brands.

COCOA NIBS These crunchy bits of roasted cocoa beans are the essence of pure chocolate without any added sugar. They remain especially crisp even when folded into ice cream. Cocoa nibs are available at specialty shops and well-stocked supermarkets. See Resources (page 259) for online purchasing.

COCOA POWDER All recipes that call for cocoa powder mean you should use unsweetened cocoa powder. Do not use cocoa drink mixes or products labeled "powdered chocolate," which contain sugar and other ingredients. In most cases, I specify Dutch-process cocoa powder, which has been acid-neutralized and is darker in color than natural cocoa powder. I find it more flavorful and prefer it for my ice creams and sorbets, although in the United States there are a few artisan brands of natural cocoa powder that are better than some of the Dutch-processed cocoa powders you find in supermarkets. If your cocoa powder has been "Dutched," it should say so somewhere on the packaging, or it will list an alkalizing agent in the ingredients list. Most European brands of cocoa powder are likely to be Dutch processed, whether the label says so or not.

MILK CHOCOLATE Milk chocolate is chocolate that's been mellowed by the addition of milk. In the United States, milk chocolate must contain a minimum of 10 percent cocoa solids, but you should search out a premium brand with at least 30 percent cocoa solids; this type is sometimes called "dark milk chocolate." Avoid using mass-marketed candy bars. They contain the minimum amount of cocoa solids and are often very sweet. Milk chocolate will keep for about one year if stored in a cool, dark place.

WHITE CHOCOLATE Real white chocolate is made with pure cocoa butter. It's ivory colored, and not truly white; bars or products labeled "white coating" that are pure white in color are not real white chocolate and shouldn't be used. Quality is very important when selecting white chocolate, and buying a premium brand is always worth it. White chocolate will keep for about one year if stored in a cool, dark place.

CHOPPING CHOCOLATE

The most effective tool for chopping chocolate is a long, serrated bread knife. If you buy chocolate in a big block, you'll find it is easier to tackle if you start to chop at one corner. As you cut a wider swath, turn the block and start chopping from another corner. If a recipe calls for finely chopped chocolate, the pieces should be no larger than ¼ inch (6mm). Coarsely chopped chocolate means pieces that are about ¾ inch (2cm).

Coconut and Coconut Milk

I prefer to use unsweetened dried coconut rather than sweetened flakes from the supermarket, which contain preservatives. Dried unsweetened coconut is available in some grocery stores as well as in natural and specialty food stores.

If you can't find unsweetened coconut, soak sweetened coconut in hot water for 15 minutes. Rinse it afterward, then wring it firmly with your hands. Let it dry before using.

Coconut milk is the extracted liquid from coconut meat. Very good canned brands are available in Asian and multicultural markets, as well as in well-stocked supermarkets. Do not substitute low-fat coconut milk, which has the deliciously rich (and flavorful) coconut cream removed, and don't use the heavily sweetened Coco López or similar products labeled "cream of coconut."

Coffee and Espresso

Much of the success of any coffee-flavored ice cream or granita depends upon the quality and strength of the coffee beans, coffee, or espresso you use. The recipes in this book call for strong, freshly brewed coffee or espresso. There are some "premium" instant espresso and coffee powders, which work in a pinch. Bialetti brand, or "moka" type, coffee pots are inexpensive and make excellent espresso or very strong coffee on the stove top. (I like them so much, I have them in practically every size.) The substitution ratio for these recipes is a rounded 1 teaspoon of top-quality instant coffee or espresso powder to ¼ cup (60ml) of hot water.

Corn Syrup

An invert sugar, corn syrup helps keep ice creams and sorbets softer and more scoopable when frozen. Corn syrup also helps prevent sugar crystallization in candy recipes and is used to keep sauces from becoming grainy. Note that the corn syrup you buy in the supermarket is different than industrial high-fructose corn syrup. You can buy natural brands in health food stores and well-stocked supermarkets. I use it judiciously when I want to give extra body and thickness to sauces.

All recipes calling for corn syrup in this book use light corn syrup. Don't substitute dark corn syrup. If you live in an area where light corn syrup is unavailable, you can substitute a very mild-flavored honey, cane syrup, or golden syrup (except for Marshmallow Sauce, page 182, and Marshmallows, page 232, where these substitutes would discolor the results). Bakers outside the United States can substitute glucose, which is available at professional pastry-supply shops and online.

READ THE RECIPE THOROUGHLY BEFORE BEGINNING

There's nothing more frustrating than getting halfway through a recipe and finding that you neglected to prepare an ingredient or need to unearth your mesh strainer. Have all your ingredients ready and all your equipment lined up before you start cooking.

Dairy

HALF-AND-HALF Half-and-half is a dairy hybrid, a mixture of milk and cream, and is between 11 and 18 percent fat. Don't use nonfat half-and-half.

HEAVY CREAM American heavy cream is roughly 36 percent butterfat. Although there is a slight difference between products labeled "whipping cream" and those labeled "heavy cream," they are interchangeable in this book. Look for cream that has not been ultrapasteurized (UHT). This process involves heating the cream to a very high temperature to prolong shelf life. Unfortunately, it also destroys much of the flavor. If your grocery store doesn't stock it, request that they do.

MILK My tastes have changed over the years, and I now prefer ice creams made with whole milk in combination with heavy cream rather than ones made with all heavy cream. But don't substitute low-fat or skim milk for the whole milk in these recipes; the result will be icy or grainy ice cream.

SOUR CREAM Sour cream has a fresh, tangy taste due to the addition of lactic acid. Buy brands with the fewest (and most natural) ingredients. Although I advise you to use regular sour cream, you can substitute low-fat sour cream in any recipe if you wish, but do not use nonfat sour cream. Crème fraîche is higher in fat than sour cream and can be used as a substitute.

YOGURT Use only plain, whole-milk yogurt. Greek-style yogurt, which has a higher butterfat content, can be used if you wish (see "It's Not All Greek to Me," page 55).

THE SKINNY ON FAT

Yes, ice cream contains a rather high amount of fat—that's why we crave it! If you're concerned, try to eat a French-style portion: one perfect scoop. You'll find most of the frozen desserts in this book are so full of flavor that a little goes a long way.

My ice creams often contain less cream and egg yolks than others because I don't believe you need to overdose on fat to make food enjoyable, and too much fat can obliterate other flavors, especially those of fresh fruits. (Many of the fresh fruits I bring home find their way into sorbets, rather than ice creams.) So you'll find a number of the recipes have milk added where cream used to be, and that instead of whisking a chicken coop's worth of egg yolks to make ice cream custards, I've used a more modest amount.

Dried Fruits

Look for dried fruits that are plump and moist, as they'll have the best flavor. Store them in an airtight container away from light to preserve their moisture and taste. Natural food stores, supermarkets, and farmers' markets are often the best places to find high-quality dried fruits, but Trader Joe's pretty much wins the prize for the most variety of well-priced dried fruit. Although some people prefer unsulfured dried fruits, their dark color will affect the look of the finished ice cream.

In recipes calling for dried apricots, please use only fruit from California. The imported varieties may be cheaper, but they have a less-concentrated flavor and you'll be disappointed in the results. Prunes, available pitted or unpitted, are sometimes labeled "dried plums." Be sure to use ones that are not flavored with anything.

Eggs

All of the recipes in this book call for large eggs. If you're unsure what size your eggs are, a large egg in the shell weighs approximately 2 ounces (60g). One yolk equals 1 tablespoon (20g), and one white equals 2 tablespoons (30g). Use the freshest eggs you can find and store them in the refrigerator.

Custard-based ice cream recipes require just the yolks, not the whites. You'll find it easier to separate

eggs that are very cold rather than ones at room temperature. Extra egg whites can be refrigerated or frozen, or used to make Marshmallow Sauce (page 182), Meringue Nests (page 256), or Ice Cream Cones (page 250).

Egg safety means cooking eggs to 160°F (71°C), which can be easily verified with an instant-read thermometer. If you have health concerns, you can find pasteurized eggs in their shell or liquid egg whites sold in some supermarkets, although if you're using them for beating into a meringue, check the package to make sure they're suitable for whipping.

Extracts, Flavorings, and Oils

Good-quality extracts cost slightly more per use than inferior-quality ones and are always worth the price. To preserve their aroma, store extracts in a cool, dark place because light and heat will cause their flavors to deteriorate quickly. Some manufacturers use the word *flavoring* rather than extract, so be sure to read the list of ingredients to confirm the purity of what you're buying. Avoid anything with the word *artificial* on the label.

ALMOND EXTRACT Always purchase pure almond extract, not the stuff labeled "imitation." When using it, remember that a little goes a very long way. If a recipe calls for a few drops of extract, pour some into the cap of the bottle first, then dribble it carefully into the mixture.

CITRUS OILS These oils are made by pricking citrus fruits, such as lemons and oranges, to release the intensely flavored oil found in the peels. See Resources (page 259) for online sources.

MINT OIL AND EXTRACT Mint oil is made by steeping mint in a base of unflavored oil, whereas mint extract has a base of alcohol. Different brands vary significantly in strength, which makes calculating their use in recipes a challenge. You may want to begin by adding a smaller quantity than called for in the recipe. Taste, then add more until you're satisfied. Look for mint oil and extract at natural or specialty food stores.

VANILLA BEANS Vanilla beans should be plump and moist. To split a bean in half and obtain the seeds, use a paring knife to cut the bean lengthwise and then scrape out the seeds with the knife. Both the seeds and the pod have a great deal of flavor. After using, the pods can be reused if rinsed well in water. Let the pods dry completely and then store them buried in sugar, or conserve them in a vial of bourbon, rum, or vodka.

VANILLA EXTRACT It's imperative to use pure vanilla extract. Shop by quality, not by price. You won't regret it once you open the bottle and take a sniff. I use vanilla extract from Mexico (the real stuff) and Bourbon vanilla from Madagascar. Tahitian vanilla has a sweet, floral aroma, and I like it with tropical fruits, but it can be harder to find.

Flour

Use all-purpose flour in all recipes calling for flour, such as the brownies, cookies, cones, and some mix-ins. You can use bleached or unbleached flour. Measure flour using the method listed under Measuring Cups on page 20, or by weight.

Fresh Fruits and Citrus

Choose fruit-based recipes to make depending on which fruits are in season; that's when they're at their peak of flavor. The quality of sorbets and other fruit-based frozen desserts depends entirely on the quality of the fruit you start with. Fruit that's not going to be peeled should be rinsed and towel dried. This includes apricots, plums, and nectarines. Fruits such as mangoes, peaches, pears, and pineapples don't need to be washed, although some experts advise washing melons before slicing, as the rind can carry microorganisms.

You may notice that in recipes calling for fresh fruits I usually specify a quantity (such as 3 large peaches) instead of a weight (1 pound, 450g). Because most people shop by quantity, I've chosen to use those measurements in the ingredients list. Yet in a few instances, I do call for measuring fruit by weight because sizes can vary rather substantially and affect the recipe outcome.

For most bush berries, like raspberries and blueberries, I've chosen to use cups (and metric weights) because baskets of berries can differ in size. If using frozen berries, be sure to measure them before thawing, because they shrink considerably as they thaw. Because strawberries are irregular in size, I find it easier to measure them by weight.

When selecting citrus, choose fruits that are heavy for their size. (I usually pick up about twenty in order to find the four or five I go home with.) Grapefruits with flatter ends, rather than rounded, are usually sweeter and juicier. To get the maximum juice from any citrus fruit, make sure the fruits are at room temperature before squeezing. Rolling them firmly on the counter will rupture the juice sacs, which will help release the juices when squeezed.

ZEST Zest is the oil-rich, colorful part of the citrus peel. The best tool for grating zest from the rind is a rasp-style zester. Seek out organic or unsprayed citrus if you can, and scrub all citrus well before zesting.

ARE WE ON THE SAME PLANE?

I use a rasp-style zester to grate citrus zest. It is frequently referred to as a Microplane, which is a brand name, although other companies (such as Oxo) make similar zesters and graters. These ultra-sharp zesters really do make a difference, and you'll find that they remove almost twice as much of the flavorful peel as your grandmother's old metal box grater does.

My recipes usually call for grating the zest of one or more citrus fruits, rather than specifying a measured amount of zest. When you zest citrus, the aromatic oils tend to spray around, so I like to zest directly into the liquid I'm infusing, to make sure the intensely flavored citrus oils go straight into the dessert—instead of seasoning the kitchen counter.

All of the recipes in this book were prepared and written for cooks using a rasp-style grater. So if you're using a box grater, you may need to double the amount of citrus that the recipe calls for to achieve the full flavor.

Gelatin

When a recipe calls for gelatin, it means unflavored powdered gelatin. If using leaf gelatin, 4 sheets equals one ¼-ounce (7g) envelope of powdered gelatin.

Whichever type you use, it's necessary to soften the gelatin in cold water first. To use powdered gelatin granules, sprinkle the powder over the cold water as indicated in the recipe and let sit for 5 minutes, until the granules are swollen and soft. Then proceed with the recipe. For leaf gelatin, soak the sheets in cold water for 5 minutes, then lift them out and wring them dry. Warm them in a small saucepan over very low heat until liquefied.

Honey

Honey is a slightly acidic ingredient, and in custard-based recipes that call for a significant amount of it, you'll be directed to warm the honey separately and then add it later. Honey-based ice creams will have a smoother texture due to the high concentration of sugars.

I recommend using a honey that is full-bodied, rather than the bland, thin supermarket varieties. (Buckwheat honey is a particular favorite.) Farmers' markets and specialty shops often carry good-tasting, locally produced honey that will make any honey-based ice cream far more delectable, and most producers gladly offer tastes. Honey that has crystallized can be melted gently in a saucepan or microwave oven until it returns to its liquid state.

Liquor

The phrase "cook with what you would drink" holds true for liquor used in frozen desserts, especially the frozen cocktails in this book. But you don't need to pop open a $100 bottle of champagne or a $40 bottle of rosé as there are lower-priced options that will work just fine. And in some instances, such as the Spritz Sorbet (page 146), you can use budget-friendly Italian Prosecco.

For other types of liquors, there are brands that won't break the bank but are fine to use. Don't be embarrassed to ask at your local liquor store for recommendations. If you're bashful about not wanting to buy a premium brand, tell the clerk you'll be freezing it and they should steer you to a bottle that will suit your needs.

Alcohol doesn't freeze, so the quantities used in this book are formulated to give your ice cream or frozen desserts and cocktails the best texture once frozen. If you want to omit the liquor when it's used in a recipe that calls for 1 tablespoon (15ml) or less, you can replace it with a little vanilla extract or a squirt of lemon juice.

Maple Syrup and Maple Sugar

I use only dark amber maple syrup, which used to be called Grade B but is now referred to as Grade A dark amber.

Nuts

There's nothing like the pleasant crunch of a crisp, freshly toasted nut. And there's nothing worse than biting into a rancid one. Because nuts have a relatively high amount of oil, to ensure freshness, buy them from a store that sells in high volume and turns over its stock regularly. Taste a few before using them to make sure they're still fresh. Hazelnuts, pecans, and walnuts are particularly susceptible to spoilage.

Nuts should be stored in a cool, dark place in a well-sealed container. Nuts can also be frozen in zip-top freezer bags.

Most nuts taste much better if they've been toasted, which brings out their flavors and gives them a crunchy contrast in ice cream. The only nuts I don't toast are pistachio nuts, because they lose their delicate green color. Buy fresh pistachios from a good source so they're crisp and vibrant green.

TOASTING NUTS

1. Preheat the oven to 350°F (180°C).

2. Spread the nuts in an even layer on an ungreased baking sheet.

3. Bake the nuts in the oven for about 10 minutes, but check them a few minutes sooner; stir them once or twice while baking so they toast evenly. To see whether they're done, snap a nut in half: it should be lightly golden brown throughout.

4. Let the nuts cool completely before using, unless the recipe indicates otherwise.

Peanut Butter

The recipes in this book mostly call for commercial peanut butter. Natural-style peanut butter will release too much oil when mixed with other ingredients.

Salt

Hey—what's salt doing in a book on sweet stuff? Salt keeps foods from tasting flat, and that goes for ice creams, and sometimes sorbets, too. A little pinch works to brighten flavors and provides a gentle contrast to sweetness. Although you can use ordinary table salt when a pinch is required, I advise using kosher salt or flaky sea salt, which is especially important in recipes that call for a specific quantity measured out.

In a few instances, I recommend using fleur de sel, a hand-harvested sea salt from Brittany. Although you may think, "Isn't salt just salt?" fleur de sel has a delicate taste, and once you try it you're likely to start using it more and more, despite the price. Maldon salt from England can be used in its place.

Spices

Like the windshield wipers on your car, spices should be replaced when their efficacy has diminished. Most spices begin to lose their flavor and aroma after a year. Buy spices from a source that turns over its stock frequently, and replenish yours if they lose their aroma and pungency.

Sugar

Sugar is important in ice creams and sorbets for sweetening and ensuring a nice, scoopable texture. But use too much sugar and your ice cream or sorbet won't freeze. Use too little and the ice cream or sorbet will be grainy and hard to scoop.

When a recipe calls for sugar, it means granulated white sugar. Powdered sugar (also called confectioners' sugar) is granulated sugar that's been pulverized to a powder with a bit of cornstarch added. Brown sugar is listed as either light brown or dark brown. Use what's indicated in the recipe, and always pack brown sugar firmly into the measuring cup to measure it accurately.

FINDING THE RIGHT ICE CREAM MAKER

An ice cream maker is the most important piece of equipment you'll use to make most of the recipes in this book. Happily, you don't need to spend a fortune: there are quality machines on the market for any budget. The price of a machine intended for home use can start at less than $50 and can climb to more than $1,000 for a freezer of professional quality. These recipes were tested using an inexpensive home freezer with a canister that requires prefreezing, an ice cream attachment for a stand mixer, and a more expensive (but very convenient) ice cream machine with a built-in compressor, with virtually identical results. Although much depends on the features you want and your budget, each type of machine has advantages and drawbacks.

GO BY THE BOOK

I don't blame you for not wanting to read instruction manuals. But each particular machine has specific requirements, and I advise you to become familiar with yours prior to using it. So take a few minutes to get to know your machine by reading the instruction manual thoroughly.

Ice and Rock Salt Machines

You may find that there's nothing like the pleasure of hand-churning your own ice cream and want the freedom to do it in the great outdoors. Or maybe you have a large brood and small, 1-quart (1l) machines won't churn enough ice cream for everyone at once. If so, perhaps a hand-cranked ice and rock salt freezer, or "bucket-type" freezer, may be for you.

To use an ice and rock salt machine, fill the inner metal container (the can) with your ice cream custard or sorbet mixture, close the top, and then pack layers of ice and rock salt around the container. (The rock salt lowers the temperature so that the mixture will freeze; ice alone isn't cold enough.) Some models require hand cranking, and others work with an electric motor.

PROS These machines provide lots of old-fashioned fun, but hand-cranked models require some hard work (although it beats going to the gym). Most can freeze large batches, some up to 6 quarts (5.5l) at a time. No electricity is needed for the hand-cranked models, nor is prefreezing the can necessary, so you can make ice cream spontaneously. Top-of-the-line brands tend to be very solid and well made.

CONS Hand-cranked models require effort. And in addition to having a few reliable friends to help you crank, you'll also need access to a large amount of ice cubes and rock salt. Care must be taken to make sure no grains of salt get into the ice cream when you remove the lid. Motorized models tend to be noisy and can't be opened to add mix-ins while churning. Also their cost can be high, and the cheaper models have underpowered motors that don't work well.

Self-Refrigerating Machines

These ice cream freezers have a built-in compressor, so you just pour in your mixture, press a button, and wait. Within 30 to 45 minutes, depending on the model, you'll have freshly churned ice cream. I recommend self-refrigerating machines for people who make ice cream on a regular basis; their higher price pays off in speed, power, and efficiency. When shopping around, look for a model with a removable freezing container, which will make cleanup easier.

PROS These machines are easy to use and make fast work of churning out batches of ice cream. No prefreezing of equipment is necessary, so you can make ice cream and sorbet at a moment's notice. You can freeze several batches consecutively, one right after another.

CONS These are priced higher than other machines, although prices have dropped in recent years. They take up a lot of counter or cabinet space and some people find the noise of the motor bothersome.

Machines that Require Prefreezing

For most people, a machine with a canister that requires prefreezing is the most practical for home use, because these types are affordably priced and perform very well.

The canister, which is filled with liquid coolant, needs to be placed in the freezer usually 24 hours in advance. No matter how firm or cold the canister may feel, don't try to churn anything unless the canister has been in the freezer for the amount of time recommended by the manufacturer (trust me, I've tried). People with sufficient freezer space usually store the canister in the freezer all the time.

Although it's not often mentioned in the instruction manual, you'll find some models work best if you turn the machine on and have the dasher moving before you pour in your mixture. If not, the mixture can freeze immediately against the sides of the canister, causing the dasher to stall.

PROS The reasonable cost of these machines makes them accessible to everyone. They produce good ice cream and don't take up too much cabinet space when not in use, and there's a wide variety of models and brands to choose from. Most have a large opening, which allows mix-ins to be added while churning.

CONS The canister must be prefrozen, which requires freezer space and advance planning. It needs to be completely refrozen between batches. Coolant-filled canisters shouldn't be run through the dishwasher.

WHICH ICE CREAM MACHINE SHOULD I BUY?

If you're going to make ice cream infrequently—say, once or twice a month—a unit with a canister that you prefreeze is probably your best bet. If you're tempted by the idea of churning ice cream in the great outdoors, a hand-cranked ice and rock salt model that requires no electricity and has sufficient capacity to feed a hungry crowd may be what you're looking for.

If you're serious about making ice cream and you have the space, a freezer with self-contained coolant is the way to go. These machines require no advance preparation, and you can freeze one batch right after the other. They're more expensive, but if you're a big ice cream aficionado, you'll find it a solid investment.

WHY DOES MY ICE CREAM FREEZE HARDER THAN WHAT I BUY IN THE STORE?

Commercial ice creams are made in high-speed machines, which are able to whip extra air (called overrun) into the ice cream. This, of course, is done both for reasons of economy (more air equals more profit) and to improve the texture. Sometimes a long list of unpronounceable ingredients are added, too, to make the texture more scoopable.

The majority of home ice cream machines don't churn as fast and aren't as powerful as commercial machines, so the ice cream you make at home will have less air and is invariably denser (but tastier) than what you buy in the store. In addition, the freezers in most home refrigerators are very cold and are not intended for keeping ice cream at the ideal serving temperature. For this reason, it's best to remove homemade ice creams, sorbets, and sherbets from the freezer 5 to 10 minutes prior to serving, or zap them in the microwave in 10-second intervals.

Other Devices

Making homemade ice cream has become so popular that myriad other options for freezing ice cream have become available. KitchenAid offers a snap-on canister attachment for their electric stand mixers. Once the canister is prefrozen, you pour the mixture inside and churn away with the mixer set on low speed.

Other novelties include "play and freeze" balls that you fill with ice cream custard, snap closed (don't forget!), and toss around the yard until the mixture is "churned." There are also "instant" ice cream makers, usually for single servings, where you pour the ice cream mixture into a prefrozen bowl or tub and stir or scrape it until thick. And then there are cocktail shaker–like containers for shaking up your own ice cream. I haven't tried most of these contraptions, but online reviews are often telling . . . and amusing.

EQUIPMENT

Fortunately, making ice creams and sorbets requires very little in the way of specialty equipment, aside from an ice cream maker. The following list describes a few other items used to make the recipes in this book.

Baking Dish

You'll need a shallow dish of some sort to make granitas. It should be made of a nonreactive material: stainless steel, porcelain, earthenware, and plastic are all suitable. The exact size isn't important, but it should be between 8 and 12 inches (20 and 30cm) across and should have sides that are 2 inches (5cm) high to contain the icy crystals as you stir the granita.

Blender, Food Processor, or Food Mill

Aside from your ice cream maker, a blender will be your second-most important piece of equipment and your best pal for making smooth purees. Stick or wand blenders do an effective job and can be used to puree anything directly in a saucepan or mixing bowl. You can also use a food processor with a sharp blade, or go low-tech with a food mill. Some cooks like to chop nuts in their food processor, although I find the results uneven and prefer to use a chef's knife.

Cherry Pitter

A handheld, spring-loaded metal cherry pitter is a small tool that you'll find handy when cherry season comes around. The Oxo cherry pitter has a splash guard, which helps keep the pitter (that's you) tidy.

Espresso Maker

Several recipes call for espresso. I use an Italian stove-top espresso maker—an inexpensive metal pot that makes good, strong coffee. The best of the genre is made by Bialetti, but any brand will do. If you have an automatic espresso machine, I recommend using the "long" (less-concentrated) setting.

Ice Cream Cone Maker

Although a cone maker is definitely a niche item, it's great fun to roll up your own cones and fill them with a scoop of home-churned ice cream. Most machines are relatively inexpensive and have a nonstick coating to make life easier. They come with a cone-rolling mold, and wire stands are available to hold the cones as they cool.

Machines called pizzelle irons will make smaller cones that, when rolled up, will hold one dainty scoop.

Knives

A good, sharp knife is invaluable for slicing fruit and chopping nuts. A paring knife with a 3- to 4-inch (8 to 10cm) blade and an 8-inch (20cm) chef's knife will perform most tasks required for the recipes in this book.

Measuring Cups

For measuring liquids, use a cup made of clear plastic or glass, so you can get an accurate measurement. Graduated measuring cups, the metal or plastic kind that nest within each other (¼ cup, ⅓ cup, etc.), are best for measuring dry ingredients. Flour should always be measured in a graduated measuring cup by spooning the flour into the cup, then leveling it off by sweeping over the top with a flat-edged utensil. I like to have several sets of each kind of measuring cup on hand.

Mixing Bowls

Any kind of bowl will do for ice cream making, although if you can find them, heavy plastic or stainless-steel bowls with rubber or silicone built into the bottom make stirring mixtures and tempering eggs easier, because pouring one ingredient into another while simultaneously whisking can be challenging. The rubber foot keeps the bowl from sliding around.

When a recipe calls for a small bowl, I mean one that holds 1 quart (1l). A medium bowl holds 2 to 3 quarts (2 to 3l), and a large bowl is anything bigger.

TEMPERING TANTRUMS

If you're all by yourself in the kitchen and you're trying to pour warm liquid from the saucepan into egg yolks while simultaneously whisking, chances are the bowl of egg yolks is going to want to move around a bit. This can be frustrating for the solitary cook. Here are a few strategies for stabilizing the mischievous bowl:

- Moisten a kitchen towel with water. Either lay the towel flat on the counter and place the bowl on top, or hold one corner of the towel and spin it into a long twist (like a gym towel intended for a locker-room snap). Form it into a closed circle on the countertop and nestle your bowl in the center.

- Buy mixing bowls with rubber bottoms. You'll find them available at stores specializing in cookware and online. I own several and love them.

- Set the bowl into a wok ring, if you have one.

- Set a pair of rubber dishwashing gloves on the countertop, side by side, then set your bowl on the gloves. The gloves will stabilize the bowl.

- Find a friend to help in the kitchen. Make sure you reward him or her with ice cream!

Saucepans and Skillets

Use heavy-duty pots and pans, which conduct heat well and will help ensure even heating when cooking on the stove top.

For fruit-based mixtures like many granitas and sorbets, or anything with an acidic ingredient like wine, always use nonreactive cookware. These include saucepans made of anodized aluminum, or copper-clad stainless steel. The acid in the fruit can react with other metals and affect the color and flavor.

A small saucepan means one that holds 1 to 3 quarts (1 to 3l), a medium saucepan holds around 4 quarts (4l), and a large saucepan refers to anything larger.

Scale

A scale is necessary to weigh out the correct amount of some of the ingredients called for in the recipes, such as chocolate. For dry ingredients, measurements are given in both cup measurements and metric weights so that you can measure them by weight if you prefer.

WHY WEIGHT?

In America, there's been a hesitant shift to weighing ingredients. The rest of the world waits patiently for us to toss out our measuring cups and put things on a scale, but many of us are reluctant to. I say it's because of nostalgia: I still have some of the measuring cups my mother baked with, and I'm not willing to give them up! But weighing things is more accurate, and although ingredient measurements for ice cream don't need to be as fussy as for a cake or a batch of cookies, I've provided weights for ingredients. I do recommend using a scale (you can get one for less than $10), but if you don't have one, no problem. You can still get most of your licks in using a cup or tablespoon.

Scoops

There are basically two types of ice cream scoops. Solid scoops are one-piece tools, sometimes filled with antifreeze, that boast the ability to scoop through even the firmest ice cream. Some shouldn't be run through the dishwasher, which can damage the finish and reduce the effectiveness of the antifreeze inside. Other single-piece scoops are coated with a nonstick material to help the ice cream release, and some are made of stainless steel, which can be run through the dishwasher. These kinds of scoops have no moving parts to break.

Spring-loaded scoops usually require a bit more effort when scooping but have the advantage of a thin arc of metal that helps release the ice cream into a neat, perfectly rounded scoop. Cheaper models are flimsy and tend to slip gears and break easily, so I advise purchasing professional-grade or top-quality spring-loaded scoopers.

Spatulas

Spatulas made of a heatproof material are the invention of the decade for home cooks and professionals. The flexible heads are made of silicone and can withstand temperatures well over 400°F (200°C) without melting. I keep lots of them on hand to use when baking and making ice cream.

Some ice cream makers come with specially designed plastic spatulas that fit nicely into the freezing canister for removing just-churned ice cream. Don't use them for any other purpose, because you want them to last as long as possible and they may be hard to replace.

Storage containers

My preferred containers for storage are ones that are square, plastic (BPA-free), and heavy-duty, so they can be reused. Square containers, rather than round ones, fit more neatly in the freezer if space is at a premium, and heavy-duty plastic ensures that they won't crack easily. Restaurant supply shops often carry a great selection of plastic food-safe containers if you want to buy in bulk. Tovolo makes sturdy, reusable ice cream tubs, which can be found in cookware shops or online, and several companies make cardboard frozen dessert containers that resemble classic ice cream tubs. Because most recipes in this book make about 1 quart (1l) of ice cream, I recommend containers that hold that much, or more to accommodate a couple of cups of mix-ins.

Strainers

Strainers with medium-size mesh screens are useful for removing seeds from berry purees and for straining just-cooked custards to remove any bits of cooked egg. Buy strainers with stainless-steel screens that feel sturdy and solid. You'll want ones that can stand up to firm pressure when pressing and straining purees.

Thermometer

Newbies as well as intrepid cooks might want to have an instant-read probe thermometer on hand when making custard-based ice creams. For the uninitiated, it takes much of the guesswork out of the process of making custard. You will find that digital instant-read thermometers take faster readings than the dial type. When checking the temperature, make sure the end of the probe is submerged in the liquid but is not touching the bottom of the pan, which is hotter than the liquid itself.

Vegetable peeler

Vegetable peelers made of nonreactive stainless steel are preferable for peeling fruit and shaving off wide strips of citrus zest. Make sure it is sharp.

Whisks

As with flexible spatulas, I keep several whisks on hand when cooking. Like other kitchen tools that take a beating, well-made whisks will last far longer than flimsy ones.

Zesters and graters

If you don't have a rasp-style grater, I suggest you make one your next purchase. They scrape off the most delicate, flavorful part of a citrus peel and allow you to leave behind the bitter white pith. See "Are We on the Smae Plane?" page 15, for zesting tips.

CHAPTER 2

Ice Creams, Frozen Yogurts, and Gelatos

For some, the perfect scoop is a simple dish of creamy Vanilla Ice Cream flecked with lots of aromatic vanilla seeds (pages 28 and 29). Others get their frosty fix from a cone of chocolate ice cream (see pages 30 and 32). But in between chocolate and vanilla, there's a whole world of flavors to explore, and you'll find them all in this chapter, from rosy-pink Strawberry–Sour Cream Ice Cream (page 98) to silky Lavender-Honey Ice Cream (page 76) to the liveliest Super Lemon Ice Cream (page 93) you've ever eaten. While youngsters will certainly go wild for Peanut Butter and Jelly Ice Cream (variation, page 59), few adults can resist an eye-opening scoop of Coffee Ice Cream (page 38), infused with a jolt of dark-roasted coffee beans. And if there's anyone who can refuse a scoop of Tin Roof Ice Cream (page 66), chock-full of chocolate-dipped peanuts and gooey rivers of fudge, I'd like to meet them.

In addition to the classics, there are myriad modern flavors that are sure to please. And I've included a handful of frozen yogurts and gelatos, too. Many of these recipes are simple enough to whiz up in a blender; others involve making a custard, gently cooked in a saucepan until rich and satiny smooth. If you've never made a stove-top custard before, it's quite simple, and I've offered step-by-step instructions (see page 6), with pictures and lots of pointers and tips to ensure success.

There's no reason why you can't create your own flavor combinations by adding mix-ins to your just churned ice cream—perhaps a swirl of Fudge Ripple (page 231), chewy nuggets of chocolate truffles (pages 230 and 234), chopped nuts, or chunks of buttery-soft Chocolate Chip Cookie Dough (page 235). You'll find all these and more in chapter 6, "Mix-Ins." Your imagination is the only limit.

VANILLA ICE CREAM

Makes about 1 quart (1l)

Everyone needs a great vanilla ice cream recipe in their repertoire, and here's mine. Keeping a tub of homemade vanilla ice cream in my freezer is standard policy, because I can't think of any dessert that isn't made better with a soft scoop of vanilla ice cream melting alongside.

I use two kinds of vanilla in mine; the bean lends rich, deep vanilla notes and the vanilla extract rounds out, and further deepens, the flavor.

1. Warm the milk, sugar, 1 cup (250ml) of the cream, and the salt in a medium saucepan. Scrape the seeds from the vanilla bean into the warm milk and add the bean as well. Cover, remove from the heat, and let steep at room temperature for 30 minutes.

2. Pour the remaining 1 cup (250ml) cream into a large bowl and set a mesh strainer on top. In a separate medium bowl, whisk together the egg yolks. Slowly pour the warm mixture into the egg yolks, whisking constantly, then scrape the warmed egg yolks into the saucepan. Stir the mixture constantly with a heatproof spatula over medium heat, scraping the bottom as you stir, until the mixture thickens and coats the spatula.

3. Pour the custard through the strainer and stir it into the cream. Put the vanilla bean into the custard, add the vanilla extract, and stir over an ice bath until cool.

4. Chill the mixture thoroughly in the refrigerator. When ready to churn, remove the vanilla bean, rinsing and reserving it for another use, and then freeze the mixture in your ice cream maker according to the manufacturer's instructions.

PERFECT PAIRINGS: Make Chocolate Chip Ice Cream by drizzling in one recipe of dark chocolate Stracciatella (page 230).

I may not fit the profile of a bourbon drinker, but I do like (and sometimes need) a shot or two of whiskey every now and then . . . even in my ice cream! To make Bourbon and Spiced Pecan Ice Cream, stir 3 tablespoons (45ml) bourbon (I like Jack Daniel's or Four Roses) into the custard just before freezing, then mix in one recipe coarsely chopped Spiced Pecans (page 218) just after churning the ice cream.

1 cup (250ml) whole milk

¾ cup (150g) sugar

2 cups (500ml) heavy cream

Pinch of kosher or sea salt

1 vanilla bean, split in half lengthwise

6 large egg yolks

¾ teaspoon pure vanilla extract

VANILLA ICE CREAM, PHILADELPHIA STYLE

Makes about 1 quart (1l)

Philadelphia-style ice cream is made with no eggs, so it can be put together in a New York minute. It gets its name because at one time there was a proliferation of dairy farms around Philadelphia. I've made this vanilla ice cream successfully with all heavy cream as well as with a mixture of cream and milk, and I like it both ways. All cream, of course, is richer and creamier.

1. Pour 1 cup (250ml) of the cream into a medium saucepan and add the sugar and salt. Scrape the seeds from the vanilla bean into the saucepan and add the pod as well. Warm over medium heat, stirring, until the sugar is dissolved.

2. Remove from the heat and add the remaining 2 cups (500ml) cream, or the remaining 1 cup (250ml) cream and the milk, and the vanilla extract.

3. Chill the mixture thoroughly in the refrigerator. When ready to churn, remove the vanilla bean, rinsing and reserving it for another use, and then freeze the mixture in your ice cream maker according to the manufacturer's instructions.

PERFECT PAIRING: To make Caramel–Chocolate Ripple Ice Cream, layer 1 cup (250g) each Fudge Ripple (page 231) and Salted Butter Caramel Sauce (page 189) into the just-churned ice cream.

3 cups (750ml) heavy cream, or 2 cups (500ml) heavy cream and 1 cup (250ml) whole milk

¾ cup (150g) sugar

Pinch of kosher or sea salt

1 vanilla bean, split in half lengthwise

¾ teaspoon pure vanilla extract

FRENCH VS. AMERICAN

There are two basic styles of ice cream: French style, a cooked custard made with egg yolks, and Philadelphia style, made with cream or a combination of cream and milk, without eggs.

French-style ice creams tend to be smoother and silkier, due to the emulsifying power of the egg yolks, which are cooked on the stove top, requiring a bit of custard-making prowess. Philadelphia-style ice creams can simply be mixed together, chilled thoroughly, and then churned. Philadelphia-style ice creams tend to be a bit firmer, freeze harder, and have a somewhat chewier texture than French-style ice creams. The advantage is that they're a little lighter tasting and are easier to make. Most benefit from being removed from the refrigerator a few minutes before serving.

CHOCOLATE ICE CREAM

Makes about 1 quart (1l)

My search for the ultimate chocolate ice cream ended the day I dipped a spoon into my ice cream maker and took a taste of this one. And soon, I was licking the dasher as clean as the day I bought it! (I don't know why, but homemade ice cream always tastes best when scraped—or if no one's watching, licked—directly from the machine.) Intense cocoa powder blended with dark, bittersweet chocolate results in a perfect chocolate ice cream that's so irresistible you won't be able to wait to dig in, or lick it up, either.

---

1. Warm 1 cup (250ml) of the cream with the cocoa powder in a medium saucepan, whisking to thoroughly blend the cocoa. Bring to a boil, then lower the heat and simmer for 30 seconds, whisking constantly.

2. Remove from the heat and add the chocolate, stirring until smooth. Stir in the remaining 1 cup (250ml) cream. Pour the mixture into a large bowl, scraping the saucepan as thoroughly as possible, and set a mesh strainer on top of the bowl.

3. Warm the milk, sugar, and salt in the same saucepan.

4. In a separate medium bowl, whisk together the egg yolks. Slowly pour the warm milk into the egg yolks, whisking constantly, then scrape the warmed egg yolks into the saucepan. Stir the mixture constantly with a heatproof spatula over medium heat, scraping the bottom as you stir, until the mixture thickens and coats the spatula.

5. Pour the custard through the strainer and stir it into the chocolate mixture until smooth, add the vanilla, and stir over an ice bath until cool.

6. Chill the mixture thoroughly in the refrigerator, then freeze it in your ice cream maker according to the manufacturer's instructions. (If the cold mixture is too thick to pour into your machine, whisk it vigorously to thin it out.)

VARIATION: To make Rocky Road Ice Cream, fold in 1½ cups (90g) homemade (or miniature store-bought) Marshmallows (page 232) and 1 cup (150g) roasted peanuts or toasted (see page 16), coarsely chopped almonds.

PERFECT PAIRINGS: To make Chocolate-Mint Ice Cream, stir ⅛ teaspoon mint oil or extract into the custard before freezing, then fold in one recipe of homemade Peppermint Patties (page 226) or 2 cups (250g) crumbled store-bought peppermint patties into the just-churned ice cream.

2 cups (500ml) heavy cream

3 tablespoons unsweetened Dutch-process cocoa powder

5 ounces (140g) bittersweet or semisweet chocolate, chopped

1 cup (250ml) whole milk

¾ cup (150g) sugar

Pinch of kosher or sea salt

5 large egg yolks

½ teaspoon pure vanilla extract

CHOCOLATE ICE CREAM, PHILADELPHIA STYLE

Makes about 1 quart (1l)

Unsweetened chocolate provides the maximum chocolate flavor in this non-custard-based chocolate ice cream. But bitter chocolate can be stubborn to melt, so you'll want to whiz the mixture in a blender to make sure it's silky smooth.

1. Whisk together the cream, cocoa powder, sugar, and salt in a large saucepan. Heat the mixture, whisking frequently, until it comes to a full, rolling boil (it will start to foam up). Remove from the heat and whisk in the chocolate until it's completely melted, then whisk in the milk and vanilla.

2. Pour the mixture into a blender and blend for 30 seconds, until very smooth.

3. Chill the mixture thoroughly in the refrigerator, then freeze it in your ice cream maker according to the manufacturer's instructions.

VARIATION: For Chocolate–Peanut Butter Patty Ice Cream, fold one recipe of Peanut Butter Patties (page 228) into the just-churned ice cream.

PERFECT PAIRINGS: Make Double Chocolate Ice Cream by folding in one recipe of Dark Chocolate Truffles (page 230) or White Chocolate Truffles (page 234) into the just-churned ice cream.

2¼ cups (560ml) heavy cream

6 tablespoons (50g) unsweetened Dutch-process cocoa powder

1 cup (200g) sugar

Pinch of kosher or sea salt

6 ounces (170g) unsweetened chocolate, chopped

1 cup (250ml) whole milk

1 teaspoon pure vanilla extract

WHAT'S THAT "ABOUT"?

In my recipes for ice creams and sorbets, I use the word *about* when indicating the quantity the recipe will make. In general, a custard or other mixture frozen in an ice cream machine designed for home use will increase in volume by around 25 percent once churned. The air incorporated into ice cream during churning, by the way, is called the overrun, and commercial ice cream can have up to 100 percent overrun!

Most of the recipes in this book will make 1 quart (1l) of frozen ice cream or sorbet. I tested the recipes with the most commonly used types of machines. I found that the ice cream increased in volume in proportion to the power and speed of the machine. Hence, the recipes may yield slightly more or slightly less for you depending on your machine.

AZTEC "HOT" CHOCOLATE ICE CREAM

Makes about 1 quart (1l)

The Aztecs were such trendsetters. Although it's become fashionable, from Los Angeles to London, to spice up chocolate with chile pepper, it's a custom that goes back more than a thousand years. No one has ever accused me of being particularly fashionable (especially when they see the way I dress), although I do like to spice up chocolate ice cream with a dose of chile. My preference is smoky ancho or chipotle chile powder, available in Mexican markets, but for those who like more heat, cayenne is hot . . . hot . . . hot! If you're unsure of the strength of your chile powder, add the smaller amount and let it sit for a while. Taste and decide whether you'd like to add more. The subtle warmth can heat up as it stands.

---

1. Whisk together the cream, cocoa powder, and sugar in a large saucepan. Heat the mixture, whisking frequently, until it comes to a full, rolling boil (it will start to foam up). Remove from the heat and add the chocolate, then whisk until it is completely melted. Stir in the milk, vanilla, salt, cinnamon, chile powder, and brandy.

2. Pour the mixture into a blender and blend for 30 seconds, until very smooth.

3. Chill the mixture thoroughly in the refrigerator, then freeze it in your ice cream maker according to the manufacturer's instructions.

PERFECT PAIRING: For Mexican Chocolate and Cajeta Ice Cream, layer in one recipe of Cajeta (page 188). Include some Spiced Pecans (page 218) if you'd like.

2¼ cups (560ml) heavy cream

6 tablespoons (50g) unsweetened Dutch-process cocoa powder

¾ cup (150g) sugar

3 ounces (85g) semisweet or bittersweet chocolate, chopped

1¼ cups (310ml) whole milk

1 teaspoon pure vanilla extract

Pinch of kosher or sea salt

1¼ teaspoons ground cinnamon

2 to 3 teaspoons pure chile powder

2 tablespoons brandy

CHOCOLATE–PEANUT BUTTER ICE CREAM

Makes about 1 quart (1l)

Two great tastes—creamy-smooth peanut butter and pure, unadulterated cocoa—come together in one great ice cream.

1. Whisk together the half-and-half, cocoa powder, sugar, and salt in a large saucepan. Heat the mixture, whisking frequently, until it comes to a full, rolling boil (it will start to foam up). Remove from the heat and whisk in the peanut butter, stirring until thoroughly blended.

2. Chill the mixture thoroughly in the refrigerator, then freeze it in your ice cream maker according to the manufacturer's instructions.

PERFECT PAIRING: For Chocolate Fudge Swirl Peanut Butter Ice Cream, layer in one recipe of Fudge Ripple (page 231) and mix in a batch of Peanut Butter Patties (page 228).

2 cups (500ml) half-and-half

¼ cup (25g) unsweetened Dutch-process cocoa powder

½ cup (100g) sugar

Pinch of kosher or sea salt

½ cup (130g) smooth peanut butter (not natural style)

CHOCOLATE-RASPBERRY ICE CREAM

Makes about 3 cups (750ml)

If you're one of those people who finds the combination of raspberries with dark chocolate the ultimate luxury, you'll adore this ice cream. It's the perfect indulgence: rich, dark chocolate with the bright flavor of tangy raspberries.

1. Whisk together the cream, cocoa powder, and sugar in a large saucepan. Heat the mixture, whisking frequently, until it comes to a full, rolling boil (it will start to foam up). Remove from the heat and add the raspberries. Cover and let stand for 10 minutes.

2. Puree the mixture in a food processor or blender. If you wish, press the mixture through a mesh strainer to remove the seeds.

3. Chill the mixture thoroughly in the refrigerator, then freeze it in your ice cream maker according to the manufacturer's instructions.

1½ cups (375ml) heavy cream

5 tablespoons (40g) unsweetened Dutch-process cocoa powder

⅔ cup (130g) sugar

2 cups (240g) raspberries, fresh or frozen

MILK CHOCOLATE ICE CREAM

Makes about 1 quart (1l)

I finally understood the allure of milk chocolate while writing a book exploring the world of chocolate. I was determined to get over my skepticism and taste-tested as many milk chocolates as I could. Yes, it was tough work, but someone had to do it. I became a convert after sampling premium dark milk chocolates made with a high percentage of cocoa solids, and my chocolate horizons expanded to include this once-banished member of the chocolate family.

Mixing in roasted cocoa nibs adds a crunchy counterpoint to this milky-smooth custard. I like biting into the little bits of pure, unadulterated cocoa bean. A few years back, they were hard to find, but nowadays, I've seen them in standard supermarkets and even big-box chain stores. Once you have a bag, you'll find yourself adding them to chocolate desserts all the time, like I do. (See Resources, page 259, for online sources.) If you can't get them, mini dark chocolate chips will do.

1. Combine the milk chocolate and cream in a large, heatproof bowl set over a saucepan of barely simmering water. Stir until the chocolate is melted, then remove the bowl from the saucepan. Set it aside with a mesh strainer over the top.

2. Warm the milk, sugar, and salt in a medium saucepan. In a separate medium bowl, whisk together the egg yolks. Slowly pour the warm milk mixture into the egg yolks, whisking constantly, then scrape the warmed egg yolks into the saucepan. Stir the mixture constantly with a heatproof spatula over medium heat, scraping the bottom as you stir, until the mixture thickens and coats the spatula.

3. Pour the custard through the strainer into the milk chocolate mixture, add the Cognac, and mix together. Stir over an ice bath until cool.

4. Chill the mixture thoroughly in the refrigerator, then freeze it in your ice cream maker according to the manufacturer's instructions. During the last few minutes of churning, add the cocoa nibs, if using.

PERFECT PAIRINGS: Make Milk Chocolate and Brownie Ice Cream by folding 2 cups (500g) crumbled Chewy-Dense Brownies (page 242) into the just-churned ice cream.

For Milk Chocolate and Chocolate-Covered Peanut Ice Cream, fold in one recipe of Chocolate-Covered Peanuts (page 220).

8 ounces (230g) milk chocolate (with at least 30 percent cocoa solids), finely chopped

1½ cups (375ml) heavy cream

1½ cups (375ml) whole milk

¾ cup (150g) sugar

Big pinch of kosher or sea salt

4 large egg yolks

2 teaspoons Cognac

¾ cup (120g) cocoa nibs or mini dark chocolate chips (optional)

GUINNESS–MILK CHOCOLATE ICE CREAM

Makes about 1 quart (1l)

If you like the hearty taste of Guinness stout, this is the ice cream for you. I was curious as to whether the beer flavor was too strong, so I asked my friend Heather, a knockout whose microscopic waistline belies the fact that the girl really knows her beer, to come by and taste. She gave this one a big thumbs-up, so I sent her home with the whole container. The next day the phone rang. It was Heather, telling me that she offered some to her attractive new neighbor, whom she'd been looking for an excuse to approach, and he was smitten enough to ask her out on a date between spoonfuls. While I can't promise that sharing this ice cream will wind up being an icebreaker for you, I don't see any reason not to give it a try.

---

1. Put the chocolate in a large bowl and set a mesh strainer over the top.

2. Warm the milk, sugar, and salt in a medium saucepan. In a separate medium bowl, whisk together the egg yolks. Slowly pour the warm mixture into the egg yolks, whisking constantly, then scrape the warmed egg yolks into the saucepan. Stir the mixture constantly with a heatproof spatula over medium heat, scraping the bottom as you stir, until the mixture thickens and coats the spatula.

3. Pour the custard through the strainer over the milk chocolate, then stir until the chocolate is melted. Once the mixture is smooth, whisk in the cream, then the Guinness and vanilla. Stir over an ice bath until cool.

4. Chill the mixture thoroughly in the refrigerator, then freeze it in your ice cream maker according to the manufacturer's instructions.

PERFECT PAIRING: Make Guinness-Milk Chocolate and Oatmeal Ice Cream by folding one recipe of Oatmeal Praline (page 225) into the just-churned ice cream.

7 ounces (200g) milk chocolate (with at least 30 percent cocoa solids), finely chopped

1 cup (250ml) whole milk

½ cup (100g) sugar

Pinch of kosher or sea salt

4 large egg yolks

1 cup (250ml) heavy cream

¾ cup (180ml) Guinness stout

1 teaspoon pure vanilla extract

WHITE CHOCOLATE ICE CREAM

Makes about 1 quart (1l)

Sometimes I'm afraid to admit that I love white chocolate. Sticklers want to bicker, "It's not real chocolate." Although that may technically be true, who cares? (French fries aren't really French, yet I'm not giving up those either.) So I don't compare it to dark chocolate, because it's a whole different ball game.

I appreciate white chocolate's creamy-smooth, rich cocoa butter flavor, which is perfect when melted and stirred into ice cream. The result makes a truly outstanding dessert when topped with Sour Cherries in Syrup (page 191), or paired with a bowl of mixed summer berries. And I've yet to come across any chocolate cake that couldn't be improved by a scoop of white chocolate ice cream melting seductively alongside.

8 ounces (230g) white chocolate, finely chopped

1 cup (250ml) whole milk

⅔ cup (130g) sugar

Pinch of kosher or sea salt

5 large egg yolks

2 cups (500ml) heavy cream

1. Put the chocolate in a large bowl and set a mesh strainer over the top.

2. Warm the milk, sugar, and salt in a medium saucepan. In a separate medium bowl, whisk together the egg yolks. Slowly pour the warm milk into the egg yolks, whisking constantly, then scrape the warmed egg yolks into the saucepan. Stir the mixture constantly with a heatproof spatula over medium heat, scraping the bottom as you stir, until the mixture thickens and coats the spatula.

3. Pour the custard through the strainer over the white chocolate. Stir until the white chocolate is completely melted and the mixture is smooth, then stir in the cream. Stir over an ice bath until cool.

4. Chill the mixture thoroughly in the refrigerator, then freeze it in your ice cream maker according to the manufacturer's instructions.

PERFECT PAIRINGS: Make White Chocolate–Cherry Ice Cream by folding very well-drained and coarsely chopped Sour Cherries in Syrup (page 191) or Candied Cherries (page 214) into the just-churned ice cream.

For Black and White Chocolate Ice Cream, layer one recipe of Fudge Ripple (page 231), Dark Chocolate Truffles (page 230), or Stracciatella (page 230) into the just-churned ice cream.

COFFEE ICE CREAM

Makes about 1 quart (1l)

As a kid growing up in puritanical New England, dessert was only an occasional treat. When temptation raised its devilish head, a few scoops of unadulterated ice cream were allowed without much fanfare. Curiously, our reward was often coffee ice cream, one of the few "adult" flavors that kids seem to like as much as grown-ups. There's no shortage of ice cream in my life nowadays. This coffee ice cream is often at the top of my list . . . and in the front of my freezer.

1½ cups (375ml) whole milk

¾ cup (150g) sugar

1½ cups (125g) whole, dark-roasted coffee beans

Pinch of kosher or sea salt

1½ cups (375ml) heavy cream

5 large egg yolks

¼ teaspoon pure vanilla extract

¼ teaspoon finely ground coffee

1. Warm the milk, sugar, whole coffee beans, salt, and ½ cup (125ml) of the cream in a medium saucepan. Once the mixture is warm, cover, remove from the heat, and let steep at room temperature for 1 hour.

2. Rewarm the coffee-infused milk mixture. Pour the remaining 1 cup (250ml) cream into a large bowl and set a mesh strainer on top. In a separate medium bowl, whisk together the egg yolks. Slowly pour the warm coffee mixture into the egg yolks, whisking constantly, then scrape the warmed egg yolks into the saucepan.

3. Stir the mixture constantly with a heatproof spatula over medium heat, scraping the bottom as you stir, until the mixture thickens and coats the spatula. Pour the custard through the strainer and stir it into the cream. Press on the coffee beans in the strainer to extract as much of the coffee flavor as possible, then discard the beans. Mix in the vanilla and the finely ground coffee and stir over an ice bath until cool.

4. Chill the mixture thoroughly in the refrigerator, then freeze it in your ice cream maker according to the manufacturer's instructions.

NOTE: I'm frequently asked about reusing the coffee beans for another purpose. When I make a cup of coffee, I never reuse the grounds because the flavor has been extracted from them. Similarly, with this ice cream, the flavor of the coffee beans is in the custard, so I put the used coffee beans in my compost bucket.

PERFECT PAIRING: Make Coffee Ice Cream Brownie Sundaes by topping brownies (see pages 240 and 242) with scoops of Coffee Ice Cream, then spooning Mocha Sauce (page 179) over the top, and finishing with a final flourish of French Almonds (page 205).

COFFEE FROZEN YOGURT

Makes about 1 quart (1l)

When my father was in the army, he and his bunkmates would eagerly anticipate the care packages that would arrive from home, filled with cookies and cakes. But in lieu of homemade goodies, a Brazilian bunkmate got sacks of dark-roasted coffee beans. He'd carefully prepare single, tiny cups of coffee by crushing a few of the highly prized beans between two metal spoons and then drizzling boiling water over them, creating probably the most labor-intensive cup of coffee ever. But I'm certain the flavor was worth the effort. Make sure the espresso you use for this recipe is excellent; the effort will be appreciated here as well.

1. Whisk together the yogurt, sugar, salt, cream, espresso, and ground coffee.

2. Chill for 2 hours in the refrigerator, then freeze it in your ice cream maker according to the manufacturer's instructions.

1 cup (240g) plain whole-milk yogurt

¾ cup (150g) sugar

Pinch of kosher or sea salt

¾ cup (180ml) heavy cream

1 cup (250ml) brewed espresso, cooled to room temperature

¼ teaspoon finely ground coffee

VIETNAMESE COFFEE ICE CREAM

Makes about 1 quart (1l)

Of all the cuisines in the world, Vietnamese is one of my favorites. At the start of every meal in a Vietnamese restaurant, I order a Vietnamese iced coffee. A glass with a sweet dose of condensed milk is brought to the table with a stainless-steel filter balanced on top, dripping steaming hot coffee into the thick, sweet milk. Once brewed, it all gets stirred up and ice is added. I thought the flavors would make an excellent ice cream, and I was right.

1. Whisk together the condensed milk, espresso, half-and-half, and ground coffee.

2. Chill the mixture thoroughly in the refrigerator, then freeze it in your ice cream maker according to the manufacturer's instructions.

1½ cups (600g) sweetened condensed milk

1½ cups (375ml) brewed espresso (or very strong brewed coffee)

½ cup (125ml) half-and-half

Big pinch of finely ground coffee

GREEN TEA ICE CREAM

Makes about 1 quart (1l)

I once spent a week teaching cooking classes in Japan, and on my day off, two earnest young Japanese women accompanied me around Tokyo to give me a tour of the city. When they told me the itinerary would start at Ralph Lauren, and then we'd go to Gucci, Armani, and Prada, I quickly revised the itinerary to include only food stalls, restaurants, and bakeries. I might not have been as well dressed as I could have been (or as poor), but I was well fed.

We did get some shopping in, though, at the 100-yen discount shops that I discovered on our route. The women giggled while I filled my shopping basket with the teeniest plastic storage containers I'd ever seen; natural bristle kitchen brushes woven around steel wire, each looking like an intricate Japanese sculpture; and candy—such as candy made from a 6-foot-long jellyfish, which I passed on, and green tea–flavored KitKat bars, which I didn't.

But I'm not the only one who loves green tea, which is a good thing, and luckily, matcha can easily be found in almost any shop that carries Japanese or Asian foodstuffs. Matcha has a slightly pungent, powerful taste, but its color is the real showstopper. Frothing the tea helps release the flavor and turns the custard a vivid green.

1. Warm the milk, sugar, and salt in a medium saucepan. Pour the cream into a large bowl and vigorously whisk in the matcha. Set a mesh strainer on top.

2. In a separate medium bowl, whisk together the egg yolks. Slowly pour the warm mixture into the egg yolks, whisking constantly, then scrape the warmed egg yolks into the saucepan. Stir the mixture constantly with a heatproof spatula over medium heat, scraping the bottom as you stir, until the mixture thickens and coats the spatula.

3. Pour the custard through the strainer and stir it into the cream, then whisk it vigorously until the custard is frothy to dissolve the matcha. Stir over an ice bath until cool.

4. Chill the mixture thoroughly in the refrigerator, then freeze it in your ice cream maker according to the manufacturer's instructions.

1 cup (250ml) whole milk

¾ cup (150g) sugar

Pinch of kosher or sea salt

2 cups (500ml) heavy cream

4 teaspoons matcha (green tea powder)

6 large egg yolks

PERFECT PAIRINGS: Make Green Tea and Red Bean Ice Cream by folding one recipe of drained Candied Red Beans (page 200) into the just-churned ice cream. Or prefreeze scoops of Green Tea Ice Cream and sprinkle them with *kinako* (roasted soybean powder, available in stores selling Japanese groceries) before serving.

BLACK CURRANT TEA ICE CREAM

Makes about 1 quart (1l)

There's something about the smoky, potent, and fruity flavor of black currant tea that makes it the perfect complement to chocolate (see Perfect Pairings, below). But if black currants aren't your cup of tea, substitute another aromatic infusion, such as bergamot-scented Earl Grey, floral jasmine, or smoky oolong instead.

---

1. Warm the milk, 1 cup (250ml) of the cream, the sugar, and the tea leaves in a medium saucepan. Cover, remove from the heat, and let steep at room temperature for 1 hour.

2. Rewarm the tea-infused milk. Pour the remaining 1 cup (250ml) cream into a large bowl and set a mesh strainer on top. In a separate medium bowl, whisk together the egg yolks. Slowly pour the warm mixture into the egg yolks, whisking constantly, then scrape the warmed egg yolks into the saucepan. Stir the mixture constantly with a heatproof spatula over medium heat, scraping the bottom as you stir, until the mixture thickens and coats the spatula.

3. Pour the custard through the strainer into the cream, pressing gently on the tea leaves to extract the maximum flavor from them, then discard the leaves. Stir over an ice bath until cool.

4. Chill the mixture thoroughly in the refrigerator, then freeze it in your ice cream maker according to the manufacturer's instructions.

PERFECT PAIRINGS: Make Black Currant Tea and Chocolate Truffle Ice Cream by adding Dark Chocolate Truffles (page 230) to the just-churned ice cream, or swirl this ice cream with Fudge Ripple (page 231) to make Black Currant Tea and Fudge Ripple Ice Cream.

1 cup (250ml) whole milk

2 cups (500ml) heavy cream

¾ cup (150g) sugar

¼ cup (15g) loose black currant tea leaves

5 large egg yolks

FRESH GINGER ICE CREAM

Makes about 1 quart (1l)

The cleansing zing of fresh ginger is always welcome after dinner. Its not-so-subtle spiciness is a pleasing juxtaposition to the cool creaminess of ice cream. Ginger is also reputed to aid digestion, and adding nuggets of soft Dark Chocolate Truffles (page 230) or layering the ice cream with Stracciatella (page 230) would certainly make this "medicine" go down quite easily.

3 ounces (85g) unpeeled fresh ginger

1 cup (250ml) whole milk

2 cups (500ml) heavy cream

¾ cup (150g) sugar

Pinch of kosher or sea salt

5 large egg yolks

1. Cut the ginger in half lengthwise (making it more stable for slicing), and then cut it into thin slices. Place the ginger in a nonreactive medium saucepan. Add enough water to cover the ginger by about ½ inch (12mm) and bring to a boil. Boil for 2 minutes, then drain, discarding the liquid.

2. Return the blanched ginger slices to the saucepan, then add the milk, 1 cup (250ml) of the cream, the sugar, and the salt. Warm the mixture, cover, and remove from the heat. Let steep at room temperature for 1 hour.

3. Rewarm the mixture. Remove the ginger slices with a slotted spoon and discard. Pour the remaining 1 cup (250ml) heavy cream into a large bowl and set a mesh strainer on top.

4. In a separate medium bowl, whisk together the egg yolks. Slowly pour the warm mixture into the egg yolks, whisking constantly, then scrape the warmed egg yolks into the saucepan. Stir the mixture constantly with a heatproof spatula over medium heat, scraping the bottom as you stir, until the mixture thickens and coats the spatula.

5. Pour the custard through the strainer and stir it into the cream. Stir over an ice bath until cool.

6. Chill the mixture thoroughly in the refrigerator, then freeze it in your ice cream maker according to the manufacturer's instructions.

VARIATION: To make Lemon–Fresh Ginger Ice Cream, grind the grated zest of 2 lemons with the sugar in a blender or food processor and warm it with the milk.

PERFECT PAIRINGS: Make Ginger and Candied Lemon Ice Cream by draining a handful of Candied Lemon Slices (page 213), coarsely chopping them, and folding them into the just-churned ice cream.

For Ginger-Gingersnap Ice Cream, mix in one recipe of Speculoos (page 229).

ANISE ICE CREAM

Makes about 1 quart (1l)

If you've never tasted anise and chocolate together, prepare yourself for an unexpected treat. I don't even like anise, but for some improbable reason this is one of my favorite ice creams, especially when nestled alongside a slice of dense chocolate cake or used to fill profiteroles doused in warm chocolate sauce (see the Perfect Pairings, below).

---

1. Toast the anise seeds in a medium saucepan over medium heat for 2 to 3 minutes, stirring occasionally, until fragrant. Transfer the seeds to a plate and let cool. Crush the seeds lightly (not to a powder, just enough to release their fragrance) in a mortar and pestle, or in a sturdy plastic bag with a hammer or rolling pin, and return them to the saucepan.

2. Pour 1 cup (250ml) of the cream and the milk into the saucepan. Add the sugar, honey, and salt. Heat until warm, then cover, remove from the heat, and let steep at room temperature for 1 hour.

3. Rewarm the anise-infused milk mixture. Pour the remaining 1 cup (250ml) cream into a large bowl and set a mesh strainer over the top. In a separate medium bowl, whisk together the egg yolks. Slowly pour the warm anise-infused mixture into the egg yolks, whisking constantly, then scrape the warmed egg yolks into the saucepan. Stir the mixture constantly with a heatproof spatula over medium heat, scraping the bottom as you stir, until the mixture thickens and coats the spatula.

4. Pour the custard through the strainer and stir it into the cream. Discard the anise seeds and stir over an ice bath until cool.

5. Chill the mixture thoroughly in the refrigerator, then freeze it in your ice cream maker according to the manufacturer's instructions.

2 teaspoons anise seeds

2 cups (500ml) heavy cream

1 cup (250ml) whole milk

⅔ cup (130g) sugar

1½ tablespoons good-flavored honey

Pinch of kosher or sea salt

5 large egg yolks

VARIATION: To make Biscotti Ice Cream, warm ½ cup (80g) mixed dark and light raisins with ¼ cup (60ml) Marsala, simmering until the wine is absorbed. Let cool. Coarsely chop ½ cup (65g) toasted almonds (see page 16). During the last few minutes of churning, add the soaked raisins and almonds to the ice cream.

PERFECT PAIRINGS: Make Anise Ice Cream Puffs by tucking scoops of Anise Ice Cream into airy Profiteroles (page 255), then surrounding them with Lean Chocolate Sauce (page 179). Or finely chop Candied Citrus Peel (page 193) made with orange peel and stir it in during the last few minutes of churning to make Orange-Anise Ice Cream.

CINNAMON ICE CREAM

Makes about 1 quart (1l)

Spicy cinnamon sticks give this ice cream a stronger, far more complex flavor than ground cinnamon does. Around the winter holidays, skip the bowl of whipped cream to accompany pumpkin pie or apple crisp and treat your lucky guests to this cinnamon ice cream instead. It's also very good alongside any favorite chocolate dessert, such as devil's food cake or homemade brownies (see pages 240 and 242). To break up the cinnamon sticks, put them in a zip-top freezer bag and whack them with a rolling pin or hammer.

1. Warm the milk, sugar, salt, cinnamon sticks, and 1 cup (250ml) of the cream in a medium saucepan. Once warm, cover, remove from the heat, and let steep at room temperature for 1 hour.

2. Rewarm the cinnamon-infused milk mixture. Remove the cinnamon sticks with a slotted spoon and discard them. Pour the remaining 1 cup (250ml) cream into a large bowl and set a mesh strainer on top.

3. In a separate medium bowl, whisk together the egg yolks. Slowly pour the warm mixture into the egg yolks, whisking constantly, then scrape the warmed egg yolks into the saucepan. Stir the mixture constantly with a heatproof spatula over medium heat, scraping the bottom as you stir, until the mixture thickens and coats the spatula.

4. Pour the custard through the strainer and into the cream. Stir over an ice bath until cool.

5. Chill the mixture thoroughly in the refrigerator, then freeze it in your ice cream maker according to the manufacturer's instructions.

PERFECT PAIRING: Marble (see Marbling, page 93) this ice cream with Aztec "Hot" Chocolate Ice Cream (page 33) to make Aztec Cinnamon-Chocolate Ice Cream.

---

1 cup (250ml) whole milk

¾ cup (150g) sugar

Pinch of kosher or sea salt

Ten 3-inch (8cm) cinnamon sticks, broken up

2 cups (500ml) heavy cream

5 large egg yolks

BUTTERSCOTCH ICE CREAM WITH PEANUT BUTTER, CHOCOLATE, AND PRETZEL BRITTLE

Makes about 1¼ quarts (1¼l)

There seems to be little agreement as to the origin of the word *butterscotch*. Some culinary scholars argue that its name is taken from "butter scorched," a theory worthy of consideration, because making butterscotch requires cooking butter. Yet others assert that the term is derived from the term *butter scoring*, as in "cutting"—not as in, "Dude, I scored some awesome Butterscotch Ice Cream from David!"

So I'd like to offer my own theory, one that's a bit simpler: it's because butterscotch always tastes better with a shot of Scotch in it.

---

1. To make the ice cream, melt the butter in a medium saucepan over low heat. Stir in the brown sugar and salt until well moistened. Increase the heat until the mixture starts to bubble and boil. Cook, stirring constantly, for 1½ minutes. Remove from the heat and add 1 cup (250ml) of the cream. Scrape the butterscotch into a medium to large bowl (one that can fit into a larger bowl, to make an ice bath). Set a mesh strainer over the top.

2. In the same pan, warm the remaining 1 cup (250ml) cream and the milk.

3. In a separate medium bowl, whisk together the egg yolks. Slowly pour the warm cream and milk into the egg yolks, whisking constantly, then scrape the warmed egg yolks into the saucepan. Stir the mixture constantly with a heatproof spatula over medium heat, scraping the bottom as you stir, until the mixture thickens and coats the spatula.

4. Pour the custard through the strainer, into the butterscotch. Add the vanilla and Scotch, then stir over an ice bath until cool.

5. Chill the mixture thoroughly in the refrigerator.

6. To make the brittle, start by stretching a sheet of plastic wrap over a dinner plate. Using two teaspoons, drop teaspoon-size dollops of the peanut butter onto the plate (use one spoon to scoop peanut butter and the other to help scrape it off), leaving spaces between them. Sprinkle the peanuts over and around the gobs of peanut butter, then add the pretzel pieces.

7. Melt the chocolate in a clean, dry bowl set over a pan of barely simmering water, stirring until smooth. Dry the bottom of the bowl, then scrape the chocolate over the peanut butter, peanuts, and pretzels in various places. Use a spatula to spread the chocolate over everything, then put the plate in the freezer until the chocolate is firm and everything is well chilled (which will make it easier to chop).

ICE CREAM

5 tablespoons (70g) butter, salted or unsalted

¾ cup plus 2 tablespoons (160g) packed dark brown sugar

½ teaspoon kosher or sea salt

2 cups (500ml) heavy cream

¾ cup (180ml) whole milk

6 large egg yolks

1 teaspoon pure vanilla extract

2 tablespoons Scotch whisky (or bourbon)

BRITTLE

⅓ cup (90g) crunchy or smooth peanut butter (not natural style)

⅓ cup (50g) roasted peanuts (salted, unsalted, or honey-roasted), coarsely chopped

½ cup (35g) coarsely crumbled pretzel twists

4 ounces (115g) bittersweet, semisweet, or milk chocolate, coarsely chopped

8. Freeze the butterscotch ice cream in your ice cream maker according to the manufacturer's instructions. While it's churning, remove the brittle from the freezer and remove it from the plate, peeling it off the plastic. Place the brittle chocolate-side down on a cutting board and chop it with a chef's knife into bite-size pieces. It'll be a challenge to get them all the same size due to the sticky peanut butter, so don't even try—it's fine to have irregular chunks. Put the pieces in a small bowl and place the pieces back in the freezer. (I usually run my hands through the brittle after I've put the pieces in the bowl, before putting them in the freezer, to help keep them separate. Still, you may want to have a cutting board and chef's knife ready to re-chop them before the final folding-in.)

9. When the ice cream has finished churning, fold in the pieces of brittle.

PERFECT PAIRINGS: Go all out and make Blondie Sundaes, serving this ice cream atop Blondies (page 241) and drizzling everything with Lean Chocolate Sauce (page 179) or Classic Hot Fudge (page 178). You can also use Butterscotch Ice Cream as a base for Butter Pecan Ice Cream: fold in Buttered Pecans (page 216), instead of the peanut butter, chocolate, and pretzel brittle.

DATE, RUM, AND PECAN ICE CREAM

Makes about 1¼ quarts (1¼l)

This is the perfect date ice cream. Ha ha . . . er, sorry about that.

Ahem. Anyway, sweet dates and rum make a good duo, but having lived in San Francisco for many years, where it's often whispered that there's no better way to liven up a pairing than by adding a third element, I offer you this ménage à trois of flavors in one sybaritic ice cream.

Be careful when heating the rum and dates: the rum can flame up, so keep an eye on the action before it gets too hot to handle.

1. To prepare the dates, chop them into ½-inch (2cm) pieces. Combine the date pieces with the rum in a small saucepan and bring to a boil. Remove from the heat and stir. Cover and let macerate at room temperature for at least 4 hours. (The dates can be prepared up to 1 day ahead.)

2. To make the ice cream, warm the milk, sugar, and salt in a medium saucepan. Pour the cream into a large bowl and set a mesh strainer on top.

CONTINUED

DATES

12 dates (4 ounces, 115g), pitted

¼ cup (60ml) dark rum

ICE CREAM

1 cup (250ml) whole milk

⅔ cup (130g) sugar

Big pinch of kosher or sea salt

3. In a separate medium bowl, whisk together the egg yolks. Slowly pour the warm mixture into the egg yolks, whisking constantly, then scrape the warmed egg yolks into the saucepan. Stir the mixture constantly with a heatproof spatula over medium heat, scraping the bottom as you stir, until the mixture thickens and coats the spatula.

4. Pour the custard through the strainer and stir it into the cream. Mix in the vanilla and rum, then stir over an ice bath until cool.

5. Chill the mixture thoroughly in the refrigerator, then freeze it in your ice cream maker according to the manufacturer's instructions. During the last few minutes of churning, add the nuts and date pieces.

NOTE: Feel free to substitute 1 cup (100g) Wet Pecans (variation, page 219) or 1 cup (100g) Spiced Pecans (page 218) for the toasted pecans.

1¼ cups (310ml) heavy cream

6 large egg yolks

½ teaspoon pure vanilla extract

2 tablespoons dark rum

1 cup (100g) pecans, toasted (see page 16) and coarsely chopped (see Note)

CANDIED BACON AND BOURBON ICE CREAM

Makes about 1¼ quarts (1¼l)

I had my first taste of maple-smoked bourbon in Paris, of all places. That's not as surprising as it might seem: the French are the number-one consumers of whiskey in the world. What you might not expect, however, is that there's a world-class Texas barbecue joint in Paris called The Beast. Owner and pit-master Thomas Abramowicz is an exceptionally genial Frenchman who learned his craft in Texas, then spent a couple of years tracking down a smoker before opening his place. In addition to delicious barbecue, The Beast features a world-class collection of bourbons. Thomas once offered me a shot of maple-smoked bourbon, and I was hooked.

This ice cream may sound as curious as Texas barbecue in Paris, but once you taste it, I think you'll agree that it combines the best of two worlds: bits of sweet-smoky bacon along with spoonfuls of bourbon-spiked custard.

1. To make the ice cream, melt the butter in a medium saucepan over medium-high heat. Stir in the brown sugar and salt. Let the mixture come to a low boil and cook for 1½ minutes, stirring frequently. Remove from the heat and add ⅔ cup (160ml) of the cream, stirring until smooth. Scrape the mixture into a large bowl and set a mesh strainer over the top.

ICE CREAM

3 tablespoons butter, salted or unsalted, cubed

¾ cup (135g) packed light brown sugar or maple sugar

¼ teaspoon kosher or sea salt

1⅔ cups (410ml) heavy cream

2. In the same saucepan, warm the remaining 1 cup (250ml) cream and the milk. In a separate bowl, whisk together the egg yolks. Slowly pour the warm cream and milk mixture into the egg yolks, whisking constantly, then scrape the mixture into the saucepan. Stir the mixture constantly with a heatproof spatula over medium heat, scraping the bottom as you stir, until the mixture thickens and coats the spatula.

3. Pour the custard through the strainer and stir it into the butter-cream mixture. Stir over an ice bath until cool. Add the vanilla and cinnamon, then chill the mixture thoroughly in the refrigerator.

4. To make the candied bacon, preheat the oven to 325°F (165°C). Line a baking sheet with aluminum foil and set a wire cooling rack on top.

5. In a small bowl, toss the bacon with the brown sugar, bourbon, cayenne, and several generous turns of black pepper. Line up the bacon strips on the wire rack (they can be touching, to fit them all on) and place in the oven.

6. Bake the bacon for 12 minutes. Using tongs, turn the bacon strips over and bake for another 6 minutes. Turn them again and continue to bake until the strips are a dark mahogany color but are not burnt, about 6 minutes more. Depending on the thickness of your bacon, this may take less or more time, so watch carefully near the end of the recommended baking time.

7. Remove the bacon from the oven, wait 30 seconds, then use the tongs to unstick the strips from the wire rack. Let the bacon cool completely on the wire rack, turning the strips frequently so they don't stick.

8. Add the 3 tablespoons bourbon to the chilled ice cream custard, then freeze the mixture in your ice cream maker according to the manufacturer's instructions. While it's churning, chop the cooled bacon into pea-size pieces. When the ice cream has finished churning, fold in the pieces of candied bacon.

VARIATION: To make Bourbon Pecan Ice Cream, mix one batch of chopped Spiced Pecans (page 218) into the just-churned ice cream.

PERFECT PAIRING: Give this ice cream an extra shot of bourbon by topping it with a spoonful of Whiskey Caramel Sauce (variation, page 190).

1¼ cups (310g) whole milk

6 large egg yolks

½ teaspoon pure vanilla extract

Pinch of ground cinnamon

3 tablespoons bourbon

CANDIED BACON

12 strips (6 ounces, 170g) smoked bacon

⅓ cup (60g) packed light brown sugar

1 tablespoon bourbon

¼ teaspoon cayenne pepper

Freshly ground black pepper

GIANDUJA GELATO

Makes about 1 quart (1l)

On my first visit to Torino, Italy, I arrived in rabid pursuit of gianduja, a confection made from local hazelnuts ground with milk chocolate that is a specialty of the Piedmont region. I was also looking forward to having gianduja gelato at the source. Needless to say, I did not leave disappointed: every bakery, chocolate shop, and *gelateria* offered jars of gianduja for spreading, traditional triangular tablets for nibbling, and by the scoop for licking. I was in hazelnut heaven.

Be sure to toast the hazelnuts well and use top-quality dark milk chocolate with at least 30 percent cocoa solids, for best results.

1. Rub the hazelnuts in a kitchen towel to remove as much of the papery skins as possible, then chop them into pieces the size of lemon seeds in a food processor or blender.

2. Warm the milk with 1 cup (250ml) of the cream, the sugar, and the salt in a saucepan. Once warm, remove from the heat and add the chopped hazelnuts. Cover and let steep at room temperature for 1 hour.

3. Put the milk chocolate in a large bowl. Heat the remaining 1 cup (250ml) cream in a medium saucepan until it just begins to boil. Pour it over the milk chocolate and stir until the chocolate is completely melted and smooth. Set a mesh strainer over the top.

4. Pour the hazelnut-infused milk through a strainer into a medium saucepan, squeezing the nuts firmly with your hands to extract as much of the flavorful liquid as possible. Discard the hazelnuts (see Note).

5. Rewarm the hazelnut-infused mixture. In a separate medium bowl, whisk together the egg yolks. Slowly pour the warm hazelnut mixture into the egg yolks, whisking constantly, then scrape the warmed egg yolks into the saucepan. Stir the mixture constantly with a heatproof spatula over medium heat, scraping the bottom as you stir, until the mixture thickens and coats the spatula.

6. Pour the custard through the strainer and stir it into the milk chocolate mixture. Add the vanilla and stir over an ice bath until cool.

7. Chill the mixture thoroughly in the refrigerator, then freeze it in your ice cream maker according to the manufacturer's instructions.

NOTE: Most of the flavor will have been extracted from the hazelnuts after they're infused in the milk, but if you wish to reuse them, to add crunch to a batch of homemade granola or to mix into a batch of brownies, they can be rinsed well, spread out a baking sheet, and dried out in a low oven.

PERFECT PAIRING: Make Gianduja-Stracciatella Gelato by adding Stracciatella (page 230) to the gelato. Scoop it into Ice Cream Cones (page 250) to serve.

1½ cups (185g) hazelnuts, toasted (see page 16)

1 cup (250ml) whole milk

2 cups (500ml) heavy cream

¾ cup (150g) sugar

¼ teaspoon kosher or sea salt

4 ounces (115g) milk chocolate, finely chopped

5 large egg yolks

⅛ teaspoon pure vanilla extract

CARAMEL "CRACK" ICE CREAM

About 1½ quarts (1½l)

I don't have an addictive personality, except when it comes to caramel. In that case, all bets are off.

The "crack" that makes this ice cream especially crave-worthy is a chocolate-cararmel topping that I discovered more than a decade ago in a recipe by baker Marcy Goldberg. She makes it with matzoh, but I've also seen it made with saltine crackers. The saltines give the topping a slightly soft texture, while adding an extra little kick of salt. If you want a crunchier option, use matzoh.

For the best flavor, cook the caramel until it just starts to burn, then add the butter quickly to stop the cooking at just the right moment. Because of the caramel, this ice cream remains scoopably soft, so you don't need to make a custard base. Feel free to personalize your chocolate-caramel "crack" with other kinds of nuts, such as toasted pecans or roasted peanuts.

---

1. To make the caramel ice cream, warm the cream in a small saucepan, or in the measuring cup in a microwave oven. Once warm, remove from the heat and set aside.

2. In a heavy-bottomed nonreactive saucepan, spread the granulated sugar into an even layer. Set the pan over medium heat and watch it carefully as the sugar warms. When the edges start to liquefy and darken, use a heatproof spatula to gently stir the liquefied sugar toward the center. As the sugar continues to melt, stir it only enough to encourage the sugar to melt evenly; don't stir it too vigorously because you don't want it to crystallize.

3. When the sugar begins to turn a light amber color, tilt the pan or stir the sugar and continue to cook until it darkens to the color of an old penny and begins to smoke. When the caramel looks almost, but not quite, burnt, and smells a bit smoky, turn off the heat and immediately stir in the butter. Stir in the warm cream about ¼ cup (60ml) at a time, scraping the bottom and sides of the pan to dissolve any hard, stubborn bits of caramel, before adding the next ¼ cup (60ml). If the mixture has any lumps after you've added all of the cream, whisk it over low heat until smooth. Stir in the milk, vanilla, and kosher salt and chill thoroughly in the refrigerator.

CARAMEL ICE CREAM

1½ cups (375ml) heavy cream

1⅓ cups (265g) granulated sugar

4 tablespoons (60g) butter, salted or unsalted, cubed, at room temperature

1½ cups (375ml) whole milk

1 teaspoon pure vanilla extract

Big pinch of kosher or sea salt

4. To make the caramel "crack," preheat the oven to 350°F (180°C). Line a rimmed baking sheet with aluminum foil, making sure it goes up and over the sides. Line the bottom of the foil-lined baking sheet with parchment paper.

5. Cover the bottom of the baking sheet with a single layer of matzoh, breaking the crackers into pieces as necessary so they fit as snugly as possible.

6. In a saucepan over medium-high heat, combine the butter and brown sugar and bring the mixture to a boil, stirring until the butter is melted. Turn the heat to low and simmer for 3 minutes. Remove the pan from the heat, stir in the vanilla and kosher salt, then quickly pour the mixture over the matzoh, spreading it evenly with an offset spatula.

7. Bake the matzoh for 15 minutes; if patches are getting too dark, rotate the pan or lower the heat. Remove the baking sheet from the oven and scatter the chocolate chips evenly over the crackers. Let the chocolate melt for 2 minutes, then use an offset spatula to spread it evenly over the matzoh. Sprinkle the top with a gentle flurry of flaky sea salt, then add the almonds evenly over the top. Put the baking sheet in the refrigerator until the chocolate hardens. Once cooled, chop the "crack" into bite-size pieces, about the size of hazelnuts.

8. Freeze the caramel ice cream in your ice cream maker according to the manufacturer's instructions. Once churned, stir in 3 cups (290g) chopped caramel "crack." (You'll have extra "crack," which you can snack on or store in an airtight container in the freezer for up to 2 months.)

NOTE: You'll notice there's an overdose of mix-ins in this ice cream. The strong caramel base stands up well to such a large quantity.

CARAMEL "CRACK"

4 to 6 sheets matzoh, or about 55 saltine crackers (about 175g of either)

1 cup (8 ounces, 230g) unsalted butter

1 cup (180g) packed light brown sugar

½ teaspoon pure vanilla extract

Big pinch of kosher or sea salt

1½ cups (240g) bittersweet or semisweet chocolate chips (or chopped chocolate)

Flaky sea salt

1 cup (80g) sliced almonds, toasted

MAPLE WALNUT ICE CREAM WITH WET WALNUTS

Makes about 1 quart (1l)

I once visited a sugar shack in Canada, a magical place where sticky maple sap was boiled down into glistening maple syrup. I watched the process until I could stand it no more, and then my wildest dreams came true: we sat down to a lunch where everything came to the table drenched with pure, precious maple syrup. And in case there wasn't enough, a big pitcher of warm maple syrup, filled to the brim, also sat within reach so we could help ourselves to as much as we wanted. If my shoulder bag had been syrup-proof, I would have been very tempted to take some of the obvious overflow off their hands.

Maple syrup is graded dark amber or light amber. The darker the syrup, the deeper the flavor, so I always use the darker type, because there's no such thing in my book as "too much maple syrup flavor." Add Wet Walnuts for a double-delivery of the delectable maple flavor, if you can handle it. (Note: I can.)

1. Warm the milk and sugar in a medium saucepan. Pour the cream into a large bowl and set a mesh strainer on top.

2. In a separate medium bowl, whisk together the egg yolks. Slowly pour the warm mixture into the egg yolks, whisking constantly, then scrape the warmed egg yolks into the saucepan. Stir the mixture constantly with a heatproof spatula over medium heat, scraping the bottom as you stir, until the mixture thickens and coats the spatula.

3. Pour the custard through the strainer and stir it into the cream. Add the maple syrup, salt, and vanilla and stir over an ice bath until cool.

4. Chill the mixture thoroughly in the refrigerator, then freeze it in your ice cream maker according to the manufacturer's instructions. During the last few minutes of churning, add the Wet Walnuts.

PERFECT PAIRING: Use Salted Butter Caramel Sauce (page 189) to make Maple Walnut Ice Cream Sundaes, resting the ice cream on Chewy-Dense Brownies (page 242) and topping them off with Candied Cherries (page 214).

1½ cups (375ml) whole milk

2 tablespoons sugar

1½ cups (375ml) heavy cream

5 large egg yolks

¾ cup (180ml) dark amber maple syrup

⅛ teaspoon kosher or sea salt

¼ teaspoon pure vanilla extract

1 batch Wet Walnuts (page 219)

VANILLA FROZEN YOGURT

Makes about 1 quart (1l)

I'm a fan of frozen yogurt, but only if it's homemade. Don't expect this to taste like the frozen yogurt that squirts out of the machine at the airport or a chain shop. That kind is loaded with so much other stuff that any similarity to real yogurt is purely coincidental. Homemade frozen yogurt has a delightful tanginess and is lighter than traditional ice cream. I choose to keep mine pure, relying on good whole-milk yogurt to provide much of the flavor. If you do want to make a denser, richer frozen yogurt, see the variation below that uses strained or Greek yogurt.

1. Mix together the yogurt, sugar, and vanilla. Stir until the sugar is completely dissolved.

2. Chill the mixture for 1 hour in the refrigerator, then freeze it in your ice cream maker according to the manufacturer's instructions.

3 cups (720g) plain whole-milk yogurt

1 cup (200g) sugar

1 teaspoon pure vanilla extract

VARIATION: To make Rich Vanilla Frozen Yogurt, substitute 3 cups (720g) strained yogurt (see box) or Greek-style yogurt for half of the plain whole-milk yogurt called for in the recipe and reduce the amount of sugar to ¾ cup (150g).

PERFECT PAIRING: Yes, you can have yogurt and granola for dessert. Just top a scoop of Vanilla Frozen Yogurt with Honey Crunch Granola (page 204).

IT'S NOT ALL GREEK TO ME

Over the past decade, Greek yogurt has become popular, and widely available. It is thicker and richer than regular whole-milk yogurt and is traditionally made by straining whole-milk yogurt to separate out the watery whey. (Some "Greek yogurts" are thickened with starches or gums, which would be listed in the ingredients. I avoid those.)

When *The Perfect Scoop* was first published, Greek yogurt was something you had to practically go to Greece (or a Greek specialty store) to get. Nowadays it's available in every supermarket, made by a variety of producers, in all sorts of styles and flavors.

I was sure that Greek yogurt would change my frozen-dessert life, and I tested the recipes in this revised edition of the book with it. But I was wrong. After many side-by-side experiments pitting Greek yogurt against regular plain yogurt, I found that once the yogurt base was frozen, it lacked the tangy taste of plain yogurt. Frozen yogurt made with 100 percent Greek yogurt was also overly thick, dense, and chewy, and I didn't prefer it. (The Labneh Ice Cream recipe, page 60, does use strained or Greek yogurt, but I formulated that recipe with honey, which lightens up the texture.)

So I prefer plain whole-milk yogurt for these recipes, but if you wish to use strained yogurt, follow these directions: To make 1 cup (250g) strained yogurt, line a mesh strainer with a few layers of cheesecloth and place the strainer over a deep bowl. Scrape 2 cups (16 ounces, 500g) plain whole-milk yogurt into the cheesecloth. Gather the ends and fold them over the yogurt, then refrigerate for 6 hours.

S'MORES ICE CREAM

Makes about 1½ quarts (1½l)

My first, and only, attempt at being a Boy Scout ended with me kneeling on rocks by a stream, scrubbing burned pots after a campfire dinner while the senior scouts relaxed and ate s'mores. I didn't trek ten miles into the woods weighted down by an overloaded backpack to wash dishes, so I turned in my kerchief.

But these days, I'd walk that far for S'mores Ice Cream, which combines melted chocolate, marshmallows, and spiced cookies or crackers, in each merit badge–worthy scoop. (If the Scouts had offered merit badges for making ice cream, I might have stayed!)

1. To make the ice cream, warm the milk, sugar, and salt in a medium saucepan. Pour the cream into a large bowl and set a mesh strainer on top.

2. In a separate medium bowl, whisk together the egg yolks. Slowly pour the warm mixture into the egg yolks, whisking constantly, then scrape the warmed egg yolks into the saucepan. Stir the mixture constantly with a heatproof spatula over medium heat, scraping the bottom as you stir, until the mixture thickens and coats the spatula.

3. Pour the custard through the strainer and stir it into the cream. Mix in the vanilla, then stir over the ice bath until cool.

4. Chill the mixture thoroughly in the refrigerator, then freeze it in your ice cream maker according to the manufacturer's instructions. Put a large (at least 1½-quart, 1½l) container in the freezer for storing the ice cream.

5. To prepare the mix-ins, while the custard is churning, spread the mini marshmallows on a silicone baking mat, or another heat-resistant surface that's nonstick. Carefully wave a blowtorch over the marshmallows, just enough to brown them. Turn them over with a spatula and continue to torch them until they're as well browned as possible but not burnt. (It's inevitable that a few will get charred.) If you don't have a blowtorch, you can brown the marshmallows under the broiler, turning them as they toast.

6. Spoon some of the Fudge Ripple on the bottom of the chilled container. Strew some of the graham cracker bits and toasted marshmallows over the chocolate, then spread some of the just-churned ice cream over the mix-ins. Continue to layer the ingredients until the container is full. If necessary, stir very, very, gently, just to incorporate the ingredients but not enough to mash everything together. Freeze the ice cream for a few hours until firm enough to scoop.

ICE CREAM

1 cup (250ml) whole milk

⅔ cup (130g) sugar

Pinch of kosher or sea salt

2 cups (500ml) heavy cream

5 large egg yolks

1 teaspoon pure vanilla extract

MIX-INS

4 cups (185g) mini marshmallows (page 232)

Fudge Ripple (page 231), chilled

1 cup (95g) crumbled graham crackers (about 10 crackers), gingersnaps, or Speculoos (page 229)

CARAMEL CORN ICE CREAM

Makes about 1½ quarts (1½l)

Like most Americans, I'm used to popcorn served with melted butter and a flurry of salt, but in France, popcorn is always sugared, even in movie theaters. While pondering why the French don't embrace popcorn with butter and salt—two ingredients they are particularly well-known for—I realized that Americans do eat sweetened popcorn, although we usually coat ours with a sticky layer of toffee and add toasted nuts for crunch. My childhood memories of munching away on caramel corn inspired this ice cream.

Until I mastered this technique for popping every single kernel of popcorn—from my friend Elise Bauer of Simplyrecipes.com (who learned it from her mom)—I had a few dentally detrimental experiences of biting down on unpopped kernels hiding in the bowl. Although I use this caramel corn as the base for ice cream, it's also great for snacking with most of the other ice creams in this book.

---

1. To make the caramel corn, heat the oil in a 4-quart (4l) saucepan with a lid over medium-high heat. Add 3 popcorn kernels. Once they pop, add the remaining kernels, cover the saucepan, and turn off the heat. Let the covered saucepan sit for 30 seconds, then turn the heat back to medium-high. Keep the lid slightly ajar and shake the pan continuously. Once all the kernels have popped, pour the popcorn into a very large heatproof bowl and set the saucepan aside. Add the peanuts to the bowl.

2. Preheat the oven to 200°F (95°C). Lightly grease a rimmed baking sheet with vegetable oil or nonstick cooking spray.

3. Wipe the saucepan clean with paper towels and place it over medium-high heat. Add the butter to the saucepan. Once the butter has melted, stir in the brown sugar, corn syrup, and molasses and let the mixture come to a boil. Boil for 5 minutes, using a heatproof spatula to stir just once or twice to combine the ingredients (don't overstir).

4. Remove the saucepan from the heat and stir in the salt, baking soda, and vanilla. Pour the toffee-like mixture over the popcorn and nuts and fold it in with the spatula until well combined. (The outside of the bowl can get quite hot, so be careful.) Spread the popcorn mixture into an even layer on the prepared baking sheet and bake for 1 hour, stirring every 15 minutes so it doesn't stick.

CONTINUED

CARAMEL CORN

3 tablespoons unflavored vegetable oil (preferably peanut or canola)

⅓ cup (65g) popcorn kernels

1 cup (140g) roasted peanuts (or another type of toasted nuts, such as almonds, pecans, or cashews), salted or unsalted

½ cup (115g) unsalted butter, cubed

1¼ cups (225g) packed light brown sugar

⅓ cup (100g) light corn syrup

1 tablespoon molasses

¾ teaspoon kosher or sea salt

½ teaspoon baking soda

1 teaspoon pure vanilla extract

5. Remove the baking sheet from the oven and let the mixture cool completely on the pan. Once cooled, break the caramel corn into pieces. The caramel corn can be made up to 3 days in advance and stored in an airtight container at room temperature.

6. To make the ice cream, combine the milk, 1 cup (250ml) of the cream, 2 cups (120g) of broken-up caramel corn, and the brown sugar in a saucepan, until the milk is warm and the brown sugar is dissolved. Remove the mixture from the heat, let it cool slightly, then cover and refrigerate for at least 8 hours or up to overnight.

7. Once the mixture is chilled, briskly stir the milk–caramel corn mixture to break up any butterfat on the surface and thin it out slightly. Place the saucepan over medium heat and rewarm the mixture. Strain it through a mesh strainer into a large bowl, pressing on the popcorn to extract as much liquid (and flavor) as possible, then pour the infused milk back into the saucepan. Discard the popcorn, but reserve the bowl and strainer. Add the granulated sugar and salt to the milk in the pan.

8. Pour the remaining 1 cup (250ml) of cream into the large bowl (the same one you strained the caramel corn–infused milk into) and set the mesh strainer on top. In a separate bowl, whisk together the egg yolks. Slowly pour the warm milk mixture into the egg yolks, whisking constantly, then scrape the warmed egg yolks into the saucepan. Stir the mixture constantly with a heatproof spatula over medium heat, scraping the bottom as you stir, until the mixture thickens and coats the spatula.

9. Pour the custard through the strainer and stir it into the cream. Add the vanilla and stir over an ice bath until cool.

10. Chill the mixture thoroughly in the refrigerator, then freeze it in your ice cream maker according to the manufacturer's instructions. While the custard is churning, chop 2 cups (120g) of the caramel corn into bite-size pieces. When the ice cream is finished churning, stir in the chopped caramel corn.

11. Serve the ice cream topped with extra clusters of caramel corn.

PERFECT PAIRINGS: Lean Chocolate Sauce (page 179) or Marshmallow–Hot Fudge Sauce (page 183) are always welcome, ladled generously over the top.

ICE CREAM

1 cup (250ml) whole milk

2 cups (500ml) heavy cream

½ cup (90g) packed light brown sugar

3 tablespoons granulated sugar

Big pinch of kosher or sea salt

6 large egg yolks

½ teaspoon pure vanilla extract

PEANUT BUTTER ICE CREAM

Makes about 1 quart (1l)

Kids love this ice cream. And it's easy enough that they can put it together themselves, with minimal help from Mom or Dad. To make it even more fun, layer in a swirl of grape jam (see variation).

1. Puree the peanut butter, sugar, half-and-half, salt, and vanilla in a blender or food processor until smooth.

2. Chill the mixture thoroughly in the refrigerator, then freeze it in your ice cream maker according to the manufacturer's instructions.

VARIATION: To make Peanut Butter and Jelly Ice Cream, as you transfer the just-churned ice cream from the machine to the storage container, layer it with ¾ cup (240g) of your favorite jam or jelly. (I prefer Concord grape, because I'm sort of a big kid when it comes to this ice cream.)

¾ cup (180g) smooth peanut butter (not natural style)

¾ cup plus 2 tablespoons (180g) sugar

2⅔ cups (660ml) half-and-half

Pinch of kosher or sea salt

⅛ teaspoon pure vanilla extract

ORANGE POPSICLE ICE CREAM

Makes about 1 quart (1l)

This ice cream is for those who are nostalgic for orange-and-cream-flavored Popsicles. If you miss that taste, here's your chance to discover it all over again.

1. In a blender, pulverize the sugar and orange zest until the zest is very fine. Add the orange juice, sour cream, half-and-half, and Grand Marnier and blend until the sugar is completely dissolved.

2. Chill the mixture thoroughly in the refrigerator, then freeze it in your ice cream maker according to the manufacturer's instructions.

PERFECT PAIRING: If you like oranges and cream, dip small scoops of Orange Popsicle Ice Cream into melted white chocolate, following the directions for Tartufi on page 258.

⅔ cup (130g) sugar

Grated zest of 3 oranges, preferably unsprayed

1¼ cups (310ml) freshly squeezed orange juice (from 4 or 5 large oranges)

1 cup (240g) sour cream

½ cup (125ml) half-and-half

2 teaspoons Grand Marnier or another orange liqueur

LABNEH ICE CREAM WITH PISTACHIO-SESAME BRITTLE

Makes about 1¼ quarts (1¼l)

I've been eternally fond of Middle Eastern food ever since my hippie-dippie days of spreading hummus on honey-sweetened whole-wheat pita bread topped with alfalfa sprouts. Once I discovered the cookbooks written by Yotam Ottolenghi and Sami Tamimi, Anissa Helou, and Claudia Rodin, I realized that Middle Eastern cusine is a spectacular world of vibrant foods seasoned with herbs like za'atar, sumac, and saffron; drizzled with olive oil or nutty tahini; and served with tangy labneh (a heavenly dive into a thick cloud of housemade cheese).

I've been fortunate to visit the Middle East, but you can get a taste of the region's signature flavors just by visiting your nearest Middle Eastern grocer. Most sell labneh, which is soft enough to spread on bread (and is especially delicious with olive oil and za'atar) but is sometimes rolled into tight, bite-size rounds. Because store-bought labneh varies in thickness and richness, for this recipe I advise you to make your own, which is easy.

1. To make the ice cream, whisk together the labneh, cream, honey, sugar, and salt. Chill the mixture thoroughly in the refrigerator.

2. To make the pistachio-sesame brittle, line a baking sheet with a silicone baking mat or grease it lightly with vegetable oil. Mix the pistachios and sesame seeds in a small bowl.

3. Spread the sugar in a medium, heavy-bottomed skillet and cook over medium heat, watching it carefully. When it begins to liquefy and darken at the edges, use a heatproof spatula to stir it very gently, encouraging the liquefied sugar around the edges to moisten and melt the sugar crystals in the center.

4. Tilt the pan and stir gently until all the sugar is melted and the caramel begins to smoke. Once it has a deep golden color, remove it from the heat and immediately stir in the nuts and seeds. Scrape the mixture onto the prepared baking sheet and spread it with a spatula into an even layer. Let cool completely. Once cooled, chop the brittle into bite-size pieces with a chef's knife. Store in an airtight container until ready to use.

5. Freeze the labneh mixture in your ice cream maker according to the manufacturer's instructions.

CONTINUED

ICE CREAM

2½ cups (620ml) homemade labneh (see Note) or plain Greek yogurt

1 cup (250ml) heavy cream

6 tablespoons (90ml) good-flavored honey, slightly warmed

¼ cup (50g) sugar

Pinch of kosher or sea salt

PISTACHIO-SESAME BRITTLE

¼ cup plus 2 tablespoons (45g) shelled pistachios

3 tablespoons sesame seeds

½ cup (100g) sugar

NOTE: Make your own labneh by straining 1 quart (1l) plain whole-milk yogurt in a cheesecloth-lined mesh strainer set over a deep bowl for 4 hours in the refrigerator, but no longer. The labneh can be made up to 2 days in advance.

VARIATION: Add a few drops of orange flower water or rose water to the labneh mixture just before freezing, or sprinkle a few drops on top. You can also reserve a little of the chopped brittle to sprinkle on the top of the ice cream when serving.

PERFECT PAIRINGS: Drizzle scoops with chamomile-infused honey: Warm ½ cup (125ml) honey with 2 teaspoons crushed dried chamomile flowers. Remove from the heat and let steep for 15 minutes, or until the flavor is to your satisfaction. Rewarm the honey and strain out the chamomile. Chamomile flowers can be found at natural food stores or Middle Eastern markets. Another option is to replace the chamomile with a little pinch of saffron threads. No need to strain out the saffron threads, which will add a nice color contrast to the flavored honey.

MALTED MILK ICE CREAM

Makes about 1½ quarts (1½l)

I froze lots and lots and lots of ice cream when I wrote the first edition of this book. It was a treat having freshly made ice cream every day, but space in my freezer quickly became an issue. Consequently, I started passing off lots of ice cream to friends, neighbors, local shopkeepers, and, occasionally, a startled delivery man. (I kept a supply of colorful Italian ice cream spoons on hand, to sweeten the deal.) Everyone was more than happy to take a quart off my hands. But I guarded this Malted Milk Ice Cream, saving it all for myself.

The recipe calls for malt powder, which is usually found in the ice cream aisle of your supermarket. Sometimes, however, it's stocked alongside chocolate drink mixes like Ovaltine, which isn't the same thing and shouldn't be used here. The most common brands of malt powder are Carnation and Horlicks. (See Resources, page 259, for online sources.)

1. Warm the half-and-half, sugar, and salt in a medium saucepan. In a large bowl, whisk together the cream, vanilla, and malt powder and set a mesh strainer on top.

2. In a separate medium bowl, whisk together the egg yolks. Slowly pour the warm mixture into the egg yolks, whisking constantly, then scrape the warmed egg yolks into the saucepan. Stir the mixture constantly with a heatproof spatula over medium heat, scraping the bottom as you stir, until the mixture thickens and coats the spatula.

3. Pour the custard through the strainer and whisk it into the malted milk mixture. Stir over an ice bath until cool.

4. Chill the mixture thoroughly in the refrigerator, then freeze it in your ice cream maker according to the manufacturer's instructions. As you remove the ice cream from the machine, fold in the chopped malted milk balls.

PERFECT PAIRINGS: Add crumbled Chewy-Dense Brownies (page 242) or Dark Chocolate Truffles (page 230) for Chocolate–Malted Milk Ice Cream.

1 cup (250ml) half-and-half

¾ cup (150g) sugar

Pinch of kosher or sea salt

2 cups (500ml) heavy cream

¼ teaspoon pure vanilla extract

⅔ cup (90g) malt powder

6 large egg yolks

2 cups (350g) malted milk balls, coarsely chopped

OATMEAL-RAISIN ICE CREAM

Makes about 1 quart (1l)

This ice cream tastes just like a big, moist, chewy oatmeal cookie, thanks to the winning combination of plump raisins and crunchy oatmeal praline folded into a custard made with just the right touch of brown sugar.

1. To prepare the raisins, heat the water and granulated sugar in a small saucepan. Add the raisins and cook over low heat, stirring frequently, until all but about 2 tablespoons (30ml) of the liquid has been absorbed, about 5 minutes. Remove from the heat and add the whiskey. Cover until ready to use.

2. To make the ice cream, warm the milk, granulated sugar, and salt in a medium saucepan. Whisk the cream, brown sugar, and cinnamon together in a large bowl and set a mesh strainer on top.

3. In a separate medium bowl, whisk together the egg yolks. Slowly pour the warm milk mixture into the egg yolks, whisking constantly, then scrape the warmed egg yolks into the saucepan. Stir the mixture constantly with a heatproof spatula over medium heat, scraping the bottom as you stir, until the mixture thickens and coats the spatula.

4. Pour the custard through the strainer and stir it into the cream. Mix in the vanilla and stir over an ice bath until cool.

5. Chill the mixture thoroughly in the refrigerator, then freeze it in your ice cream maker according to the manufacturer's instructions. During the last few minutes of churning, add the raisins and the Oatmeal Praline.

PERFECT PAIRING: Sandwich this ice cream between oatmeal cookies (see page 244) for double-delicious Oatmeal Cookie Ice Cream Sandwiches.

RAISINS

¼ cup (60ml) water

2 tablespoons granulated sugar

½ cup (80g) raisins

2 teaspoons whiskey

ICE CREAM

1 cup (250ml) whole milk

½ cup (100g) granulated sugar

Pinch of kosher or sea salt

2 cups (500ml) heavy cream

⅓ cup (70g) packed light brown sugar

¼ teaspoon ground cinnamon

5 large egg yolks

½ teaspoon pure vanilla extract

1 batch Oatmeal Praline (page 225)

RUM RAISIN ICE CREAM

Makes about 1 quart (1l)

The first time I discovered "gourmet" ice cream, the flavor was rum raisin, made by one of those premium brands that has lots of vowels in its name. Aside from all those vowels, it also had lots and lots of raisins plumped in real, honest-to-goodness rum, and I had never had store-bought ice cream that was so smooth and so creamy. Coincidentally, at about the same time I discovered those little round pints of premium ice cream, I learned a new way to eat ice cream: right from the little round pint container. Which, by strange coincidence (or shrewd marketing), fit perfectly in my hand.

---

1. Heat the raisins, rum, and orange zest in a small saucepan. Let simmer for 2 minutes, then remove from the heat. Cover and let stand for a few hours. (The raisins can be macerated up to 1 day in advance.)

2. Warm the milk, sugar, ½ cup (125ml) of the cream, and salt in a medium saucepan. Pour the remaining 1 cup (250ml) cream into a large bowl and set a mesh strainer on top.

3. In a separate medium bowl, whisk together the egg yolks. Slowly pour the warmed milk into the egg yolks, whisking constantly, then scrape the warmed egg yolks into the saucepan. Stir the mixture constantly with a heatproof spatula over medium heat, scraping the bottom as you stir, until the mixture thickens and coats the spatula.

4. Pour the custard through the strainer and into the cream. Stir over an ice bath until cool, then chill the mixture thoroughly in the refrigerator.

5. When you're ready to freeze the ice cream, drain the raisins over a bowl and reserve the rum. Discard the orange zest. Measure the drained rum and add more, if necessary, so that you have a total of 3 tablespoons (45ml). Stir the rum into the custard.

6. Freeze the mixture in your ice cream maker according to the manufacturer's instructions. During the last few minutes of churning, add the raisins.

PERFECT PAIRING: Make Rum Raisin Vacherins, filling Meringue Nests (page 256) with Rum Raisin Ice Cream topped with Whipped Cream (page 184) and thin strips of Candied Citrus Peel (page 193) made with orange zest.

⅔ cup (100g) raisins

½ cup (125ml) dark rum

1-inch (3cm) strip of orange or lemon zest

¾ cup (180ml) whole milk

⅔ cup (130g) sugar

1½ cups (375ml) heavy cream

Pinch of kosher or sea salt

4 large egg yolks

TIN ROOF ICE CREAM

Makes about 1¼ quarts (1¼l)

Do you know how tin roof ice cream got its name? Neither do I. Nor does anyone else, it seems. I've tried my best to find out but have always come up empty-handed. I do know that it's one of my favorite ice cream combinations, and I've learned to be content with that. Tin roof sundaes are traditionally made of vanilla ice cream topped with chocolate sauce and a scattering of red-skinned Spanish peanuts. I couldn't resist using chocolate-covered peanuts instead and folding them into the ice cream, where they become embedded between layers of gooey fudge ripple.

1. Warm the milk, sugar, salt, and ½ cup (125ml) of the cream in a medium saucepan. With a sharp paring knife, scrape the flavorful seeds from the vanilla bean and add them, along with the pod, to the hot milk mixture. Cover, remove from the heat, and let steep at room temperature for 30 minutes.

2. Rewarm the vanilla-infused mixture. Pour the remaining 1 cup (250ml) cream into a large bowl and set a mesh strainer on top. In a separate medium bowl, whisk together the egg yolks. Slowly pour the warm mixture into the egg yolks, whisking constantly, then scrape the warmed egg yolks into the saucepan. Stir the mixture constantly with a heatproof spatula over medium heat, scraping the bottom as you stir, until the mixture thickens and coats the spatula.

3. Pour the custard through the strainer and stir it into the cream to cool. Remove the vanilla bean, wipe it clean of any egg bits, and add it back to the custard. Add the vanilla extract and stir over an ice bath until cool. Chill the mixture thoroughly in the refrigerator.

4. When you're ready to churn the ice cream, remove the vanilla bean (it can be rinsed and reused). Freeze the ice cream in your ice cream maker according to the manufacturer's instructions. While the ice cream is freezing, chop the peanuts into bite-size pieces. Fold the peanut pieces into the just-churned ice cream and layer it with Fudge Ripple.

PERFECT PAIRING: To make Tin Roof Sundaes, serve this ice cream with plenty of Marshmallow–Hot Fudge Sauce (page 183) and Salt-Roasted Peanuts (page 207), topped off with Candied Cherries (page 214).

¾ cup (180ml) whole milk

¾ cup (150g) sugar

Pinch of kosher or sea salt

1½ cups (375ml) heavy cream

½ vanilla bean, split in half lengthwise

4 large egg yolks

¼ teaspoon pure vanilla extract

¾ cup (100g) Chocolate-Covered Peanuts (page 220)

Fudge Ripple (page 231)

ZABAGLIONE GELATO

Makes about 1 quart (1l)

Zabaglione—a foamy custard of egg yolks, wine, and sugar—is made to order in Italian restaurants. While you wait, you'll hear the frenetic "clang-clack-clang" of the whisk hitting the copper bowl in the kitchen, which adds to the anticipation. Once it's reached a billowy peak, it's heaped into a glass quickly but not necessarily neatly (speed trumps presentation with zabaglione) and brought out to your table, served straight up and warm. In season, you'll often find sliced strawberries buried underneath all that delicious froth. Zabaglione Gelato captures the taste of a true zabaglione in a cool scoop of ice cream without the last-minute flurry of activity, and it's just as good served with lots of juicy strawberries.

1. Warm the milk, sugar, and salt in a medium saucepan. Zest half of the lemon directly into the warm milk. Pour the cream into a large bowl and set a mesh strainer on top.

2. In a separate medium bowl, whisk together the egg yolks. Slowly pour the warm lemon-infused milk into the egg yolks, whisking constantly, then scrape the warmed egg yolks into the saucepan. Stir the mixture constantly with a heatproof spatula over medium heat, scraping the bottom as you stir, until the mixture thickens and coats the spatula.

3. Pour the custard through the strainer and stir it into the cream. Add the Marsala and stir over an ice bath until cool.

4. Chill the mixture thoroughly in the refrigerator, then freeze it in your ice cream maker according to the manufacturer's instructions.

PERFECT PAIRING: Pair Zabaglione Gelato with Mixed Berry Coulis (page 198), or spoon lots of sugared strawberries into a wine goblet and top with a scoop of the ice cream.

1 cup (250ml) whole milk

⅔ cup (130g) sugar

Big pinch of kosher or sea salt

1 lemon, preferably unsprayed

1½ cups (375ml) heavy cream

6 large egg yolks

½ cup (125ml) dry Marsala wine

CHARTREUSE ICE CREAM

Makes about 1 quart (1l)

Maybe I'm not the sharpest knife in the drawer. When I visited the Chartreuse distillery in the French Alps, our guide told us that the precise recipe for the famed herbal liqueur was a closely guarded secret, known only by three brothers who worked at the monastery.

Astounded, I spoke up. "Wow, that's incredible. What is the likelihood of three brothers going into the same business together, as well as becoming monks at the same monastery?" The other guests on the tour simply stopped and looked at me, their mouths agape. Then our guide enlightened me about the "brothers" and we moved on, but not before I overheard a few hushed conversations evaluating my intellect.

This is a very light ice cream, and it's so simple that anyone, regardless of his intelligence level, can put it together easily.

1. Puree the milk, sour cream, sugar, and Chartreuse in a blender or food processor until smooth. Taste, and add a bit more Chartreuse, if desired.

2. Chill the mixture thoroughly in the refrigerator, then freeze it in your ice cream maker according to the manufacturer's instructions.

VARIATION: Substitute another liquor or liqueur for the Chartreuse, such as dark rum, Cognac, or Grand Marnier.

PERFECT PAIRING: Fill Profiteroles (page 255) with Chartreuse Ice Cream, then ladle warm Lean Chocolate Sauce (page 179) over them, and top them with a shower of crisp French Almonds (page 205).

2⅔ cups (660ml) whole milk

1⅓ cups (320g) sour cream

¾ cup (150g) sugar

3 tablespoons (45ml) green Chartreuse liqueur, or to taste

EGGNOG ICE CREAM

Makes about 1 quart (1l)

If you need to liven things up around your holiday table, this tipsy ice cream will do the trick. Warm apple crisp, cranberry upside-down cake, or the ever-popular pumpkin pie—all are improved with a scoop of this frozen version of eggnog melting on top. This will definitely make those obligatory family get-togethers a bit less traumatic . . . and that I can personally attest to.

The simplest way to measure freshly grated nutmeg, which is the only kind you should use, is to fold a sheet of paper in half, reopen it, and grate the nutmeg over the paper. Then fold the paper again to direct the nutmeg into the measuring spoon.

---

1. Warm the milk, sugar, and salt in a medium saucepan. Pour the cream into a large bowl and set a mesh strainer on top.

2. In a separate medium bowl, whisk together the egg yolks. Slowly pour the warm mixture into the egg yolks, whisking constantly, then scrape the warmed egg yolks into the saucepan. Stir the mixture constantly with a heatproof spatula over medium heat, scraping the bottom as you stir, until the mixture thickens and coats the spatula.

3. Pour the custard through the strainer and stir it into the cream. Mix in the nutmeg, brandy, rum, and vanilla and stir over an ice bath until cool.

4. Chill the mixture thoroughly in the refrigerator. Once it's cold, taste it, and grate in more fresh nutmeg if you wish. Freeze in your ice cream maker according to the manufacturer's instructions.

PERFECT PAIRING: Make Eggnog Ice Cream Cups by serving scoops of Eggnog Ice Cream in punch cups, drizzled with Whiskey Caramel Sauce (variation, page 190) and dusted with freshly grated nutmeg.

1 cup (250ml) whole milk

⅔ cup (130g) sugar

Pinch of kosher or sea salt

2 cups (500ml) heavy cream

6 large egg yolks

1 teaspoon freshly grated nutmeg, or to taste

2 tablespoons brandy

2 tablespoons dark rum

2 teaspoons pure vanilla extract

TOASTED ALMOND AND CANDIED CHERRY ICE CREAM

Makes about 1½ quarts (1½l)

Crack open a cherry pit or an apricot pit and you'll discover a tender kernel inside with the pronounced scent of almonds. I took a cue from whatever higher power designed these two flavors together and paired cherries with almonds in one heavenly ice cream.

Be sure to drain the cherries very well in a strainer before folding them into the ice cream. They should be dry and sticky before you chop them up and mix them in.

1. Warm the milk, sugar, salt, and 1 cup (250ml) of the cream in a medium saucepan. Finely chop 1 cup (135g) of the almonds and add them to the warm milk. Cover, remove from the heat, and let steep at room temperature for 1 hour.

2. Strain the almond-infused milk into a separate medium saucepan. Press with a spatula or squeeze with your hands to extract as much flavor from the almonds as possible. Discard the almonds.

3. Rewarm the almond-infused milk. Pour the remaining 1 cup (250ml) cream into a large bowl and set a mesh strainer on top. In a separate medium bowl, whisk together the egg yolks. Slowly pour the warm mixture into the egg yolks, whisking constantly, then scrape the warmed egg yolks into the saucepan. Stir the mixture constantly with a heatproof spatula over medium heat, scraping the bottom as you stir, until the mixture thickens and coats the spatula.

4. Pour the custard through the strainer and stir it into the cream. Stir in the almond extract and stir over an ice bath until cool.

5. Chill the mixture thoroughly in the refrigerator, then freeze it in your ice cream maker according to the manufacturer's instructions. During the last few minutes of churning, add the remaining 1 cup (135g) chopped almonds. When you remove the ice cream from the machine, fold in the chopped cherries.

PERFECT PAIRINGS: Try layering this ice cream with Fudge Ripple (page 231) for Almond, Cherry, and Chocolate Ice Cream, or add Dark Chocolate Truffles (page 230) or Stracciatella (page 230) instead.

1 cup (250ml) whole milk

¾ cup (150g) sugar

Pinch of kosher or sea salt

2 cups (500ml) heavy cream

2 cups (270g) whole almonds, toasted (see page 16) and coarsely chopped

5 large egg yolks

¼ teaspoon pure almond extract

1 cup (200g) well-drained Sour Cherries in Syrup (page 191) or Candied Cherries (page 214), coarsely chopped

CRÈME FRAÎCHE ICE CREAM

Makes about 1 quart (1l)

Crème fraîche is the cultured French cousin to American sour cream, although it's far richer, with a distinct, nutty-tangy-sweet flavor. It was rarely found in the United States until a few years ago, when small-scale cheesemakers and dairies starting making their own.

   This ice cream is made in a slightly different manner than other recipes, because mixing the crème fraîche with the other ingredients too far in advance can cause the whole batch to turn into a whole lot of crème fraîche, perhaps more than you bargained for. So whisk in the crème fraîche right before churning.

1. Place a mesh strainer over a medium bowl and set the bowl in an ice bath.

2. Warm the milk, sugar, and salt in a medium saucepan. In a separate medium bowl, whisk together the egg yolks. Slowly pour the warm milk into the egg yolks, whisking constantly, then scrape the warmed egg yolks into the saucepan. Stir the mixture constantly over medium heat with a heatproof plastic spatula, scraping the bottom as you stir, until the mixture thickens and coats the spatula.

3. Pour the custard through the strainer and stir over the ice bath until cool. Chill the mixture thoroughly in the refrigerator.

4. Once cooled, whisk in the crème fraîche, then freeze the mixture in your ice cream maker according to the manufacturer's instructions.

1 cup (250ml) whole milk

¾ cup (150g) sugar

Big pinch of kosher or sea salt

5 large egg yolks

2 cups (480g) crème fraîche (see Note)

NOTE: Crème fraîche is available at cheese shops and in well-stocked supermarkets. You can make your own version by stirring together 2 cups (500ml) heavy cream and ¼ cup (60ml) buttermilk. Let stand at room temperature for 24 hours, until thick. Refrigerate until ready to use.

VARIATION: If crème fraîche is your refined cousin from France, mascarpone is the rugged Italian uncle from New Jersey that no one in the family likes to talk about. To make Mascarpone Ice Cream, substitute 2 cups (480g) mascarpone for the crème fraîche. Mascarpone Ice Cream makes a terrific affogato: douse a couple of scoops with a shot of warm espresso.

PERFECT PAIRING: Make Cherries Jubilee by warming Candied Cherries (page 214) with 2 tablespoons (30ml) kirsch or curaçao (or another liqueur), and then spoon the warmed cherries over scoops of Crème Fraîche Ice Cream.

TURRÓN ICE CREAM

Makes about 1¼ quarts (1¼l)

While navigating my way through the Barcelona train station, I was suddenly surrounded by a squadron of Spanish police, guns drawn, barking orders at me in Spanish. Armed and ready, they gestured to me to open up the suspiciously overstuffed valise I was hauling behind me.

I carefully unzipped my bulky suitcase, revealing rows and rows of peculiar brown paper–wrapped bundles, neatly lined up inside. An officer demanded that I unwrap one of the rectangular packages, so I slowly tore the paper off the first one, holding it high for all to see. The policemen let down their guns and had a good laugh. My crime? Smuggling home blocks of crispy Spanish *turrón* (nougat).

This ice cream duplicates the taste of turrón with crispy almonds, honey, and a touch of candied orange, and it can be made, without raising any suspicions, in your ice cream maker at home.

---

1. Warm the half-and-half, sugar, honey, and salt in a medium saucepan. Zest the orange directly into the mixture. Pour the cream into a large bowl and set a mesh strainer on top.

2. In a separate medium bowl, whisk together the egg yolks. Slowly pour the warm mixture into the egg yolks, whisking constantly, then scrape the warmed egg yolks into the saucepan. Stir the mixture constantly with a heatproof spatula over medium heat, scraping the bottom as you stir, until the mixture thickens and coats the spatula.

3. Pour the custard through the strainer and stir it into the cream. Add the orange flower water and stir over an ice bath until cool.

4. Chill the mixture thoroughly in the refrigerator, then freeze it in your ice cream maker according to the manufacturer's instructions. As you remove it from the machine, fold in the candied orange peel, almonds, and pistachios.

NOTE: I recommend using thick-cut candied orange peel, which is roughly ¼ inch (6mm) thick. It's available in well-stocked supermarkets and online. You can also use Candied Citrus Peel (page 193) using orange zest, which is finer.

1½ cups (375ml) half-and-half

½ cup (100g) sugar

¼ cup (60ml) good-flavored honey

Pinch of kosher or sea salt

1 orange, preferably unsprayed

1½ cups (375ml) heavy cream

5 large egg yolks

1 teaspoon orange flower water

2 tablespoons chopped candied orange peel (see Note)

⅔ cup (75g) almonds, toasted (see page 16) and very coarsely chopped

¼ cup (30g) shelled unsalted pistachios, very coarsely chopped

GOAT CHEESE ICE CREAM

Makes about 3 cups (750ml)

The first time I ever saw fresh goat cheese was when we started serving it on salads at Chez Panisse in the 1980s. Being in California, and especially being in Berkeley, most of the customers thought it was tofu. Nowadays, goat cheese is far more familiar, and popular, especially in food-fixated Berkeley. Adding goat cheese to ice cream gives it the surprising taste of a blue-ribbon cheesecake. Use a moist, fresh goat cheese rather than an aged one.

1½ cups (375ml) whole milk

⅔ cup (130g) sugar

8 ounces (230g) fresh goat cheese

6 large egg yolks

A few drops freshly squeezed lemon juice (optional)

1. Warm the milk and sugar in a medium saucepan. While the milk is warming, crumble the goat cheese into a large bowl and set a mesh strainer on top.

2. In a separate medium bowl, whisk together the egg yolks. Slowly pour the warm mixture into the egg yolks, whisking constantly, then scrape the warmed egg yolks into the saucepan. Stir the mixture constantly with a heatproof spatula over medium heat, scraping the bottom as you stir, until the mixture thickens and coats the spatula.

3. Pour the custard through the strainer and stir it into the goat cheese. Keep stirring until the cheese is melted, then stir over an ice bath until cool. Taste, and add a few drops of lemon juice if you want more tang.

4. Chill the mixture thoroughly in the refrigerator, then freeze it in your ice cream maker according to the manufacturer's instructions.

PERFECT PAIRING: Mix the cheese course and dessert by serving Goat Cheese Ice Cream with Honey and Walnuts. Toast some very delicious walnut halves (see page 16) and let cool. To serve, drizzle a scoop of Goat Cheese Ice Cream with strongly flavored honey (I like chestnut or lavender honey), then scatter the toasted walnut halves over the top.

CHEESECAKE ICE CREAM

Makes about 3 cups (750ml)

When I began to visit France regularly and locals found out that I was American, they would rhapsodize, "Oh . . . *j'adore le* Philadelphia!" I like Philadelphia just fine, but was puzzled as to why the French had taken to this city so much. It took me a while to realize they were enthralled with our cream cheese, which is indeed worthy of international acclaim. They've adopted cheesecake too, calling it *le gâteau fromage* or simply *le cheesecake.*

1. Cut the cream cheese into small pieces. Zest the lemon directly into a blender or food processor. Add the cream cheese, sour cream, half-and-half, sugar, and salt and puree until smooth.

2. Chill the mixture thoroughly in the refrigerator, then freeze it in your ice cream maker according to the manufacturer's instructions.

PERFECT PAIRING: For Blueberry Cheesecake Ice Cream, layer the ice cream with Blueberry Sauce (page 198).

8 ounces (230g) cream cheese

1 lemon, preferably unsprayed

1 cup (240g) sour cream

½ cup (125ml) half-and-half

⅔ cup (130g) sugar

Pinch of kosher or sea salt

TIRAMISÙ ICE CREAM

Makes about 1¼ quarts (1¼l)

I used to live in Paris above a *huilerie*, a shop that sold top-quality olive oils from all over the world. Because Colette, the owner, had such good taste and an excellent palate, I decided that she would be my primary ice cream taste tester. I also knew that, being French, she'd have absolutely no problem expressing her opinions—good or bad. This was her favorite of all the ice creams I brought her. Her eyes rolled back in her head when she slipped the first spoonful into her mouth. "*Ooh la la,*" she exclaimed, in perfect French.

1. Puree the mascarpone, half-and-half, sugar, salt, liqueur, and brandy together in a blender or food processor until smooth and the sugar is dissolved.

2. Chill thoroughly in the refrigerator, then freeze it in your ice cream maker according to the manufacturer's instructions. As you remove it from the machine, alternate layers of Mocha Ripple with the frozen ice cream in the storage container.

PERFECT PAIRING: Make a classic affogato, which means "drowned" in Italian, by pouring warm espresso over Tiramisù Ice Cream served in a small bowl.

2 cups (450g) mascarpone

1 cup (250ml) half-and-half

⅔ cup (130g) sugar

Pinch of kosher or sea salt

¼ cup (60ml) coffee-flavored liqueur, such as Kahlúa

3 tablespoons brandy or dark rum

Mocha Ripple (variation, page 231)

LAVENDER-HONEY ICE CREAM

Makes about 1 quart (1l)

The Marché d'Aligre is the liveliest market in Paris. In the center, there's a marvelous *épicerie* with bins brimming with things familiar and unusual: various grains and exotic spices, plump dried fruits, organic honey, bars of chocolate, and artisan candies from all over France. It's my one-stop shop for anything *délicieux*!

When I stopped by to get some lavender flowers, José Ferré, the proprietor of La Graineterie du Marché, shooed me away from the display basket in his sunny window and stepped into the back room. A minute later he returned hefting a burlap sack of dark-purple lavender that had just arrived from Provence. He gestured toward the bag, so I stuck my head in and inhaled deeply. The perfumed bouquet of the freshly harvested lavender was ethereal. Of course, those flowers made amazing ice cream.

Try to find the most fragrant lavender flowers you can, wherever you live, and be sure to use flowers that are intended for consumption.

---

1. Heat the honey and 2 tablespoons (4g) of the lavender in a small saucepan. Once warm, remove from the heat and set aside to steep at room temperature for 1 hour.

2. Warm the milk, sugar, and salt in a medium saucepan. Pour the cream into a large bowl and set a mesh strainer on top. Pour the lavender-infused honey through the strainer into the cream and press on the flowers to extract as much flavor as possible. Discard the lavender and set the strainer back over the bowl.

3. In a separate medium bowl, whisk together the egg yolks. Slowly pour the warm mixture into the egg yolks, whisking constantly, then scrape the warmed egg yolks into the saucepan. Stir the mixture constantly with a heatproof spatula over medium heat, scraping the bottom as you stir, until the mixture thickens and coats the spatula.

4. Pour the custard through the strainer and stir it into the cream. Add the remaining 2 tablespoons (4g) lavender flowers and stir over an ice bath until cool.

5. Chill the mixture overnight in the refrigerator. The next day, before churning, strain the mixture, again pressing on the lavender flowers to extract their flavor. Discard the flowers, then freeze the mixture in your ice cream maker according to the manufacturer's instructions.

VARIATION: To make Honey-Sesame Ice Cream, omit the lavender and the steps for infusing lavender flowers in the honey and the custard. Crumble one recipe of Honey-Sesame Brittle (page 224) into the ice cream during the last few minutes of churning.

½ cup (125ml) good-flavored honey

¼ cup (8g) dried or fresh lavender flowers

1½ cups (375ml) whole milk

¼ cup (50g) sugar

Pinch of kosher or sea salt

1½ cups (375ml) heavy cream

5 large egg yolks

PERFECT PAIRING: To make Figs Roasted in Pernod, for 4 to 6 servings, slice 10 fresh figs in half and place them in a baking dish. Drizzle with 3 tablespoons (45ml) good-quality honey (such as lavender honey) and 2 tablespoons (30ml) Pernod. Cover with aluminum foil and bake in a preheated 375°F (190°C) oven for 20 minutes, until tender. Serve the figs warm or at room temperature, along with some of the sauce and a scoop of Lavender-Honey Ice Cream. Top with a few strips of Candied Citrus Peel (page 193) if you like.

ROQUEFORT-HONEY ICE CREAM
Makes about 3 cups (750ml)

This curious combination of flavors will surprise you, as it did the unsuspecting friends I invited over for dinner one night. One guest was so enamored of it that she dug her spoon into the container over and over again, until it was scraped clean. I like to serve this ice cream with warm oven-baked pears. Not only do they taste very good together, but the combination does double duty as the cheese course and dessert.

A few helpful tips: You can replace the Roquefort with your favorite blue cheese. Also, if your honey is very strong, you may wish to use the smaller amount indicated. Be a bit careful when making the custard; because it has no sugar, it will cook quickly.

1. Warm the honey in a small saucepan, then set aside. Crumble the cheese into a large bowl and set a mesh strainer over the top.

2. Warm the milk in a medium saucepan. In a separate medium bowl, whisk together the egg yolks. Slowly pour the warm milk into the egg yolks, whisking constantly, then scrape the warmed egg yolks into the saucepan. Stir the mixture constantly with a heatproof spatula over medium heat, scraping the bottom as you stir, until the mixture thickens and coats the spatula.

3. Pour the custard through the strainer and stir it into the cheese until most of the cheese is melted (some small bits are fine and are rather nice in the finished ice cream, I think). Add the cream and the honey, then stir over an ice bath until cool.

4. Chill the mixture thoroughly in the refrigerator, then freeze it in your ice cream maker according to the manufacturer's instructions.

PERFECT PAIRING: The flavors of this ice cream are enhanced when drizzled with warm honey and served with toasted pecans or walnuts scattered over the top.

6 to 8 tablespoons (90 to 125ml) good-flavored honey

4 ounces (115g) Roquefort or other blue cheese

1 cup (250ml) whole milk

4 large egg yolks

1 cup (250ml) heavy cream

SWEET POTATO ICE CREAM WITH MAPLE-GLAZED PECANS

Makes about 1 quart (1l)

I've spent many a summer night enjoying an ice cream cone, flanked by Mexican and Filipino families and other San Franciscans, at Mitchell's Ice Cream in the city's lively Mission District. This ice cream is inspired by ube, the sweet potato ice cream they serve up in addition to the other exotic flavors. Mitchell's is so popular that the place is just as packed when the inevitable summer fog rolls in and chills the city down as it is when the sun is shining. There's always a line.

Although some of their flavors might be unfamiliar to you (purple yam and lucuma, for example), don't think for a minute that the flavor of this one is too adventurous. Imagine a wedge of creamy spiced pumpkin pie; this ice cream delivers that classic flavor in one neat scoop.

The best sweet potatoes to use have vivid orange flesh. It's sometimes hard to know, so I scrape a bit of the skin off one, just to be sure, before I put them in my shopping basket.

1. Cut the sweet potatoes into 1-inch (3cm) cubes. Place the cubed potatoes in a medium saucepan and cover with water. Bring to a boil, lower the heat to a simmer, and cook for 20 minutes, or until tender when poked with a sharp knife. Drain the sweet potatoes and let cool to room temperature.

2. Pour the milk into a blender and add the brown sugar, sweet potatoes, cinnamon, vanilla, and salt. Puree until very smooth, about 30 seconds. Add lemon juice to taste. Using a flexible rubber spatula, press the mixture through a mesh strainer.

3. Chill the mixture thoroughly in the refrigerator, then freeze it in your ice cream maker according to the manufacturer's instructions. During the last few minutes of churning, add the pecans and their syrup.

PERFECT PAIRINGS: Top with Whiskey Caramel Sauce (variation, page 190) or Pecan-Praline Sauce (page 195).

1 pound (450g) sweet potatoes, peeled

1 cup plus 2 tablespoons (280ml) whole milk

⅔ cup (120g) packed light brown sugar

¼ teaspoon ground cinnamon

½ teaspoon pure vanilla extract

Pinch of kosher or sea salt

A few drops freshly squeezed lemon juice

1 batch Wet Pecans (variation, page 219)

PANFORTE ICE CREAM

Makes about 1 quart (1l)

Fortunately, I once worked with pastry chef Mary Canales. Unfortunately, our time together didn't last long. I was ending my tenure at Chez Panisse, and she was just beginning hers. But I liked her instantly, and we kept in touch. Years later, she opened an ice cream shop, Ici, in Berkeley, and I was thrilled when her ice creams became legendary in the Bay Area. Here's the most popular flavor from her vast repertoire. *Panforte* is an Italian confection, a Tuscan specialty that's dense and delicious. Like the best *panforte*, Mary's ice cream has the perfect balance of spices, toasted almonds, and candied citrus peel.

1. Warm the half-and-half, sugar, and spices in a medium saucepan. Cover, remove from the heat, and let steep at room temperature for 30 minutes.

2. Rewarm the spice-infused mixture. Pour the cream into a large bowl and set a mesh strainer on top. In a separate medium bowl, whisk together the egg yolks. Slowly pour the warm mixture into the egg yolks, whisking constantly, then scrape the warmed egg yolks into the saucepan. Stir the mixture constantly with a heatproof spatula over medium heat, scraping the bottom as you stir, until the mixture thickens and coats the spatula.

3. Pour the custard through the strainer and mix it into the cream. Discard the cinnamon stick. Stir the custard over an ice bath until cool. While it's cooling, warm the honey in a small saucepan, then stir it into the custard.

4. Chill the mixture thoroughly in the refrigerator, then freeze it in your ice cream maker according to the manufacturer's instructions. During the last few minutes of churning, add the candied citrus peel and almonds.

NOTE: I recommend using a mix of thick-cut candied orange, grapefruit, and lemon peel, which is roughly ¼ inch (6mm) thick. They're available in well-stocked supermarkets and online. You can also use Candied Citrus Peel (page 193), made with lemons and oranges.

PERFECT PAIRING: Pair Panforte Ice Cream with a drizzle of Hot Honey (page 202) in the spirit of *panpepato*, the peppy version of panforte.

1 cup (250ml) half-and-half

⅔ cup (130g) sugar

1 cinnamon stick, broken in half

¼ teaspoon ground cloves

¼ teaspoon freshly grated nutmeg

2 cups (500ml) heavy cream

4 large egg yolks

3 tablespoons full-flavored honey

¼ cup (30g) mixed candied citrus peel (see Note)

½ cup (65g) almonds, toasted (see page 16) and coarsely chopped

FRESH APRICOT ICE CREAM

Makes about 1 quart (1l)

If you're lucky enough to live in an area where fresh apricots are bountiful in the summer, be sure to take advantage of their fleeting season by churning up a batch of this ice cream. Don't be put off by apricots that are übersoft, as plump and fragile as an overfilled water balloon, seemingly ready to burst at the slightest touch. Those are the best-tasting fruits.

---

1. Slice open the apricots and remove the pits, then cut each apricot into sixths. Place the apricot pieces with the water in a medium, nonreactive saucepan. Cover and cook over medium heat, stirring occasionally, until the apricots are tender, about 8 minutes. Remove from the heat and stir in the sugar until dissolved. Let cool to room temperature.

2. Once cooled, puree the apricots and any liquid in a blender or food processor until smooth. Taste a big spoonful; if there are any small fibers, press the mixture through a mesh strainer to remove them. Stir in the cream, almond extract, and lemon juice.

3. Chill the mixture thoroughly in the refrigerator, then freeze it in your ice cream maker according to the manufacturer's instructions.

PERFECT PAIRING: It's easy to assemble Apricot Vacherins with Sour Cherries in Syrup. Fill Almond Meringue Nests (page 256) with Fresh Apricot Ice Cream and top with Sour Cherries in Syrup (page 191). You might want to finish them with some Whipped Cream (page 184) and candied French Almonds (page 205).

1 pound (450g) squishy-ripe fresh apricots (10 to 15, depending on size)

½ cup (125ml) water

½ cup (100g) sugar

1 cup (250ml) heavy cream

3 drops pure almond extract

A few drops freshly squeezed lemon juice

ROASTED BANANA ICE CREAM

Makes about 1 quart (1l)

You never know which of your recipes is going to be the one that especially stands out in a cookbook. I didn't know either, until a reader noted that a recipe uncannily similar to this one won a $100,000 grand prize in a magazine cooking contest. I didn't know an ice cream recipe could be worth a hundred thousand dollars. But sure enough, there it was.

Fortunately, you don't have to pay that much to have the recipe. You've already got this book, so for the price of some bananas and a few other groceries, you can have the six-figure goodness without breaking the bank.

---

1. Preheat the oven to 400°F (200°C).

2. Slice the bananas into ½-inch (12mm) pieces and toss them with the brown sugar and butter in a 2-quart (2l) baking dish. Bake for 40 minutes, stirring just once, until the bananas are browned and cooked through.

3. Scrape the bananas and the thick syrup in the baking dish into a blender or food processor. Add the milk, granulated sugar, vanilla, lemon juice, and salt and puree until smooth.

4. Chill the mixture thoroughly in the refrigerator, then freeze it in your ice cream maker according to the manufacturer's instructions. If the chilled mixture is too thick to pour into your machine, whisking will thin it out.

PERFECT PAIRING: Roasted Banana Ice Cream makes a terrific foundation for an updated banana split. Drench the ice cream with warm Classic Hot Fudge (page 178) and add ripe banana slices and Whipped Cream (page 184) or Marshmallow Sauce (page 182). Top it off with a Candied Cherry (page 214), of course!

3 medium ripe bananas, peeled

⅓ cup (60g) packed light brown sugar

1 tablespoon butter, salted or unsalted, cut into small pieces

1½ cups (375ml) whole milk

2 tablespoons granulated sugar

½ teaspoon pure vanilla extract

1½ teaspoons freshly squeezed lemon juice

¼ teaspoon kosher or sea salt

SOUR CHERRY FROZEN YOGURT

Makes about 3 cups (750ml)

What do you say when a nice Jewish boy gives up a promising career as a lawyer to become a self-appointed "amateur gourmet"? "Oy!" his mom probably said.

When the audacious amateur himself, Adam Roberts, used my recipe for Strawberry Frozen Yogurt (page 99) as inspiration for churning up a batch of Sour Cherry Frozen Yogurt, he posted a picture of the results on his blog, amateurgourmet.com. It was an idea too delicious not to include in this book. However, when pressed for minor details like, say, a recipe or exact quantities, Adam played the amateur card and feigned ignorance, forcing a certain professional to do his duty.

Adam now writes sitcoms in sunny Southern California, where sour cherries are probably more abundant than in his former home, New York City. They're different from their sweeter counterparts and sometimes require a bit of foraging to find. Their tiny little pits can easily be slipped out by squeezing the cherries with your fingers or with the help of a cherry pitter.

1. Stem and pit the cherries. Put them in a medium, nonreactive saucepan with the sugar. Cover, bring to a boil, then lower the heat and simmer for 5 minutes, stirring frequently to encourage the juices to flow, until the cherries are tender and cooked through. Remove from the heat and let cool to room temperature.

2. Puree the cooked sour cherries and any liquid in a blender or food processor with the yogurt and the almond extract until slightly chunky but almost smooth.

3. Chill for 2 hours in the refrigerator, then freeze in your ice cream maker according to the manufacturer's instructions.

PERFECT PAIRING: Make Sour Cherry Profiteroles by filling Profiteroles (page 255) with Sour Cherry Frozen Yogurt and topping them off with a few Sour Cherries in Syrup (page 191) and a scribble of Lean Chocolate Sauce (page 179).

1 pound (450g) fresh sour cherries (about 3 cups, measured unpitted)

¾ cup (150g) sugar

1 cup (240g) plain whole-milk yogurt

2 drops pure almond extract

DRIED APRICOT–PISTACHIO ICE CREAM

Makes about 3 cups (750ml)

I love, love, love dried apricots. They're one of my favorite foods on Earth, as long as they're from California. People are often tempted by Turkish and Chinese dried apricots because they're more colorful and fatter (and cheaper), but I find them too sweet, and ice cream made with them lacks the flavor and intensity of their California-grown counterparts.

The combination of pistachio nuts and apricots is particularly good. Don't toast the pistachios or they'll lose their appealing green color. Make sure the ones you're using are fresh and crisp.

1. In a small saucepan, warm the apricots in the wine. Simmer for 5 minutes, cover, remove from the heat, and let stand for 1 hour. Coarsely chop the pistachios.

2. In a blender, puree the apricots with the wine, sugar, half-and-half, and lemon juice until smooth.

3. Chill the mixture thoroughly in the refrigerator, then freeze it in your ice cream maker according to the manufacturer's instructions. During the last few minutes of churning, add the chopped pistachios.

PERFECT PAIRING: You can make Apricot-Pistachio Ice Cream Crêpes by warming Crêpes (page 253) and serving them, folded, on plates, topped with scoops of this ice cream, a drizzling of honey, and a scattering of chopped pistachios.

5 ounces (140g) dried California apricots, quartered

¾ cup (180ml) white wine, dry or sweet

½ cup (70g) shelled unsalted pistachio nuts

⅔ cup (130g) sugar

2 cups (500ml) half-and-half

A few drops freshly squeezed lemon juice

PLUM ICE CREAM

Makes about 1 quart (1l)

For many years, I worked with Lindsey Shere, the founding pastry chef at Chez Panisse in Berkeley, California. She was constantly surprising us with amazing fruits and berries from neighbors' backyards and nearby farms. Without fail, Lindsey would come in one weekend each summer carrying a plastic Tupperware container that, due to its distinctive rounded shape, left no question that it was designed to hold a canned ham. But instead of a ham, inside would be a jumble of tiny, tender, smushed wild plums she had picked. Eaten raw, they were puckery-tart, but once stewed, they made an incredibly flavorful plum ice cream. The canned ham container always gave me a chuckle, and the highlight of my summer was poking fun at her when she walked through the kitchen door with it. Although wild plums may be hard to come by, you can use whatever plums are available with equal success. (And you can store them in whatever kind of container you want. I won't judge.)

1. Slice the plums in half and remove the pits. Cut the plums into eighths and put them in a medium, nonreactive saucepan with the water. Cover and cook over medium heat, stirring occasionally, until the plums are tender, about 8 minutes. Remove from the heat and stir in the sugar until dissolved. Let cool to room temperature.

2. Once cooled, in a blender or food processor, puree the plums with the cream and the kirsch until smooth.

3. Chill the mixture thoroughly in the refrigerator, then freeze it in your ice cream maker according to the manufacturer's instructions.

PERFECT PAIRINGS: To make Plum–Raspberry Swirl Ice Cream, layer the just-churned Plum Ice Cream with Raspberry Swirl Ice Cream (page 100) as you transfer it to a storage container, or make Plum–Blackberry Swirl Ice Cream by substituting blackberries for the raspberries.

1 pound (450g) plums
(about 8 medium plums)

⅓ cup (80ml) water

¾ cup plus 2 tablespoons
(180g) sugar

1 cup (250ml) heavy cream

1 teaspoon kirsch or vodka

PEAR-CARAMEL ICE CREAM

Makes about 1 quart (1l)

This ice cream combines the best of two worlds: deeply caramelized sugar and sweet, juicy pears. Use the ripest, most flavorful pears you can find, because you want the flavor of the pears to stand up to the slightly burnt taste of the caramel. I recommend Comice or Bartlett pears, which have a heady, roselike aroma when ripe. Don't be alarmed if the sugar hardens and crackles when you add the pears. Keep cooking. The liquid from the pears will dissolve any bits of the caramelized sugar that may, at first, seem stubborn. Any resistance will soon melt away.

1. Dice the pears into ¼-inch (6mm) pieces.

2. Spread the sugar in a large, nonreactive, heavy-bottomed saucepan. Cook over medium heat, watching it carefully. When the sugar begins to liquefy and darken at the edges, use a heatproof spatula to very gently stir, encouraging the heat of the liquefied sugar around the edges to moisten and melt the sugar crystals in the center.

3. Once the sugar becomes deep amber, stir in the pear pieces. Some of the caramel will seize and harden; use a heatproof utensil to stir the pears and melt any bits of hard caramel. Continue to cook the pears for 10 minutes, until the pieces are cooked through.

4. Remove from the heat and stir in ½ cup (125ml) of the cream, then mix in the remaining 1½ cups (375ml) cream, along with the salt and lemon juice.

5. Let cool to room temperature, then puree in a blender or food processor until smooth. To remove any tough pear fibers, use a flexible rubber spatula to press the mixture through a mesh strainer.

6. Chill the mixture thoroughly in the refrigerator, then freeze it in your ice cream maker according to the manufacturer's instructions.

3 medium ripe pears, peeled and cored

¾ cup plus 2 tablespoons (180g) sugar

2 cups (500ml) heavy cream

⅛ teaspoon kosher or sea salt

A few drops freshly squeezed lemon juice

VARIATION: For Pear, Caramel, and Ginger Ice Cream, add ⅓ cup (35g) very finely chopped candied ginger during the last few minutes of churning.

PERFECT PAIRING: Make Pear-Caramel Cream Puffs with Salted Butter Caramel and Chocolate Sauces and Buttercrunch Toffee Bits: Fill Profiteroles (page 255) with Pear-Caramel Ice Cream, and set them on a pool of Salted Butter Caramel Sauce (page 189). Scribble Lean Chocolate Sauce (page 179) over the cream puffs, then top with bits of well-crumbled Buttercrunch Toffee (page 223).

FRESH FIG ICE CREAM

Makes about 3 cups (750ml)

Quite a lot of people have never seen a fresh fig. When they do, they invariably ask, "What is that?" Indeed, a majority of the fig harvest gets dried and pureed into filling for the famous bar cookies. But fresh figs have a sweet succulence that can't be matched by their dried counterparts. A fig is ripe when the sides crack and split and a dewy drop of syrupy juice begins to ooze from the hole in the bottom. Once picked, figs don't ripen much further, so try to find figs that are dead-ripe. For best results, use Black Mission figs, which will give the ice cream a lovely violet color.

---

1. Remove the hard stem ends from the figs, then cut each fig into eight pieces. Put the figs in a medium, nonreactive saucepan with the water, and zest the lemon directly into the saucepan. Cover and cook over medium heat, stirring occasionally, until the figs are tender, 8 to 10 minutes. Remove the lid, add the sugar, and continue to cook, stirring frequently, until the figs have a jamlike consistency.

2. Remove from the heat and let cool to room temperature. Once cooled, puree the fig paste in a blender or food processor with the cream and the lemon juice. Taste, then add more lemon juice if desired.

3. Chill the mixture thoroughly in the refrigerator, then freeze it in your ice cream maker according to the manufacturer's instructions.

2 pounds (1kg) fresh figs (about 20 figs)

½ cup (125ml) water

1 lemon, preferably unsprayed

¾ cup (150g) sugar

1 cup (250ml) heavy cream

½ teaspoon freshly squeezed lemon juice, or to taste

PRUNE-ARMAGNAC ICE CREAM

Makes about 1 quart (1l)

One winter I visited my friend Kate Hill, who lives in Gascony, a region in France famous for its tasty prunes, *les pruneaux d'Agen*. As a means of prying me away from her cozy kitchen hearth, where I could happily eat cassoulet and drink Armagnac all day by the fire, we decided to do something cultural and visit the local prune museum. It was all rather exciting: an entire museum full of educational displays on the history of prunes, including informative dioramas showing the various phases of prune production. We ended our visit with a thrilling film explaining prune cultivation and harvesting, which was a real nail-biter.

On our way out, near the prune-filled gift shop (where there was a comic book about a prune-fueled superhero . . . I'm not kidding), was a shrine with a jar holding what they claimed was the world's oldest prune, dating back to the mid-1800s. For this recipe, you should use prunes that are wrinkled but not necessarily that old, and be alert that it's become *au courant* to call them dried plums in America.

---

1. To prepare the prunes, put the prune pieces in a small saucepan with the Armagnac and the sugar. Heat until the Armagnac starts bubbling. Let cook at a low boil for about 1 minute, until most of the Armagnac is absorbed, then remove from the heat and cover. Let stand for at least 2 hours. (The prunes can be macerated a few days in advance.)

2. To make the ice cream, puree the prunes and any liquid in a food processor or blender along with the sour cream, milk, sugar, lemon juice, and vanilla. Pulse the mixture until it's almost smooth, with a few bits of prune remaining.

3. Chill the mixture thoroughly in the refrigerator, then freeze it in your ice cream maker according to the manufacturer's instructions.

PERFECT PAIRING: If you've never had prunes and chocolate together, try studding this ice cream with Dark Chocolate Truffles (page 230).

PRUNES

6 ounces (170g) pitted prunes (about 20 large prunes), cut into quarters

½ cup (125ml) Armagnac

2 tablespoons sugar

ICE CREAM

1 cup (240g) sour cream

1 cup (250ml) whole milk

½ cup (100g) sugar

1½ teaspoons freshly squeezed lemon juice

½ teaspoon pure vanilla extract

OLIVE OIL ICE CREAM

Makes about 1 quart (1l)

My well-meaning hostess, knowing that I had come to Italy to sample chocolate and gelato, planned a special dinner in my honor. As we drove to the restaurant, she turned to me and said, "We've arranged a special dinner just for you. Each and every course is going to have chocolate in it!" Gulp.

Dinner was, um, interesting, and chocolate was indeed incorporated into each and every course—except for dessert! However, the chef presented us with a reassuring selection of house-made ice creams, including one flavored with a fruity, locally pressed olive oil.

Olive oil ice cream pairs remarkably well with summer fruits such as strawberries or roasted apricots, and if you use a fruity Spanish Arbequina olive oil, you'll find this ice cream is sublime drizzled with Lean Chocolate Sauce (page 179). Or just serve it with a few threads of extra-virgin olive oil scribbled over the top, flecked with a few grains of flaky sea salt.

---

1. Warm the milk, sugar, and salt in a medium saucepan. Pour the cream into a large bowl and set a mesh strainer on top.

2. In a separate medium bowl, whisk together the egg yolks. Slowly pour the warm mixture into the egg yolks, whisking constantly, then scrape the warmed egg yolks into the saucepan. Stir the mixture constantly with a heatproof spatula over medium heat, scraping the bottom as you stir, until the mixture thickens and coats the spatula.

3. Pour the custard through the strainer and stir it into the cream. Vigorously whisk the olive oil into the custard until it's well blended, then stir over an ice bath until cool.

4. Chill the mixture thoroughly in the refrigerator, then freeze it in your ice cream maker according to the manufacturer's instructions.

1⅓ cups (330ml) whole milk

½ cup (100g) sugar

Pinch of kosher or sea salt

1 cup (250ml) heavy cream

6 large egg yolks

½ cup (125ml) fruity extra-virgin olive oil

VARIATION: For Lemon–Olive Oil Ice Cream, very, very finely grate the zest of 1 lemon, preferably unsprayed, into the olive oil and warm it gently. Remove from the heat and let it infuse while you make the custard. Whisk the oil along with the zest into the ice cream custard.

PERFECT PAIRING: To make Honey-Roasted Apricots to serve alongside, for 6 servings, halve 12 fresh apricots and remove the pits. Arrange them cut-side down in a baking dish and drizzle with 3 tablespoons (45ml) honey, ⅓ cup (90ml) white wine, and ½ vanilla bean, split lengthwise. Bake uncovered in a 400°F (200°C) oven for 15 to 20 minutes, until the apricots are tender, basting them with their juices during baking. Serve the apricots with a scoop of ice cream and some French Almonds (page 205).

ORANGE–SZECHWAN PEPPER ICE CREAM

Makes about 1 quart (1l)

After a big meal, when I feel like I can't eat another bite, my taste buds seem to come back to life if I'm presented with a dessert that's been infused with an intriguing flavor, such as Szechwan pepper. Curiosity has a way of perking up my appetite. This ice cream starts off comfortably, with the familiar flavor of orange, and then comes alive with a spritzy kick from the Szechwan peppercorns. If you want to give them even more flavor, toast the peppercorns in a dry skillet over medium heat, stirring frequently, until they become fragrant. Let cool before grinding.

1. Coarsely grind the Szechwan peppercorns in a mortar and pestle, or place them in a heavy-duty freezer bag and crack them with a rolling pin or hammer.

2. Heat the milk, ½ cup (125ml) of the cream, and the sugar with the crushed Szechwan peppercorns in a medium saucepan. Zest the oranges directly into the saucepan. Once warm, cover, remove from the heat, and let steep at room temperature for 1 hour.

3. Rewarm the Szechwan pepper–infused mixture. Pour the remaining 1 cup (250ml) heavy cream into a large bowl and set a mesh strainer on top.

4. In a separate medium bowl, whisk together the egg yolks. Slowly pour the warm mixture into the egg yolks, whisking constantly, then scrape the warmed egg yolks into the saucepan. Stir the mixture constantly with a heatproof spatula over medium heat, scraping the bottom as you stir, until the mixture thickens and coats the spatula.

5. Pour the custard through the strainer and stir it into the cream. Stir over an ice bath until cool.

6. Chill the mixture thoroughly in the refrigerator, then freeze it in your ice cream maker according to the manufacturer's instructions.

VARIATIONS: For Orange-Cardamom Ice Cream, substitute 2 teaspoons cardamom seeds, crushed, for the Szechwan pepper. For Orange-Clove Ice Cream, substitute 10 to 15 crushed whole cloves (depending on how clovey you want your ice cream) for the Szechwan pepper.

PERFECT PAIRING: Serve with Mixed Berry Coulis (page 198).

3 tablespoons (10g) Szechwan peppercorns

1½ cups (375ml) whole milk

1½ cups (375ml) heavy cream

1 cup (200g) sugar

4 oranges, preferably unsprayed

6 large egg yolks

BLUEBERRY FROZEN YOGURT

Makes about 1 quart (1l)

When I wrote my first baking book, I told the story of the blueberry bush my father planted when I was growing up. As soon as the berries would ripen, the wily and evil blackbirds would come and snag any and all berries before I got to taste even one. It was an early lesson in disappointment (there were many more to come, but that was the first).

When I returned home, just after my sister sold the house and was moving away, I noticed that the lone berry bush was still there, still devoid of berries. Although I gave up hope a long time ago, I considered warning the family moving in not to get their hopes up for any ripe blueberries. But I decided to let them find out on their own. They'll learn the same lesson I did, and end up buying blueberries at the store, where the blackbirds can't get them.

---

1. In a blender or food processor, blend together the yogurt, sugar, and blueberries. Press the mixture through a mesh strainer to remove the seeds. Stir in the kirsch and lemon juice.

2. Chill the mixture for 1 hour in the refrigerator, then freeze it in your ice cream maker according to the manufacturer's instructions.

VARIATION: To make a richer version, substitute 1½ cups (360g) Greek-style yogurt or strained yogurt (see page 55) for the plain yogurt.

To make Raspberry Frozen Yogurt, puree 2 cups (480g) plain whole-milk yogurt, ¾ cup (150g) sugar, and 2 cups (240g) fresh or frozen raspberries with 1 teaspoon freshly squeezed lemon juice. Press the mixture through a mesh strainer to remove the seeds. Chill for 1 hour, then freeze in your ice cream maker.

PERFECT PAIRING: Serve scoops of Blueberry Frozen Yogurt in Honey-Cornmeal Ice Cream Cones (variation, page 252).

1½ cups (360g) plain whole-milk yogurt

¾ cup (150g) sugar

3 cups (340g) blueberries, fresh or frozen

1 teaspoon kirsch

2 teaspoons freshly squeezed lemon juice

SUPER LEMON ICE CREAM

Makes about 1 quart (1l)

This recipe comes from Barbara Tropp, the woman who introduced many Americans to the wonders of Chinese cooking. She was deservedly popular in the food community and left us too soon, leaving many great recipes as her legacy, including this famous lemon ice cream. It was passed on to me by Susan Loomis, a dear friend we had in common. After eating my first spoonful, I immediately found another reason to love, and miss, Barbara. The flavor is superbly lemony and clean . . . and as zesty as Barbara was herself.

1. Zest the lemons directly into a food processor or blender. Add the sugar and blend until the lemon zest is very fine. Add the lemon juice and blend until the sugar is completely dissolved. Blend in the half-and-half and salt.

2. Chill the mixture for 1 hour in the refrigerator, then freeze it in your ice cream maker according to the manufacturer's instructions.

PERFECT PAIRINGS: Make Mock Lemon Meringue Pie by folding Marshmallows (page 232) into the just-churned ice cream or by topping it off with fluffy Marshmallow Sauce (page 182). Give this ice cream a tropical twist by marbling it with Mango Sorbet (page 112) or add colorful contrast with Raspberry Sherbet (pge 138).

2 lemons, preferably unsprayed

½ cup (100g) sugar

½ cup (125ml) freshly squeezed lemon juice (from about 3 lemons)

2 cups (500ml) half-and-half

Pinch of kosher or sea salt

MARBLING

Marbling together several flavors of ice cream and sorbet is a great way to multitask your scoops. Start off by picking any two (or more) flavors that sound complementary. Chocolate, vanilla, and strawberry ice creams combined will make Neapolitan ice cream, for example. Toasted Coconut Ice Cream (page 105) and Mango Sorbet (page 112), when marbled together, become a combination that's as welcome as an afternoon—or an entire week—on a tropical beach. Get the idea?

Make and churn the ice creams or sorbets you plan to marble. Once they're churned and while they're still relatively soft, take a separate container and alternate large scoopfuls of the ice creams or sorbets, one after the other, rapping the container on the counter to release any air pockets as you go. Avoid stirring, which will muddy the flavors and colors. When you're done, cover the container and freeze until solid.

If your ice cream maker requires 24 hours in the freezer between batches, remove the previously frozen ice cream from the freezer to soften a bit before marbling it with the second batch.

LEMON-SPECULOOS ICE CREAM

Makes about 1½ quarts (1½l)

Belgians have their own version of gingersnaps, called speculoos (SPEC-ou-looze). They're meant to be nibbled alongside the copious amounts of beer that Belgians drink, which was one of the many lessons I learned when I went to chocolate school there. Belgians like their beer so much that outdoor beer gardens are busy all year long, even during the freezing cold winters. We had to brush the snow off our table to put down our glasses! The good news is that you don't have to worry about your beer getting warm.

Back home, I found that speculoos go equally well with lemon ice cream when the cookies are crumbled and folded in. Like Belgian beer, this can be consumed any time of the year and it's especially good when served frosty cold.

1. Zest the lemons directly into a food processor or blender. Add the sugar and blend until the lemon zest is very fine.

2. Warm the milk with the lemon-scented sugar, ½ cup (125ml) of the heavy cream, and the salt in a medium saucepan. Cover, remove from the heat, and let infuse for 1 hour.

3. Rewarm the lemon-infused mixture. Pour the remaining 1½ cups (375ml) cream into a large bowl and set a mesh strainer on top.

4. In a separate medium bowl, whisk together the egg yolks. Slowly pour the warm lemon-infused milk into the egg yolks, whisking constantly, then scrape the warmed egg yolks into the saucepan. Stir the mixture constantly with a heatproof spatula over medium heat, scraping the bottom as you stir, until the mixture thickens and coats the spatula.

5. Pour the custard through the strainer and stir it into the cream. Discard the lemon zest and stir over an ice bath until cool.

6. Chill the mixture thoroughly in the refrigerator, then freeze it in your ice cream maker according to the manufacturer's instructions. As you remove the ice cream from the machine, fold in the crumbled speculoos.

PERFECT PAIRING: Because speculoos are meant to be enjoyed with beer, try pairing this ice cream with a fruity Belgian beer for dessert. I'm particularly fond of kriek, a sour-cherry beer, which you can find in well-stocked supermarkets and liquor stores.

3 large lemons, preferably unsprayed

¾ cup (150g) sugar

1 cup (250ml) whole milk

2 cups (500ml) heavy cream

Pinch of kosher or sea salt

5 large egg yolks

1 batch Speculoos (page 229), crumbled

PEACH ICE CREAM

Makes about 1 quart (1l)

This is the first ice cream that springs to mind when people nostalgically recall hand-cranked fruit-flavored ice creams from their past. For those of us old enough to remember a time before electric ice cream machines, we took turns churning away at the White Mountain with its wooden bucket and oversized handle that got harder to turn the closer the ice cream got to being ready. Our efforts were rewarded after we finally wiped away the salt-crusted ice, removed the lid, and dove in with spoons.

An effortless way to peel peaches is to cut an X in their bottoms and then lower them into a pot of boiling water for about 20 seconds. Using a slotted spoon, transfer the peaches to a colander and shock them by rinsing under cold water. When cool enough to handle, you'll find their fuzzy peels just slip right off.

---

1. Peel the peaches, slice them in half, and remove the pits. Cut the peaches into chunks and add them with the water to a medium, nonreactive saucepan. Cover and cook over medium heat stirring once or twice, until the peaches are soft and cooked through, about 10 minutes. Remove from the heat, stir in the sugar, and then cool to room temperature.

2. Once cooled, puree the peaches and any liquid in a blender or food processor with the sour cream, heavy cream, vanilla, and lemon juice until slightly chunky but almost smooth.

3. Chill the mixture thoroughly in the refrigerator, then freeze it in your ice cream maker according to the manufacturer's instructions.

1⅓ pounds (600g) ripe peaches (about 4 large peaches)

½ cup (125ml) water

¾ cup (150g) sugar

½ cup (120g) sour cream

1 cup (250ml) heavy cream

¼ teaspoon pure vanilla extract

A few drops freshly squeezed lemon juice

VARIATION: To make Nectarine Ice Cream, simply substitute nectarines for the peaches. There's no need to peel the nectarines, because their tender skins soften during cooking.

PERFECT PAIRING: Make a Peaches and Cream Compote. Peel and slice several peaches (allow 2 peaches for 4 people), then toss the slices with a sprinkle of sugar and let stand for about 30 minutes, until juicy. Put a scoop each of the Peach Ice Cream and Crème Fraîche Ice Cream (page 72) in bowls and pile peach slices around them.

PEACH FROZEN YOGURT

Makes about 3 cups (750ml)

I make this with plain, unstrained yogurt. The peach puree is so velvety thick, this frozen yogurt has a lovely consistency without any additional richness.

1. Peel the peaches, slice them in half, and remove the pits. Cut the peaches into chunks and add them with the water to a medium, nonreactive saucepan. Cover and cook over medium heat, stirring occasionally, until the peaches are soft and cooked through, about 10 minutes. Remove from the heat, stir in the sugar, and then chill in the refrigerator.

2. When the peaches are cool, puree them in a food processor or blender with the yogurt until slightly chunky but almost smooth. Mix in the lemon juice.

3. Freeze the mixture in your ice cream maker according to the manufacturer's instructions.

PERFECT PAIRING: Serve Peach Frozen Yogurt with a summertime Mixed Berry Coulis (page 198).

1½ pounds (675g) ripe peaches (about 5 large peaches)

½ cup (125ml) water

¾ cup (150g) sugar

1 cup (240g) plain whole-milk yogurt

A few drops freshly squeezed lemon juice

TWEAKING THE TANG

Frozen yogurt is a popular alternative to ice cream not only because it's less rich but also because it has an appealing, lively acidity. When paired with fruits, its flavors are highlighted by the contrast between sweet and tart.

After yogurt has been sweetened and churned, that tang can become less pronounced. To add a bit of extra zing to frozen yogurt, stir ¼ teaspoon of citric acid into the mix (for any recipe that yields 1 quart, 1l). Citric acid, which is naturally found in citrus fruits, is sold in crystallized form; it resembles coarse salt. You can find it online, and some pharmacists carry it. You can also use Fruit Fresh, which is used by canning enthusiasts to raise acidity and prevent browning; it is available in supermarkets. Citric acid is a prominent ingredient in Fruit Fresh, but it is not the only one. So you may want to sprinkle in a little more of it than if using pure citric acid.

STRAWBERRY–SOUR CREAM ICE CREAM

Makes about 1¼ quarts (1¼l)

Pastel-pink fresh strawberry ice cream is a classic and, along with chocolate and vanilla, is an American favorite. I'm a big fan of any kind of berries served with tangy sour cream, but I think strawberries are the most delicious, especially when frozen into a rosy scoop. Macerating the strawberries beforehand magically transforms even ho-hum berries into fruits that are brilliantly red. Try to eat this ice cream soon after it's been churned.

---

1. Slice the strawberries and toss them in a bowl with the sugar and vodka, stirring until the sugar begins to dissolve. Cover and let stand at room temperature for 1 hour, stirring every so often.

2. Pulse the strawberries and their liquid with the sour cream, heavy cream, and lemon juice in a blender or food processor until slightly chunky but almost smooth.

3. Chill the mixture for 1 hour in the refrigerator, then freeze it in your ice cream maker according to the manufacturer's instructions.

1 pound (450g) fresh strawberries, rinsed and hulled

¾ cup (150g) sugar

1 tablespoon vodka or kirsch

1 cup (240g) sour cream

1 cup (250ml) heavy cream

½ teaspoon freshly squeezed lemon juice

STRAWBERRY FROZEN YOGURT

Makes about 1 quart (1l)

This frozen yogurt is a snap to put together, and is especially welcome in the summer, when you may want to limit your time in a warm kitchen. But don't let its ease of preparation fool you—this vibrantly colored frozen yogurt provides the biggest blast of strawberry flavor imaginable.

---

1. Slice the strawberries into small pieces. Toss them in a bowl with the sugar and vodka (if using), stirring until the sugar begins to dissolve. Cover and let stand at room temperature for 1 hour, stirring every so often.

2. Puree the strawberries and their liquid with the yogurt and lemon juice in a blender or food processor until smooth. If you wish, press the mixture through a mesh strainer to remove any seeds.

3. Chill the mixture for 1 hour in the refrigerator, then freeze it in your ice cream maker according to the manufacturer's instructions.

PERFECT PAIRING: For Strawberry Frozen Yogurt Meringues, fill Meringue Nests (page 256) with Strawberry Frozen Yogurt. Add a dollop of Whipped Cream (page 184) and surround the frozen yogurt and meringue shell with lots of sliced sweetened strawberries, adding a few raspberries or mango slices if you like.

1 pound (450g) fresh strawberries, rinsed and hulled

⅔ cup (130g) sugar

2 teaspoons vodka or kirsch (optional)

1 cup (240g) plain whole-milk yogurt

1 teaspoon freshly squeezed lemon juice

RASPBERRY SWIRL ICE CREAM

Makes about 1½ quarts (1½l)

I have a particular soft spot for the very fit, young men at my local fish market who wake early each morning to unpack, debone, and clean cold fish all day long. Because their freezer has a much larger capacity than mine, and their capacity for eating ice cream follows suit, I got into the habit of bringing them lots of ice creams and sorbets that I was testing for this book. Each time I'd bring them another flavor, they'd drop whatever work they were doing, rip off the lid, and dig right in. They liked this Raspberry Swirl Ice Cream the most, and it earned me VIP status. Now, I get the quickest and most helpful service of anyone who shops at that fish store.

For best results, layer the just-churned ice cream with the raspberry swirl and avoid stirring it, to preserve the colorful contrast between the frozen vanilla custard and the gorgeous swirl of raspberries.

---

1. To make the ice cream, warm the milk, sugar, and salt in a medium saucepan. Pour the cream into a large bowl and set a mesh strainer over the top.

2. In a separate medium bowl, whisk together the egg yolks. Slowly pour the warm milk into the egg yolks, whisking constantly, then scrape the warmed egg yolks into the saucepan. Stir the mixture constantly with a heatproof spatula over medium heat, scraping the bottom as you stir, until the mixture thickens and coats the spatula.

3. Pour the custard through the strainer and stir it into the cream. Add the vanilla and stir over an ice bath until cool. Chill thoroughly in the refrigerator.

4. To make the raspberry swirl, an hour or so before churning the ice cream, using a fork, mash the raspberries (if using frozen raspberries, let them thaw a bit first), sugar, and vodka until the berries are juicy but nice-size chunks remain. Chill until ready to use.

5. Freeze the ice cream custard in your ice cream maker according to the manufacturer's instructions. As you remove it from the machine, layer it in the container with spoonfuls of the chilled raspberry swirl mixture.

VARIATION: To make Blackberry Swirl Ice Cream, substitute blackberries for the raspberries and add 1 teaspoon freshly squeezed lemon juice to the mixture.

PERFECT PAIRINGS: Sandwich Raspberry Swirl Ice Cream between Oatmeal Ice Cream Sandwich Cookies (page 244) or Chocolate Ice Cream Sandwich Cookies (page 245).

ICE CREAM
1 cup (250ml) whole milk

⅔ cup (130g) sugar

Pinch of kosher or sea salt

1½ cups (375ml) heavy cream

5 large egg yolks

½ teaspoon pure vanilla extract

RASPBERRY SWIRL
1½ cups (160g) raspberries, fresh or frozen

3 tablespoons sugar

1 tablespoon vodka

RASPBERRY ICE CREAM

Makes about 1 quart (1l)

Raspberry ice cream is one of life's most unabashed luxuries. I prefer to strain out the seeds, which interfere with the sublime smoothness and pleasure of this ice cream. To do so, puree the raspberries in a food processor, then press the puree through a mesh strainer with a flexible rubber spatula, or use a food mill. This recipe requires 1½ cups (375ml) of puree, so you'll need to begin with about 6 cups (750g) of fresh or frozen raspberries.

1. Warm the half-and-half and sugar in a medium saucepan. Pour the cream into a large bowl and set a mesh strainer over the top.

2. In a separate medium bowl, whisk together the egg yolks. Slowly pour the warm half-and-half into the egg yolks, whisking constantly, then scrape the warmed egg yolks into the saucepan. Stir the mixture constantly with a heatproof spatula over medium heat, scraping the bottom as you stir, until the mixture thickens and coats the spatula.

3. Pour the custard through the strainer and stir it into the cream. Mix in the raspberry puree and lemon juice, then stir over an ice bath until cool.

4. Chill the mixture thoroughly in the refrigerator, but to preserve the fresh raspberry taste, churn the ice cream within 4 hours.

PERFECT PAIRING: Italians dip scoops of ice cream in pure, dark chocolate, creating Tartufi (page 258), or truffles of ice cream. Serve Raspberry Ice Cream and Tartufi with White Chocolate Sauce (page 184).

1½ cups (375ml) half-and-half

1 cup (200g) sugar

1½ cups (375ml) heavy cream

4 large egg yolks

1½ cups (375ml) strained raspberry puree

1 tablespoon freshly squeezed lemon juice

PASSION FRUIT ICE CREAM

Makes about 3 cups (750ml)

As a smart shopper, I like to outwit unsuspecting produce clerks who don't know any better that mark down passion fruits that are ugly and deeply wrinkled. These "flaws" actually indicate that they're perfectly ripe and ready to use. I buy any and all, whether I need them right away or not, because the pulp freezes beautifully. You can find passion fruits in well-stocked supermarkets and Latin markets, although you can also find good-quality, unsweetened frozen passion fruit pulp in some specialty stores and online (see Resources, page 259). I like to add a drop or two of pure orange extract to augment the passion fruit flavor, but if unavailable, you can substitute a few swipes of freshly grated orange zest.

To extract the pulp, cut each passion fruit in half at the equator and scoop the pulp and seeds into a nonreactive strainer set over a bowl. Use a flexible rubber spatula to press and extract as much of the precious pulp as possible, until the seeds look dry. You can freeze the fragrant pulp or use it right away. I like to add a few seeds back to the just-churned ice cream, for looks, so be sure to save a few.

---

1. Mix together the passion fruit pulp and ½ cup (125ml) of the cream in a large bowl. Set a mesh strainer over the bowl.

2. Warm the milk, sugar, salt, and remaining ½ cup (125ml) cream in a medium saucepan. In a separate medium bowl, whisk together the egg yolks. Slowly pour the warm mixture into the egg yolks, whisking constantly, then scrape the warmed egg yolks into the saucepan. Stir the mixture constantly with a heatproof spatula over medium heat, scraping the bottom as you stir, until the mixture thickens and coats the spatula.

3. Pour the custard through the strainer and stir it into the passion fruit and cream mixture. Mix in a few drops of orange extract, if using, then stir over an ice bath until cool.

4. Chill the mixture thoroughly in the refrigerator, then freeze it in your ice cream maker according to the manufacturer's instructions. Add a spoonful of passion fruit seeds to the custard during the last few minutes of churning, if you wish.

½ cup (125ml) fresh or frozen passion fruit pulp (from 6 to 8 fresh passion fruits), plus a spoonful of passion fruit seeds (optional)

1 cup (250ml) heavy cream

6 tablespoons (90ml) whole milk

7 tablespoons (85g) sugar

Pinch of kosher or sea salt

3 large egg yolks

A few drops pure orange extract or grated zest of 1 small orange (optional)

AVOCADO ICE CREAM

Makes 1 quart (1l)

I never tasted an avocado until I was a teenager on my first trip to California. There, I was served a salad piled with chunks of avocado—which were soft, oily, and pea green. I tried to spear the offending slices to get them off my plate, but they resisted my persistent jabs and kept sliding away. Those luscious tidbits were trying to tell me something, and I regret the loss of so many avocados that I could have loved, before I finally fell for them.

If you're hesitant to try avocado ice cream, let my foolhardy prejudice be a lesson to you. The best avocados are the pebbly-skinned Hass variety. When ripe, the flesh should give just a little when pressed and the bit of stem should pop off easily. And be sure to try the *batido de aguacate con leche* in the Perfect Pairing at the end of the recipe. It is unbelievably delicious.

---

1. Slice the avocados in half and pluck out the pits. Scoop out the flesh with a spoon and cut it into little pieces. In a blender or food processor, puree the avocado pieces with the sugar, sour cream, heavy cream, lime juice, and salt until the sugar is dissolved and the mixture is smooth.

2. Freeze immediately in your ice cream maker according to the manufacturer's instructions.

PERFECT PAIRING: A great summertime refresher is *batido de aguacate con leche*, milk shakes popular in South and Central America. For each serving, put 2 scoops (4 ounces, 115g) Avocado Ice Cream in a blender along with ½ cup (125ml) milk, 2 teaspoons sugar, 3 ice cubes, and a squirt of freshly squeezed lime juice. Blend until smooth, then pour into a glass. A shot of espresso can be added as well.

3 medium ripe Hass avocados (about 1½ pounds, 675g)

¾ cup (150g) sugar

1 cup (240g) sour cream

½ cup (125ml) heavy cream

1 tablespoon freshly squeezed lime juice

Big pinch of kosher or sea salt

BASIL ICE CREAM

Makes about 1 quart (1l)

One of my favorite pastry chefs in Paris is Jacques Genin, who has earned accolades for his *tarte au citron*. When you take that first bite of it, you'll immediately understand why. For one thing, it's unusually puckery, thanks to Jacques making the filling with fresh limes, rather than lemons. The other is the hint of fresh basil in the citrusy filling, giving it a slight anise-like accent.

This ice cream is wonderful to make in the summer when bunches of fresh basil are abundantly available at the market. It goes particularly well with a slice of lemon tart, paired with Super Lemon Ice Cream (page 93), or served with Strawberries in Lemon Syrup (see Perfect Pairing, below).

1. Using a blender or small food processor, puree the basil leaves with the sugar and 1 cup (250ml) of the cream until the leaves are ground as fine as possible. Pour about half of the basil mixture into a large bowl and add the remaining 1 cup (250ml) cream. Set a mesh strainer on top.

2. Warm the remaining half of the basil mixture in a medium saucepan along with the milk and salt. In a separate medium bowl, whisk together the egg yolks. Slowly pour the warm mixture into the egg yolks, whisking constantly, then scrape the warmed egg yolks into the saucepan. Stir the mixture constantly with a heatproof spatula over medium heat, scraping the bottom as you stir, until the mixture thickens and coats the spatula.

3. Pour the custard through the strainer and stir it into the cream. Zest the lemon directly into the custard, then stir over an ice bath until cool.

4. Chill the mixture thoroughly in the refrigerator, then freeze it in your ice cream maker according to the manufacturer's instructions.

PERFECT PAIRING: Try Basil Ice Cream paired with Strawberries in Lemon Syrup. For 4 servings, in a small saucepan, combine 1 cup (250ml) water and ¼ cup (50g) sugar with the grated zest of 1 lemon. Bring to a boil and cook, stirring, until the sugar is dissolved. Remove from the heat, pour into a bowl, and let cool to room temperature. Hull and quarter 1 pound (450g) of fresh strawberries. Add them to the lemon syrup and let macerate in the refrigerator for 1 to 4 hours. To serve, spoon the strawberries and some lemon syrup into shallow bowls and float a scoop of Basil Ice Cream in the center.

1 cup (25g) packed fresh basil leaves

¾ cup (150g) sugar

2 cups (500ml) heavy cream

1 cup (250ml) whole milk

Pinch of kosher or sea salt

5 large egg yolks

1 lemon, preferably unsprayed

TOASTED COCONUT ICE CREAM

Makes about 1 quart (1l)

I'll admit that my favorite selection from the shiny white Good Humor truck that cruised our neighborhood was simply called "coconut": vanilla ice cream on a stick, coated with lots of sweet shredded coconut. Just hearing the bells as the truck rounded the corner to our street sent me racing to my mother, to cajole 35¢ out of her, so I could buy one.

On the last fateful day that I'd ever see the Good Humor man, the bully next door decided to spray him with water from a garden hose as he circled our block. For safety reasons, the trucks were outfitted so they couldn't drive very fast so even though the driver repeatedly floored the gas pedal, he couldn't outrun the bully who followed him with the water-spewing hose.

The driver beat hasty retreat and never came back. Being blackballed by the Good Humor man made that the worst summer of my life. I don't know what happened to the neighborhood bully, but now that I'm an adult I can have coconut-flavored ice cream whenever I want. And I do.

---

1. Preheat the oven to 350°F (175°C). Spread the coconut on a rimmed baking sheet and bake for 5 to 8 minutes, stirring frequently so it toasts evenly. Remove from the oven when it's nice and fragrant and golden brown.

2. In a medium saucepan, warm the milk, 1 cup (250ml) of the cream, the sugar, and the salt, then add the toasted coconut. Use a paring knife and scrape all the vanilla seeds into the warm milk, then add the pod as well. Cover, remove from the heat, and let steep at room temperature for 1 hour.

3. Rewarm the coconut-infused mixture. Set a mesh strainer over another medium saucepan and strain the coconut-infused liquid through the strainer into the saucepan. Press down on the coconut very firmly with a flexible rubber spatula to extract as much of the flavor from it as possible. Remove the vanilla bean pieces (rinse and reserve them for another use) and discard the coconut.

4. Pour the remaining 1 cup (250ml) heavy cream into a large bowl and set the mesh strainer on top. In a separate medium bowl, whisk together the egg yolks. Slowly pour the warm coconut-infused mixture into the egg yolks, whisking constantly, then scrape the warmed egg yolks into the saucepan. Stir the mixture constantly with a heatproof spatula over medium heat, scraping the bottom as you stir, until the mixture thickens and coats the spatula.

5. Pour the custard through the strainer and stir it into the cream. Mix in the vanilla extract and stir over an ice bath until cool.

6. Chill the mixture thoroughly in the refrigerator, then freeze it in your ice cream maker according to the manufacturer's instructions.

1 cup (70g) dried shredded coconut, preferably unsweetened

1 cup (250ml) whole milk

2 cups (500ml) heavy cream

¾ cup (150g) sugar

Big pinch of kosher or sea salt

1 vanilla bean, split in half lengthwise

5 large egg yolks

½ teaspoon pure vanilla extract or 1 teaspoon rum

FRESH MINT ICE CREAM

Makes about 1 quart (1l)

Standing in front of an immense, intricately carved wooden door in Fez, Morocco, my guide handed me a big bunch of fresh mint, shoving it firmly under my nose and telling me not to move it from there . . . or I'd be sorry. Sure enough, when the gate swung open and we entered the tannery, I kept my face deeply buried in the mint, as advised, and was happy for the good advice. Afterward, I didn't want to part with the bunch because I love the aroma of mint so much.

Even better than using it as an air freshener, mint makes a wonderfully invigorating ice cream. I've planted mint in gardens, against the warnings of friends who say it'll take over before I know it, but I never had a problem using it all. And they've never had a problem eating the ice cream I made from it, either.

1. Warm the milk, sugar, 1 cup (250ml) of the cream, and the salt in a small saucepan. Add the mint leaves and stir until they're immersed in the liquid. Cover, remove from the heat, and let steep at room temperature for 1 hour.

2. Strain the mint-infused mixture through a mesh strainer into a medium saucepan. Press on the mint leaves to extract as much of the flavor as possible, then discard the mint leaves. Pour the remaining 1 cup (250ml) heavy cream into a large bowl and set the strainer on top.

3. Rewarm the mint-infused mixture. In a separate medium bowl, whisk together the egg yolks. Slowly pour the warm mint liquid into the egg yolks, whisking constantly, then scrape the warmed egg yolks into the saucepan. Stir the mixture constantly with a heatproof spatula over medium heat, scraping the bottom as you stir, until the mixture thickens and coats the spatula.

4. Pour the custard through the strainer and stir it into the cream. Stir over an ice bath until cool.

5. Chill the mixture thoroughly in the refrigerator, then freeze it in your ice cream maker according to the manufacturer's instructions.

PERFECT PAIRINGS: Make Girl Scout–Style Ice Cream Sandwiches by using Chocolate Ice Cream Sandwich Cookies (page 245) to surround scoops of Fresh Mint Ice Cream. You can also get that same chocolate-mint cookie effect by layering the just-churned ice cream with a swirl of Fudge Ripple (page 231), Stracciatella (page 230), or crumbled bits of Chewy-Dense Brownies (page 242).

---

1 cup (250ml) whole milk

¾ cup (150g) sugar

2 cups (500ml) heavy cream

Pinch of kosher or sea salt

2 cups (80g) lightly packed fresh mint leaves

5 large egg yolks

CHAPTER 3

Sorbets and Sherbets

No matter how full I am, I'm always ready to dig in to a bowl of ice-cold sorbet after dinner. There's something both cleansing and exhilarating about a spoonful of homemade sorbet—the pure flavor of spectacular fresh fruit ends any meal on a perfect note. The best fruit sorbets heighten the taste of the fresh fruit. By adding a touch of sweetness, and perhaps a squeeze of lemon juice, you can brighten fruit flavors, making them "pop" with even more intensity than the fruit itself.

You'll find no better inspiration for churning out a superb sorbet than your local market. When I see fragrant, tree-ripened peaches, tangy limes, or blood oranges with their deep-scarlet juice, I can't resist turning them into sorbet, capturing their essence in each perfect scoop. The best-tasting fruit sorbets are made from fruits at their peak of ripeness.

You'll notice that my sorbets have just a few ingredients. Many are made with fruit and just enough sugar to augment their natural sweetness and to keep them smooth once frozen. I use their simplicity as a springboard for ideas to dress them up and create desserts that I find work just as well after a casual supper as they do after a more elaborate feast. One of my very favorite desserts to bring to the table is chilled soup bowls cradling seasonal fruit—slices of peaches, plums, nectarines, or pears, or citrus segments perhaps mixed with mango, pineapple, passion fruit pulp, and fresh berries—with a scoop of sorbet or sherbet resting in the middle. You can be creative and pair whatever fruits you like. But be sure to offer some nice cookies alongside, or dress the sorbet up with a tangle of Candied Citrus Peel (page 193) on top.

The difference between a sorbet and a sherbet can be elusive. Technically, sorbets have no milk or cream, but sherbets often have milk or buttermilk added. (Some versions may have beaten egg whites folded in.) But these definitions are not set in stone, and I've seen the terms used interchangeably, even by professionals.

Most sorbets and sherbets will benefit by being taken out of the freezer about 5 minutes before you plan to serve them, to soften them up to just the right serving temperature. Sorbets tend to freeze much harder than ice cream because they have very little fat and fruit is composed primarily of water. Of course, you could eat them right out of the machine as well, which I've been known to do.

MANGO SORBET

Makes about 1 quart (1l)

One evening, after wasting the afternoon on the sofa flipping through the television channels, I stopped when I came across a not-very-well-choreographed procession of statuesque, exotically beautiful women parading across a stage. After a few minutes of riveted attention, I realized that I'd happened upon the Miss Martinique pageant.

Once the glamorous gals had strutted their stuff wearing barely there bikinis, teetering around on precariously steep high heels (it seemed the smaller the swimsuit, the higher the heels), the contest concluded with the host posing the all-important question about why the pageant was so vital for promoting world peace and understanding. One of the contestants flashed her big, toothy smile, looked right into the camera, and responded, "Because beauty is the key to communication."

With a thought-provoking answer like that, awarding the crown to anyone else would have been a crime. And sure enough, she won. But maybe she got mixed up and was talking about mangoes, the other beauties of the tropics. Their vibrant red exterior and glowing orange pulp do indeed communicate that beauty and good taste aren't just on the outside, but inside as well.

---

1. Peel the mangoes and cut the flesh away from the pit. Cut the flesh into chunks and put them in a blender with the sugar, water, lime juice, rum, and salt. Squeeze the mango pits hard over the blender to extract as much of the pulp and juice as possible. Puree the mixture until smooth. Taste, then add more lime juice or rum, if desired.

2. Chill the mixture thoroughly in the refrigerator, then freeze it in your ice cream maker according to the manufacturer's instructions.

PERFECT PAIRINGS: Mango Sorbet is terrific served along with a cool scoop of Toasted Coconut Ice Cream (page 105) or marbled (see Marbling, page 93) with Raspberry Sherbet (page 138).

2 large, ripe mangoes
(about 2 pounds, 1kg)

⅔ cup (130g) sugar

⅔ cup (160ml) water

4 teaspoons freshly
squeezed lime juice,
plus more to taste

1 tablespoon dark rum,
plus more to taste

Pinch of kosher or sea salt

GREEN APPLE AND SPARKLING CIDER SORBET

Makes about 3 cups (750ml)

Years ago, I was toiling away in a restaurant kitchen when one day a widely televised celebrity chef who had a reputation for being rather, um, obnoxious stopped by. I was minding my own business, caught in a Zen-like state while peeling a case of apples and, naturally, generating a huge pile of peels, which I tossed into the garbage as I went. (This was before we started composting.) He walked by, looked in the garbage, and reprimanded me: "Don't you know you're throwing away the best part?"

My infamous sarcasm got the best of me, so I offered to wrap them up for him to take home. I'm pretty sure it was that moment that effectively killed my television cooking career. All kidding (and sarcasm) aside, the peels do indeed have a lot of flavor, so I include them when infusing the apples in this sorbet. Hopefully, this recipe will make amends to the offended chef, and who knows? Maybe someday, you'll see me peeling away on prime time, too.

1. Quarter the apples and remove the cores and seeds. Cut the unpeeled apples into 1-inch (3cm) chunks.

2. Combine the cider, sugar, and water in a medium, nonreactive saucepan and bring to a boil. Add the apples, turn the heat to low, and cover. Simmer the apple chunks for 5 minutes, then turn off the heat and let the apples steep until cooled to room temperature.

3. Pass the apples and their liquid through a food mill fitted with a fine disk, or use a coarse-mesh strainer set over a bowl and press firmly on the apples to extract all their pulp and liquid. Discard the apple peels—they've given up their flavor at this point. Add the lemon juice. Taste and add more if you wish, because sparkling apple ciders can vary in sweetness.

4. Chill the mixture thoroughly in the refrigerator, then freeze it in your ice cream maker according to the manufacturer's instructions.

4 Granny Smith or green Pippin apples (about 2 pounds, 1kg), preferably unsprayed

2 cups (500ml) sparkling dry apple cider, with or without alcohol (see Note)

⅓ cup (65g) sugar

½ cup (125ml) water

½ teaspoon freshly squeezed lemon juice, or to taste

NOTE: California-produced nonalcoholic sparkling apple cider is available at most supermarkets in the fruit juice aisle. There are also a number of French and American sparkling ciders with alcohol on the market. If buying French, brut (dry) cider is preferable to doux (sweet).

PERFECT PAIRING: Pour shots of Calvados, the powerful apple brandy from Normandy, over scoops of Green Apple and Sparkling Cider Sorbet for serving after dinner. Poire Williams, or pear eau de vie, also works well.

APPLE-GINGER SORBET

Makes about 1 quart (1l)

Few folks are as opinionated about all things apple as Frank Browning, whom I've dubbed the Apple Autocrat. Frank grew up on an apple farm in Kentucky, which nurtured his headstrong, Southern-style convictions regarding apples. He offered this recipe from *An Apple Harvest*, which he cowrote with Sharon Silva, but absolutely insisted that I make it only in the fall, when good-tasting, red-skinned apples are in abundance. So wait I did.

Okay . . . I didn't wait. But please don't tell Frank. I made this during the spring using Jonagold apples, which worked great. And although Frank insisted I use Gewürztraminer, I made it with a dry Riesling instead (blame my rebellious Yankee spirit). So feel free to use any tasty red-skinned apple, but don't use the bland Red Delicious variety or you might get yourself a Kentucky-style comeuppance.

1. Cut the unpeeled apples, cores and all, into 1-inch (3cm) chunks. Put the apples and the wine in a large, nonreactive saucepan. Crush the piece of ginger with the side of a cleaver and add it to the apples. Cover and bring to a boil. Lower the heat and simmer for 15 minutes, stirring once or twice, until the apples are tender.

2. Remove the knob of ginger and pass the apples and their liquid through a food mill fitted with a fine disk, or use a coarse-mesh strainer and press firmly on the apples to extract all their pulp and liquid into a container. Discard the peels and seeds.

3. Stir the sugar into the warm apple mixture until dissolved.

4. Chill the mixture thoroughly in the refrigerator, then freeze it in your ice cream maker according to the manufacturer's instructions.

4 red-skinned apples (about 2 pounds, 1kg), preferably unsprayed

2 cups (500ml) Riesling or Gewürztraminer

½-ounce (15g) piece fresh ginger, about 1 inch (3cm)

⅔ cup (130g) sugar

PEAR SORBET

Makes about 1 quart (1l)

Use fragrant pears that are buttery ripe and slightly soft to the touch. You'll be glad you did when you taste how good this simple sorbet is. Pears are one of the only fruits that ripen off the tree, so if your pears are rock hard when you buy them, chances are they'll transform into sweet, sorbet-worthy fruits in a few days. When ripe and ready to use, pears exude a strong, unmistakable sweet pear fragrance at the bottom end. Bartlett, Comice, and French butter pears are varieties that I recommend.

4 ripe pears (about 2½ pounds, 1.25kg), peeled and cored

1¼ cups (310ml) water

⅔ cup (130g) sugar

1 teaspoon freshly squeezed lemon juice

1. Cut the pears into 1-inch (3cm) chunks. Put them in a large, nonreactive saucepan along with ½ cup (125ml) of the water. Cover and cook over medium-high heat for 15 minutes, stirring occasionally, until the pears are cooked through and tender when poked with a paring knife.

2. Transfer the cooked pears to a blender and add the remaining ¾ cup (180ml) water, the sugar, and the lemon juice. Puree until smooth. You should have 2 cups (500ml) of puree.

3. Chill the mixture thoroughly in the refrigerator, then freeze it in your ice cream maker according to the manufacturer's instructions.

VARIATION: For Pear-Ginger Sorbet, add ¼ cup (25g) very finely chopped candied ginger to the sorbet during the last few minutes of churning.

PERFECT PAIRINGS: Serve Pear Sorbet with a scoop of Chocolate Sorbet (page 126) or chocolate ice cream (see pages 30 and 32).

CANTALOUPE SORBET

Makes about 2 cups (500ml)

My friend, and cookbook author, Susan Loomis says that finding a perfect melon is like finding love—you need to try many before you land on the right one. The best way to pick a cantaloupe is to find one that has lots of netting around the outside and a sweet, compelling scent that makes you want to slice it open and dive right in. Follow those tips and there's no doubt that you'll fall head over heels for this simple sorbet that makes excellent use of the bounty of melons that are usually most abundant during the summer months.

1. Peel the rind from the melon, removing any traces of green. Split the melon in half and scrape out the seeds. Cut the melon into 1-inch (3cm) pieces. Puree in a blender with the sugar, salt, and lime juice until smooth. Taste and add more lime juice, if desired, and the wine, if using.

2. Chill the mixture thoroughly in the refrigerator, then freeze it in your ice cream maker according to the manufacturer's instructions.

PERFECT PAIRING: Cantaloupe Sorbet goes remarkably well with port, either tippled over the top or sipped from a glass alongside.

One 2-pound (1kg) ripe cantaloupe

½ cup (100g) sugar

Pinch of kosher or sea salt

1 teaspoon freshly squeezed lime juice, plus more to taste

2 tablespoons dry or sweet white wine or champagne (optional)

GRAPE SORBET

Makes about 1 quart (1l)

Grapes that are very robust, such as Concord or Muscat, make a fine, full-flavored grape sorbet. Grapes are usually at their best in autumn. If you have access to wine grapes, the qualities that make them good for wine also make them wonderful for sorbet. Don't use seedless table grapes such as Thompson or Red Flame; they're fine for snacking, but don't make a very tasty sorbet.

1. Rinse the grapes and remove them from the stems (see No Separation Anxiety, page 159). Cut them in half if they're large or have thick skins. Place them in a large, nonreactive pot, add the water, and cover. Cook the grapes over medium heat, stirring occasionally, until the skins have burst and the grapes are soft and cooked through.

2. Remove from the heat and pass the warm grapes through a food mill fitted with a fine disk, or, if you wish to remove the grape solids, use a flexible spatula to press them through a mesh strainer. Stir the sugar, corn syrup, and vodka into the grape juice.

3. Chill the mixture thoroughly in the refrigerator, then freeze it in your ice cream maker according to the manufacturer's instructions.

PERFECT PAIRING: Serve Grape Sorbet alongside Peanut Butter Ice Cream (page 59).

2¼ pounds (1.75kg) grapes, preferably Concord or Muscat

¼ cup (60ml) water

3 tablespoons sugar

2 tablespoons light corn syrup

1 tablespoon vodka

WATERMELON SORBETTO

Makes about 1 quart (1l)

I wouldn't dream of visiting the vast Mercato Centrale in Florence without my friend Judy Witts, known throughout town as the Divina Cucina. With Judy as my guide, butchers and cheese merchants greet us like given-up-for-lost family members; and everywhere we turn, another oversize platter appears, heaped with Tuscan delights: sheep's milk pecorino, candied fruits spiced with mustard seeds, fresh raspberries dotted with syrupy balsamic vinegar, and juicy tripe sandwiches (which I haven't yet built up the courage to try). And because we're in Italy, it all ends with shots of grappa taken straight from little glass vials, *obbligatorio* after all that sampling.

This *sorbetto* is adapted from Judy's recipe. One of her favorite parts is the little chocolate "seeds" it contains. Because watermelons have a lot of water, take the *sorbetto* out of the freezer long enough ahead of serving to make it scoopable, 5 to 10 minutes. To pass the time, serve shots of grappa, and if there's any left by serving time, splash some over the *sorbetto*, too.

1. In a small, nonreactive saucepan, heat ½ cup (125ml) of the watermelon puree with the sugar and salt, stirring until the sugar is dissolved. Transfer to a medium bowl and stir in the remaining 2½ cups (625ml) watermelon puree. Mix in the lime juice and the vodka, if using.

2. Chill the mixture thoroughly in the refrigerator, then freeze it in your ice cream maker according to the manufacturer's instructions. During the last minute of churning, add the mini chocolate chips.

NOTE: I find that I get about 3 cups (750ml) watermelon puree from a 3-pound (1.4kg) chunk of watermelon. Cut away the rind, remove any seeds, and then cut the juicy, pink flesh into cubes and puree them in a blender or food processor. Any extra puree can be frozen for another use, such as watermelon margaritas.

VARIATION: This sorbetto makes excellent Watermelon Popsicles. Simply pour the just-churned mixture into plastic Popsicle molds and freeze until firm.

3 cups (750ml) watermelon puree (from a 3-pound, 1.4kg, watermelon; see Note)

½ cup (100g) sugar

Big pinch of kosher or sea salt

1 tablespoon freshly squeezed lime juice

1 to 2 tablespoons vodka (optional)

1 to 2 tablespoons mini semisweet chocolate chips

LIME SORBET

Makes about 1 quart (1l)

Whenever I pass a bin of colorful limes at the market, I can't resist running my hands over their glossy emerald skins. I don't know why, but I'm always hypnotized when I see big, overflowing bins of shiny limes, and I just can't stop myself from buying a bag of them. Maybe it's because fresh limes transport us to somewhere far away, suggesting sitting on a hot beach full of sexy, half-dressed folks, lounging in the sun? If that doesn't give you impetus to make this sorbet, I don't know what will.

1. In a medium, nonreactive saucepan, mix 1 cup (250ml) of the water with the sugar. Grate the zest of the lime directly into the saucepan. Heat, stirring frequently, until the sugar is completely dissolved. Remove from the heat and add the remaining 1¼ cups (310ml) water, then chill thoroughly in the refrigerator.

2. Mix in the lime juice and the champagne, if using. Freeze in your ice cream maker according to the manufacturer's instructions.

PERFECT PAIRING: To make Lime Sorbet more festive, prepare the recipe but omit the champagne. Serve scoops in frosty cocktail glasses with shots of tequila poured over them. Top each off with a few flecks of flaky sea salt.

2¼ cups (560ml) water

¾ cup (150g) sugar

1 lime, preferably unsprayed

¾ cup (180ml) freshly squeezed lime juice (from about 9 limes)

6 tablespoons (90ml) champagne or dry sparkling wine (optional)

CRANBERRY-ORANGE SORBET

Makes about 1 quart (1l)

One of the few fruits native to North America is the cranberry. They are hollow, which is why you can bounce them (go ahead, try it . . . I'll wait) and also explains why they float, which turns out to be an advantage at harvest time. Farmers flood the areas where cranberries are cultivated, causing the berries to rise to the surface, where it's a cinch to scoop 'em up.

Predictably, the majority of cranberries are purchased just before Thanksgiving, but I stock up the day after, when they're on sale, and freeze them to use during the next few months. Their tangy taste brightens up my winter.

1. Heat the cranberries, water, sugar, and orange zest in a medium, nonreactive saucepan until the liquid begins to boil. Boil for 1 minute, then remove from the heat, cover, and let stand for 30 minutes.

2. Pass the cranberries and their liquid through a food mill fitted with a fine disk, or puree them in a blender or food processor and then press the puree through a mesh strainer to remove any large bits of cranberry skin. Stir in the orange juice and the liqueur, if using.

3. Chill the mixture thoroughly in the refrigerator, then freeze it in your ice cream maker according to the manufacturer's instructions.

PERFECT PAIRING: Dress up Cranberry-Orange Sorbet by serving scoops nestled in Lemon–Poppy Seed Cookie Cups (page 249), topped with pieces of Candied Citrus Peel (page 193) made with orange zest.

1½ cups (180g) cranberries, fresh or frozen

1 cup (250ml) water

¾ cup (150g) sugar

Grated zest of 1 orange

1½ cups (375ml) freshly squeezed orange juice (from 5 or 6 oranges)

2 teaspoons Grand Marnier or Cointreau (optional)

LEMON SORBET

Makes about 1 quart (1l)

Anyone who's been to New York City in August knows that one of the best ways to cool down is by spooning up the ubiquitous Italian ice sold by pushcart vendors. Unfortunately, it's mostly disappointing and is never as good as what you can easily make at home. This sorbet captures the taste of fresh lemons better than anything you'll find on the street.

1. In a medium, nonreactive saucepan, mix ½ cup (125ml) of the water and the sugar. Grate the zest of the lemons directly into the saucepan. Heat, stirring frequently, until the sugar is completely dissolved. Remove from the heat and add the remaining 2 cups (500ml) water, then chill thoroughly in the refrigerator.

2. Stir the lemon juice into the sugar syrup, then freeze the mixture in your ice cream maker according to the manufacturer's instructions.

NOTE: I like my Lemon Sorbet tangy. If you prefer it sweeter, you can add another ¼ cup (50g) sugar.

PERFECT PAIRING: Freshly made Raspberry Granita (page 168) makes a lively partner and stands up well to the puckery lemon flavor.

2½ cups (625ml) water

1 cup (200g) sugar (see Note)

2 lemons, preferably unsprayed

1 cup (250ml) freshly squeezed lemon juice (from about 6 lemons)

LEMON SHERBET

Makes about 1 quart (1l)

If you're looking for a light, simple, lemony frozen dessert, here it is. It's a bit more substantial than Lemon Sorbet (page 121) and every bit as good.

1. In a medium, nonreactive saucepan, mix 1 cup (250ml) of the milk with the sugar. Grate the zest of the lemon directly into the saucepan. Heat, stirring frequently, until the sugar is dissolved. Remove from the heat and add the remaining 2 cups (500ml) milk, then chill thoroughly in the refrigerator.

2. Stir the lemon juice into the milk mixture. If it curdles a bit, whisk it vigorously to make it smooth again. Freeze in your ice cream maker according to the manufacturer's instructions.

PERFECT PAIRINGS: Lemon Sherbet is good with anything berry, including Raspberry Ice Cream (page 101) or Strawberry Sorbet (page 134). Or simply serve it with lots of lightly sweetened berries.

3 cups (750ml) whole milk

¾ cup (150g) sugar

1 lemon, preferably unsprayed

6 tablespoons (90ml) freshly squeezed lemon juice (from 2 to 3 lemons)

LEMON-BUTTERMILK SHERBET

Makes about 1 quart (1l)

While teaching classes in the American heartland a few years back, as I started to measure out a cup of buttermilk, I stopped and gasped, horrified to see tiny yellow flecks floating on top. Being a city slicker, I figured there was something wrong with the buttermilk and was ready to toss it out. But on closer inspection, I noticed that those flecks were little bits of real, honest-to-goodness butter, something you don't see often anymore, because most buttermilk is cultured rather than a by-product of the butter-making process. The crowd got a good laugh at my startled reaction to my first encounter with the real deal. And I promised them that I'd never dismiss the country's midsection as "flyover states" again, because there's very good buttermilk over there.

1. In a medium, nonreactive saucepan, mix the water and sugar. Grate the zest of the lemon directly into the saucepan. Heat, stirring frequently, until the sugar is dissolved. Remove from the heat and let stand until the syrup cools to room temperature, then chill thoroughly in the refrigerator.

2. Whisk the buttermilk into the syrup, then whisk in the lemon juice. Freeze in your ice cream maker according to the manufacturer's instructions.

PERFECT PAIRING: A scoop of Lemon-Buttermilk Sherbet is pretty and delicious resting on a pool of Creamy Caramel Sauce (page 186).

⅓ cup (80ml) water

⅔ cup (130g) sugar

1 lemon, preferably unsprayed

2 cups (500ml) buttermilk

¼ cup (60ml) freshly squeezed lemon juice (from about 2 lemons)

PINK GRAPEFRUIT–CHAMPAGNE SORBET

Makes about 1 quart (1l)

Long before svelte supermodels and well-heeled tycoons made it chic to do so, relatives of mine would make their annual winter pilgrimage to Miami, Florida, to get some sun, and, God willing . . . a bit of a schvitz. A week later, we'd greet a deeply bronzed Uncle Myron and Aunt Sophie at the airport, schlepping mesh nylon sacks bulging with yellow-skinned grapefruits, a bit of sunshine for those of us without the chutzpah to escape the dreary Northeast winter.

Nowadays grapefruits are everywhere, but they're at their best during the winter months. Choose fruits that are heavy for their size, with ends that are a bit flat, an indication they'll be juicy and sweet.

1. In a medium, nonreactive saucepan, heat about half of the champagne with the sugar, stirring frequently, until the sugar is completely dissolved. Remove from the heat and stir in the remaining champagne and the grapefruit juice.

2. Chill the mixture thoroughly in the refrigerator, then freeze it in your ice cream maker according to the manufacturer's instructions.

PERFECT PAIRING: Although any fruit granita would go well with this Pink Grapefruit–Champagne Sorbet, Raspberry Granita (page 168) makes the most stunning complement. Another option is to turn it into a frosty version of a Kir Royale by drizzling it lightly with crème de cassis (blackcurrant liqueur).

1⅓ cups (330ml) champagne or dry sparkling wine

1 cup (200g) sugar

2½ cups (625ml) freshly squeezed pink grapefruit juice (from about 3 grapefruits)

TANGERINE SORBET

Makes about 1 quart (1l)

It's easy to forget that citrus fruits do have a specific season, because they seem abundant all year-round. The one exception is tangerines, which are rarely seen except during the winter. My favorite varieties for making this sorbet are the oddly shaped tangelos, whose juice is mischievously tart, and squat honey tangerines, whose protruding belly signals the bright-colored and exceptionally sweet juice within.

1. Zest the tangerine into a small, nonreactive saucepan. Add ½ cup (125ml) of the tangerine juice and the sugar. Warm over low heat until the sugar is dissolved, then stir the syrup into the remaining 2½ cups (625ml) tangerine juice in a medium bowl.

2. Chill the mixture thoroughly in the refrigerator, then freeze it in your ice cream maker according to the manufacturer's instructions.

PERFECT PAIRINGS: Mixed Berry Coulis (page 198) served alongside Tangerine Sorbet makes for a truly eye-popping, colorful dessert, or try the sorbet with a scattering of French Almonds (page 205).

1 tangerine, preferably unsprayed

3 cups (750ml) freshly squeezed tangerine juice (from 12 to 15 tangerines, depending on size)

¾ cup (150g) sugar

CHOCOLATE-TANGERINE SORBET

Makes about 1 quart (1l)

There are folks who can't imagine dessert without chocolate, while others aren't happy unless they get something with citrus. Sometimes I can't decide which I want. Am I in the mood for something citrusy? Or am I having a chocolate craving that needs to be satisfied? Here's a happy truce that marries the two flavors in perfect harmony and is guaranteed to please everyone.

1. In a medium, nonreactive saucepan, heat the water and sugar, stirring frequently, until the sugar is completely dissolved. Remove from the heat.

2. Add the chocolate and whisk until it's melted. Whisk in the tangerine juice. Puree the mixture in a blender until smooth.

3. Chill the mixture thoroughly in the refrigerator, then freeze it in your ice cream maker according to the manufacturer's instructions.

PERFECT PAIRINGS: Almond Butterscotch Cookie Cups (page 248) are good vessels for Chocolate-Tangerine Sorbet. Drizzle a bit of Lean Chocolate Sauce (page 179) over the top, or serve with Candied Citrus Peel (page 193) made with orange zest.

1½ cups (375ml) water

¾ cup (150g) sugar

6 ounces (170g) bittersweet or semisweet chocolate, finely chopped

1½ cups (375ml) freshly squeezed tangerine juice (from 6 to 8 tangerines, depending on size)

MOCHA SHERBET

Makes about 1 quart (1l)

This frozen delight is perfect in the summer when you need a brisk perk-me-up. It combines two of my favorite flavors, coffee and chocolate, in one scoop. Although, to be honest, I can never stop myself at just one.

---

1. Whisk together the coffee, sugar, cocoa powder, and salt in a large saucepan. Bring the mixture to a boil and allow it to boil for 30 seconds, whisking constantly. Remove from the heat and stir in the milk.

2. Chill the mixture thoroughly in the refrigerator, then freeze it in your ice cream maker according to the manufacturer's instructions.

PERFECT PAIRING: To make a Mocha Freeze, for each serving, put 2 scoops of Mocha Sherbet (4 ounces, 115g) in a blender along with ½ cup (125ml) very strongly brewed coffee or espresso, 1½ tablespoons sugar, and 3 ice cubes. Blend until almost smooth. Pour into a glass and top with Whipped Cream (page 184) and top with shaved chocolate.

2¼ cups (560ml) very strongly brewed top-quality, coffee

¾ cup (150g) sugar

6 tablespoons (50g) unsweetened Dutch-process cocoa powder

Pinch of kosher or sea salt

¾ cup (180ml) whole milk

CHOCOLATE SORBET

Makes about 1 quart (1l)

This is the perfect chocolate sorbet—it's very rich, dense, and full of bittersweet chocolate flavor, and it's one of my all-time favorites. Use a top-quality cocoa powder; it will make a huge difference. Be sure to use a large saucepan, because the mixture will bubble up as it boils, and be sure to blend it before churning, which ensures the finished sorbet will be silky smooth.

---

1. In a large saucepan, whisk together 1½ cups (375ml) of the water with the sugar, cocoa powder, and salt. Bring to a boil, whisking frequently. Let it boil, continuing to whisk, for 45 seconds.

2. Remove from the heat and stir in the chocolate until it's melted, then stir in the vanilla and the remaining ¾ cup (180ml) water. Transfer the mixture to a blender and blend for 15 seconds.

3. Chill the mixture thoroughly, then freeze it in your ice cream maker according to the manufacturer's instructions. If the mixture has become too thick to pour into your machine, whisk it vigorously to thin it out.

2¼ cups (555ml) water

1 cup (200g) sugar

¾ cup (75g) unsweetened Dutch-process cocoa powder

Pinch of kosher or sea salt

6 ounces (170g) bittersweet or semisweet chocolate, finely chopped

½ teaspoon pure vanilla extract

CHOCOLATE-COCONUT SORBET

Makes about 1 quart (1l)

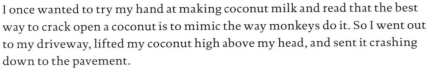

I once wanted to try my hand at making coconut milk and read that the best way to crack open a coconut is to mimic the way monkeys do it. So I went out to my driveway, lifted my coconut high above my head, and sent it crashing down to the pavement.

Suddenly, I began to feel wet from my knees down, and I realized that the watery liquid had splashed everywhere, saturating my shoes, socks, and trousers. I suppose I should have followed those instructions more literally. Because monkeys don't wear clothing, I should have removed mine first. So if you see a scantily clad man hurling coconuts around in your neighborhood, don't call the police. It's probably me preparing the ingredients for this tropically tinged sorbet, which combines two of my favorite flavors: dark, bittersweet chocolate and sweet coconut. On second thought, in the name of public decency, I think I'll stick to store-bought coconut milk from now on.

1. Warm the water, sugar, and salt in a medium saucepan, stirring, until the sugar is dissolved. Remove from the heat. Add the chocolate and whisk until it's melted. Whisk in the coconut milk and vanilla.

2. Chill the mixture thoroughly in the refrigerator, then freeze it in your ice cream maker according to the manufacturer's instructions. If a layer of coconut milk fat has firmed up on top, simply whisk in it before churning.

NOTE: Thai coconut milk can be found in well-stocked supermarkets or Asian markets. Do not substitute Coco López, which is heavily sweetened.

PERFECT PAIRINGS: Serve Chocolate-Coconut Sorbet atop a Blondie (page 241), topped with a spoonful of Dulce de Leche (page 185) or Cajeta (page 188), and sprinkled with some toasted shredded coconut.

1 cup (250ml) water

1 cup (200g) sugar

Pinch of kosher or sea salt

8 ounces (230g) bittersweet or semisweet chocolate, finely chopped

2 cups (500ml) Thai coconut milk (see Note)

½ teaspoon pure vanilla extract

HAVING A MELTDOWN?

Sorbets can become icy and crystallized if neglected in the freezer for too long. If this happens, simply remove them from the freezer and leave in the refrigerator until melted. You can rechurn any fruit sorbet in your ice cream machine, which will make them look, and taste, as good as new.

NECTARINE SORBET

Makes about 1 quart (1l)

There's a custom in Gascony, a region in the southwest of France known for its full-bodied red wines (its famous neighbor is Bordeaux). When locals have just about finished their soup, they tip a little bit of the red wine from their glass into their soup bowl, mingling the wine with the last few spoonfuls of the broth.

I discovered that this custom is equally good with a goblet of sorbet when I was scrambling to figure out a way to make this rosy nectarine treat a bit more special for an impromptu dinner party. I simply scooped sorbet into my guests' wine glasses at the table and let them pour in as little (or as much) red wine as they wished. It was a big success. If you have time to plan ahead, prepare a big bowl of sweet, juicy berries and sliced nectarines, and let your guests add some fruit to their sorbet, too.

1. Slice the unpeeled nectarines in half and remove the pits. Cut the nectarine halves into small chunks and add them along with the water to a medium, nonreactive saucepan. Cover and cook over medium heat, stirring occasionally, until the nectarines are soft and cooked through, about 10 minutes. Add a bit more water during cooking, if needed.

2. Remove from the heat and stir in the sugar. Let cool to room temperature. When cool, puree the mixture in a blender or food processor until smooth. Stir in the kirsch.

3. Chill the mixture thoroughly in the refrigerator, then freeze it in your ice cream maker according to the manufacturer's instructions.

VARIATION: For Peach Sorbet, substitute 7 large, ripe peaches for the nectarines. Remove the skins (see page 96) prior to cutting them into chunks.

PERFECT PAIRINGS: If you like the idea of red wine with Nectarine Sorbet, pair it with Raspberry-Rosé Sorbet (page 137), or simply serve it in goblets and pass a bottle of fruity red wine, such as Merlot or Pinot noir.

6 ripe nectarines (about 2 pounds, 1kg)

⅔ cup (160ml) water, plus more if needed

¾ cup (150g) sugar

1 teaspoon kirsch or ¼ teaspoon freshly squeezed lemon juice

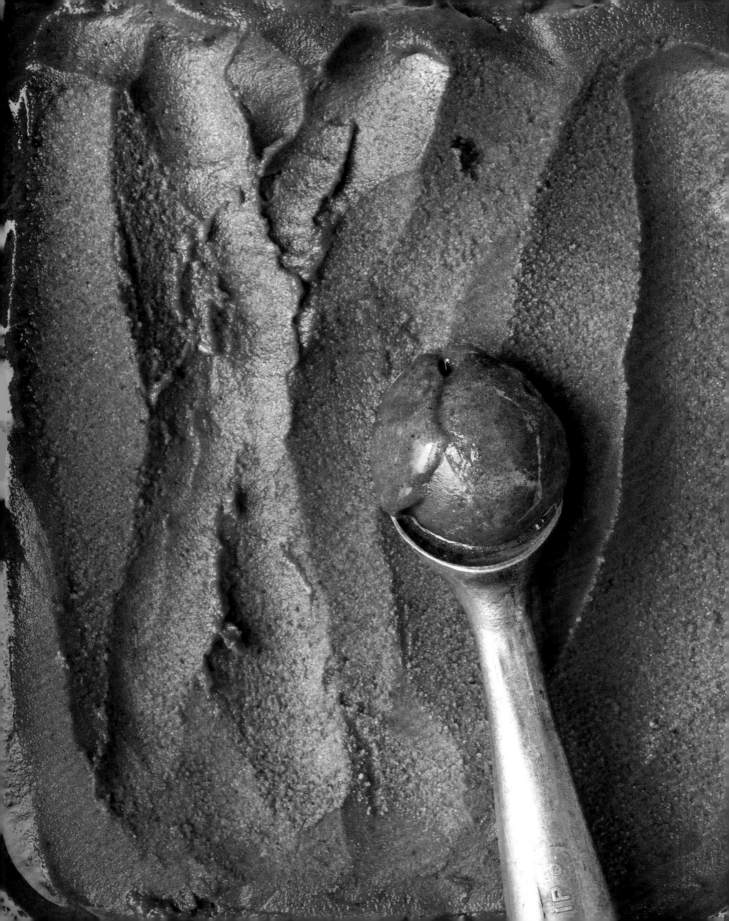

BLACKBERRY SORBET

Makes about 1 quart (1l)

When I moved into my first home in San Francisco, the backyard was teeming with blackberry bushes. Blinded by greed, I was thrilled at the prospect of having as many luscious blackberries as I wanted. But as I soon learned, blackberry bushes are a mixed blessing, and for the next few years, I spent many thorny weekends working to thwart the persistent, and prickly, shrubs from taking over my entire yard. Luckily, the bonus was indeed lots and lots of inky blackberries all summer long, which made their way into jams and sorbets. But each and every one I picked was well earned . . . and I still have a few battle scars to prove it.

1. Puree the blackberries in a blender or food processor with the water and sugar. Press the mixture through a strainer to remove the seeds. Stir in the lemon juice.

2. Chill the mixture thoroughly in the refrigerator, then freeze it in your ice cream maker according to the manufacturer's instructions.

PERFECT PAIRING: Fill Meringue Nests (page 256) with Blackberry Sorbet and top with Whipped Cream (page 184) and a flurry of crisp French Almonds (page 205).

4 cups (450g) blackberries, fresh or frozen

1 cup (250ml) water

⅔ cup (130g) sugar

2 teaspoons freshly squeezed lemon juice

BLACKBERRY-LIME SORBET

Makes about 1 quart (1l)

You can tell a lot about people by looking in their freezer. Next time you're at a friend's house, peek in theirs and you'll discover their most hidden desires. One secret I am willing to share is that I'm hopelessly frugal and it's impossible for me to throw anything away, no matter how trivial. One day when I had lots of blackberries on hand, I pulled out one of my buried treasures, a small container of frozen lime juice left over from an overanxious lime-buying spree. I was curious about how the tart lime juice would play against the sweet blackberries. Happily, it was a great combination, and it's one secret I don't want to keep to myself. Although I recommend that you use freshly squeezed juice, frozen lime juice that you've kept well concealed is the next best thing.

CONTINUED

BLACKBERRY-LIME SORBET, *CONTINUED*

1. In a small saucepan, bring the sugar and water to a boil, stirring until the sugar is dissolved. Remove from the heat and let cool to room temperature.

2. Puree the blackberries in a blender or food processor with the sugar syrup. Press the mixture through a strainer to remove the seeds, then stir the lime juice into the sweetened puree.

3. Chill the mixture thoroughly in the refrigerator, then freeze it in your ice cream maker according to the manufacturer's instructions.

PERFECT PAIRING: Serve this sorbet with a heap of Lime Granita (page 165).

¾ cup (150g) sugar

¾ cup (180ml) water

4 cups (450g) blackberries, fresh or frozen

¾ cup (180ml) freshly squeezed lime juice (from about 9 limes)

CHERRY SORBET

Makes about 1 quart (1l)

I'm insatiable when it comes to fresh cherries, and I eat pounds and pounds of them during their ridiculously brief season, which I'm convinced is one of nature's cruelest acts. But their characteristic flavor really becomes pronounced when warmed, so for this sorbet, I sauté them first to deepen their luxurious flavor. Be sure to start with full-flavored, very dark sweet cherries, like plump Burlat cherries or blackish red Bings.

1. Stem the cherries and remove the pits. In a medium, nonreactive saucepan, warm the cherries over medium heat with the water, sugar, and lemon juice until they start becoming juicy. Cook for 10 to 15 minutes, stirring occasionally, until the cherries are very soft and cooked through. Remove from the heat and let cool to room temperature.

2. Puree the cherries and their liquid with the almond extract in a blender until smooth.

3. Chill the mixture thoroughly in the refrigerator, then freeze it in your ice cream maker according to the manufacturer's instructions.

PERFECT PAIRINGS: Any of the other summer fruit and berry sorbets make good partners for Cherry Sorbet, including Nectarine Sorbet (page 129), Cantaloupe Sorbet (page 116), or even Banana Sorbet (page 142).

2 pounds (1kg) sweet cherries

1 cup (250ml) water

¾ cup plus 2 tablespoons (180g) sugar

1 teaspoon freshly squeezed lemon juice

⅛ teaspoon pure almond extract or 1 teaspoon kirsch

APRICOT SORBET

Makes about 1 quart (1l)

It wasn't until I was twenty years old that I got a taste of my first fresh apricot. I was baking in a restaurant in upstate New York, and one day the produce person handed me a small, crinkly paper sack with a few orange orbs inside. I'd eaten many a dried apricot in my lifetime but had neither seen nor tasted a fresh one, and frankly, I didn't know what to do with them. Because I had just a handful, I made one singularly gorgeous apricot tart that I kept away from the prying hands of the line cooks (the greatest hazard for the pastry chef in any professional kitchen). I sliced it carefully so eight lucky customers were able to have a taste.

My first summer after moving to California, I was amazed at how many fresh apricots there were and thought that the stacked-up crates at the market were a one-time windfall. So I started hoarding them, making as many things as I could before they disappeared forever. Or so I thought.

When the next year rolled around and the cases of apricots started stacking up again, I learned that they were actually quite common. But to this day, when they're in season I try to use as many as I can, still mindful of how precious each and every silky-soft apricot is. And don't be put off by apricots that are so ripe they feel like they're ready to burst. That's when they're at their best.

1. Halve the apricots, remove the pits, and cut each apricot into sixths. Place the apricot pieces with the water in a medium, nonreactive saucepan. Cover and cook over medium heat, stirring occasionally, until the apricots are cooked through, about 10 minutes. Remove from the heat and stir in the sugar. Let cool to room temperature.

2. Puree the mixture in a blender or food processor until smooth. Taste a spoonful; if there are any small fibers, press the puree through a mesh strainer. Stir in the almond extract.

3. Chill the mixture thoroughly in the refrigerator, then freeze it in your ice cream maker according to the manufacturer's instructions.

PERFECT PAIRING: Turrón Ice Cream (page 73), flavored with honey and nuts, goes very nicely with the tangy taste of Apricot Sorbet.

2 pounds (1kg) squishy-ripe fresh apricots (10 to 15 apricots, depending on size)

1 cup (250ml) water

1 cup (200g) sugar

3 drops pure almond or vanilla extract

STRAWBERRY SORBET

Makes about 3 cups (750ml)

If you've ever gone shopping at the original Fairway Market on the Upper West Side of Manhattan, you know that the simple act of buying a good basket of strawberries can be a full-contact sport. Never in my life have I left a market with so many bumps and bruises! Next time I go, I'm wearing football gear to protect myself from the combative shoppers who wield their carts like modern-day jousting vehicles, taking on any and all oncoming produce shoppers who might happen to be heading toward the basket of berries they've set their sights on.

But if you think this is just an East Coast phenomenon, visit Berkeley Bowl in California, where people who've just parked their Volvos with fading "Make Love, Not War" bumper stickers are more than happy to trample you with their Birkenstocks while homing in on their berries.

No matter where you live, I recommend that you take the trouble and assume all risks to find good strawberries for this intensely flavored sorbet to enjoy at home, where you're safe and sound.

1. Slice the strawberries and toss them in a medium bowl with the sugar and kirsch, if using, stirring until the sugar begins to dissolve. Cover and let stand for 1 hour, stirring every so often.

2. Puree the strawberries and their liquid with the lemon juice and salt in a blender or food processor, until smooth. If you wish to remove the seeds, press the mixture through a mesh strainer.

3. Chill the mixture thoroughly in the refrigerator, then freeze it in your ice cream maker according to the manufacturer's instructions.

PERFECT PAIRING: Strawberry Sorbet goes well with Plum-Berry Compote. For 6 servings, slice 1 pound (450g) purple-skinned plums in half and remove the pits. Cut each plum into 8 slices. Bring 1 cup (250ml) water and ¼ cup (50g) sugar to a boil in a medium, nonreactive saucepan. Add the plum slices, lower the heat, and simmer for 5 minutes. Remove from the heat and add 1 cup (100g) fresh or frozen raspberries, blackberries, or blueberries. Cover and let stand until cooled to room temperature. Serve the compote with a scoops of this sorbet.

1 pound (450g) fresh strawberries, rinsed and hulled

¾ cup (150g) sugar

1 teaspoon kirsch (optional)

1 teaspoon freshly squeezed lemon juice

Pinch of kosher or sea salt

STRAWBERRY-RHUBARB SORBET

Makes about 1 quart (1l)

One of the funniest (albeit most excruciating) things I've ever seen was a videotaped appearance of a cookbook author making a rhubarb pie on a live morning television show. Just as the cameras began rolling, the cocky host looked at his guest and blurted out, "You want to know something? I hate rhubarb. I mean, I really, really hate it."

The poor dear continued to make her rhubarb pie, but it was easy to see that the host's constant grousing was taking its toll on her as she baked, bantered, and defended her delicious-looking pie for a few painful on-air minutes.

If it were me, I would have taken a different approach. With the cameras rolling, I would have ordered him out of the studio and pulled another person into the kitchen who looked forward to the first rhubarb in the spring with the same anticipation that I do. Look for stalks that are bright red, which will make the most enticingly colored sorbet. The flavor of gently stewed rhubarb with fresh strawberries will remind you why this combination is so beloved by everyone. Well, almost everyone.

1. Wash the rhubarb stalks and trim the stem and leaf ends. Cut the rhubarb into ½-inch (12mm) pieces.

2. Place the rhubarb, water, and sugar in a medium, nonreactive saucepan and bring to a boil. Lower the heat, cover, and simmer for 5 minutes, or until the rhubarb is tender and cooked through. Remove from the heat and let cool to room temperature.

3. Slice the strawberries and puree them with the cooked rhubarb mixture and lemon juice until smooth.

4. Chill the mixture thoroughly in the refrigerator, then freeze it in your ice cream maker according to the manufacturer's instructions.

12 ounces (325g) rhubarb

⅔ cup (160ml) water

¾ cup (150g) sugar

10 ounces (280g) fresh strawberries, rinsed and hulled

½ teaspoon freshly squeezed lemon juice

PERFECT PAIRING: To make a Red Wine–Poached Rhubarb Compote that goes beautifully with this sorbet, use cookbook author Susan Loomis's recipe. For 6 servings, cut 1 pound (450g) rhubarb into green bean–size strips. In a nonreactive saucepan, combine the rhubarb with 2 cups (500ml) red wine, ½ cup (100g) sugar, 1 tablespoon honey, 1 cinnamon stick, and a pinch of ground cloves. Bring to a boil, then simmer until the wine is reduced by about one-third. Once the compote is cool, divide it among six bowls and serve a scoop of Strawberry-Rhubarb Sorbet in the middle.

PLUM-RASPBERRY SORBET

Makes about 1 quart (1l)

Plums are the last of the summer fruits to arrive, and they stay around long enough to welcome in the fall. Having a batch of plum sorbet in the freezer is the perfect way to extend the warm glow of summer just a few more weeks.

1. Slice the plums in half and remove the pits. Cut the plums into eighths and put them in a medium, nonreactive saucepan with the water. Cover and cook over medium heat, stirring occasionally, for about 8 minutes, or until tender. Remove from the heat and stir in the sugar and raspberries. Let cool to room temperature.

2. Once cool, puree the mixture in a blender or food processor until smooth. If you wish to remove the seeds, press the puree through a mesh strainer. Stir in the kirsch, if using.

3. Chill the mixture thoroughly in the refrigerator, then freeze it in your ice cream maker according to the manufacturer's instructions.

PERFECT PAIRING: Serve scoops of Plum-Raspberry Sorbet in Gingersnap Ice Cream Cones (variation, page 252).

1 pound (450g) plums (about 8 plums)

1 cup (250ml) water

⅔ cup (130g) sugar

¾ cup (90g) raspberries, fresh or frozen

1 teaspoon kirsch or vodka (optional)

TO SEED OR NOT TO SEED

Normally I'm a fan of leaving things as close to their natural state as possible. Yet in many frozen desserts with berries, I choose to strain out the seeds. Why? Much of the pleasure of eating ice creams, sorbets, and sherbets is in the smooth, creamy mouthfeel, and crunching on seeds, or getting them stuck between your teeth, can be somewhat unpleasant if there are a lot of them. (Especially if you don't have a toothpick handy afterward.) If you do wish to keep the seeds in your mixtures, by all means do so. Or compromise by straining out most of the seeds, but reserving a few for stirring back in.

RASPBERRY-ROSÉ SORBET

Makes about 1 quart (1l)

Creating a whole book with lots of recipes for sorbets means that you run the risk of using the word *refreshing* too often. But this sorbet is truly the most refreshing of them all, so I saved that word to describe it here. Each bite is pure, frosty bliss.

I use a rosé wine that's bold and fruity. Because of the quantity of wine in this sorbet, it will not freeze very firmly in your ice cream machine and will be somewhat soft when you scrape it out. But don't worry. When you go to serve it a few hours later, you'll find that it's the perfect texture, and, yup—very refreshing.

1. In a medium, nonreactive saucepan, bring the rosé and sugar to a boil. Remove from the heat, add the raspberries, and let cool to room temperature. Pass the mixture through a food mill fitted with a fine disk, or puree in a blender or food processor, then press the puree through a strainer to remove the seeds.

2. Chill the mixture thoroughly in the regrigerator, then freeze it in your ice cream maker according to the manufacturer's instructions.

VARIATION: To make Strawberry-Rosé Sorbet, substitute 1 pound (450g) fresh strawberries, rinsed, hulled, and sliced, for the raspberries.

PERFECT PAIRING: Raspberry-Rosé Sorbet is so perfect on its own that you don't need to serve it with anything except a handful of luscious fresh raspberries.

2 cups (500ml) rosé wine

⅔ cup (130g) sugar

3 cups (340g) raspberries, fresh or frozen

RASPBERRY SHERBET

Makes about 1 quart (1l)

The flavor of raspberries is so intense that they can simply be blended with milk and sugar and *voilà*! . . . you've got a sumptuous, full-flavored sherbet. The mixture is best frozen right after you've blended the ingredients because freezing preserves the vivid taste of the raspberries.

4 cups (450g) raspberries, fresh or frozen

2 cups (500ml) whole milk

1 cup (200g) sugar

1½ teaspoons freshly squeezed lemon juice

1. Put the raspberries, milk, and sugar in a blender or food processor. Puree until smooth, then strain the mixture to remove the seeds. Stir in the lemon juice.

2. Freeze the mixture in your ice cream maker according to the manufacturer's instructions.

PERFECT PAIRINGS: White Chocolate Ice Cream (page 37) or Fresh Apricot Ice Cream (page 81) makes a good partner for Raspberry Sherbet.

RASPBERRY-CHAMPAGNE SORBET

Makes about 2 cups (500ml)

Although made with champagne, I invite you to improvise, and economize, on this recipe by substituting a sparkly cava from Spain, a crémant from France, or Prosecco from Italy, all of which provide a lively sparkle without draining your wallet. Have a tasting to find one that you like. (Tip: Freixenet, in the black bottle, is a reliable budget option.)

Note that this recipe makes a small quantity, as the sorbet is better when it's soft and freshly churned, and doesn't improve with age.

1¼ cups (310ml) champagne or dry sparkling wine

¼ cup (60ml) water

½ cup (100g) sugar

2 cups (220g) raspberries, fresh or frozen

1. Combine the champagne, water, and sugar in a medium, nonreactive saucepan. Bring to a boil. Add the raspberries, remove from the heat, and cover. Let stand for 10 minutes.

2. Pass the mixture through a food mill with a fine disk, or use a flexible rubber spatula to firmly press it through a mesh strainer.

3. Chill the mixture thoroughly in the refrigerator, then freeze it in your ice cream maker according to the manufacturer's instructions.

PERFECT PAIRINGS: A pool of White Chocolate Sauce (page 184) makes Raspberry-Champagne Sorbet more festive and luxurious. You also can't go wrong pairing it with colorful Peach Ice Cream (page 96) or Passion Fruit Ice Cream (page 102).

RASPBERRY FROZÉ

Makes about 1 quart (1l)

I had trouble tracking down the definitive source for the idea of frozé, but it could have been a bartender who poured a bottle of rosé into one of those frozen margarita machines churning away in spring break–ready bars. I'll admit that I used to covet one so I could have frozen cocktails on tap at home, anytime I wanted. Then I realized it was probably a better idea to admire them from a respectable distance.

This was inspired by a strawberry-based frozen rosé recipe that appeared in *Bon Appétit*, although I swapped out raspberries, which have a stronger flavor than strawberries. Go with a strongly flavored rosé, if you can, but you don't need to use a fancy one. A French chef once advised me when I was using wine to make fruit-based apértifs, "Use the cheapest wine you can find. The stuff in the box works great." Like the frugal folks of Provence, in the south of France, I'll confess to having rosé on tap in the summer. And when I do, at least one bottle's worth gets frozen into frozé.

1. Pour the rosé into a wide plastic container so it is about 1 inch (3cm) deep. (You can divide it between several containers if you don't have one that'll hold the full bottle.) Place the rosé in the freezer until frozen, at least 4 hours.

2. While the rosé is freezing, heat the water and sugar together in a small saucepan until the sugar is dissolved. Remove from the heat, add the raspberries, and cover. Let steep for 15 minutes.

3. Pass the raspberries and the liquid through a food mill, or use a flexible rubber spatula to firmly press the mixture through a mesh strainer.

4. Scrape the raspberry syrup into a blender and add the vodka and lemon juice. Remove the frozen rosé from the freezer, break it into chunks, add it to the blender along with 4 cups (520g) ice cubes, and blend until smooth.

5. Transfer the mixture back to the plastic container and freeze for at least 4 hours, or up to overnight. When ready to serve, blend the mixture again, until it's slushy and smooth. Spoon into glasses.

PERFECT PAIRING: A sunny day!

1 750ml bottle rosé wine

½ cup (125ml) water

½ cup (100g) sugar

¾ cup (90g) raspberries, fresh or frozen

2 tablespoons vodka

1 teaspoon freshly squeezed lemon juice

CUCUMBER-GIN SORBET

Makes about 2 cups (500ml)

While discussing my list of proposed recipes with Julie, my editor, to add to this updated edition of *The Perfect Scoop*, I heard a barely concealed squeal on the other end of the line when we got to this one. I'm not sure why it was so close to her heart, but maybe she had a stockpile of gin left over from working with me before—I fear most editors that work with me keep a bottle of something handy in their office—and she was gearing up to work with me again?

So I moved the recipe to the top of my list, and was glad I did. Because who doesn't need a batch of Cucumber-Gin Sorbet in their freezer? Whether you're my editor or not.

This makes a smaller batch of sorbet than the other recipes in this book. Feel free to double it, if you wish (or if you have a lot of gin to use up). I like to use a fuller-flavored gin, like Tanqueray or Beefeater, and although I prefer premium brands of tonic water, such as Fever-Tree or Q Tonic with my gin, any tonic water will work well in this recipe.

⅔ cup (160ml) tonic water

⅓ cup (65g) sugar

6 tablespoons (90ml) gin

6 fresh mint leaves

1½ cups (210g) peeled, seeded cucumber pieces

1 tablespoon freshly squeezed lime juice, plus more to taste

1. In a small saucepan, heat ⅓ cup (80ml) of the tonic water and the sugar, stirring until the sugar is dissolved. Let the syrup cool to room temperature.

2. Pour the syrup into a blender and add the gin, mint leaves, cucumber pieces, and lime juice. Blend until smooth. Add the remaining ⅓ cup (80ml) tonic water, taste, and add more lime juice, if desired.

3. Chill the mixture thoroughly in the refrigerator, then freeze it in your ice cream maker according to the manufacturer's instructions.

BANANA-BLUEBERRY SORBET

Makes about 1 quart (1l)

When I was a professional baker, foodies would walk into the kitchen, look down their noses at my heaped-up flats of cultivated blueberries, and sneer, "Oh . . . I only like wild blueberries." Then they'd stand there making idle chat while grabbing fistfuls of cultivated blueberries and gobbling them up.

Wild blueberries are indeed wonderful, but they can be hard to find (unlike annoying food snobs), so you can use any kind of blueberry here. Just don't gobble them all up, or let anyone else do so, before you get a chance to use them.

1. Cut the banana into chunks and puree in a blender or food processor along with the blueberries, water, sugar, and lemon juice. Puree until smooth and few discernible bits of blueberry skins remain.

2. Chill the mixture thoroughly in the refrigerator, then freeze it in your ice cream maker according to the manufacturer's instructions.

VARIATION: To make Banana-Blackberry Sorbet, substitute 2 cups (240g) fresh or frozen blackberries for the blueberries and pass the mixture through a food mill or mesh strainer to remove the seeds.

PERFECT PAIRING: Make a fruit salad combining pineapple, tangerines, bananas, and any available berries, tossing the fruits with a good sprinkle of sugar and a splash of dark rum. Serve with a scoop of Banana-Blueberry Sorbet.

1 medium ripe banana, peeled

2 cups (360g) blueberries, fresh or frozen

¾ cup (180ml) water

½ cup (100g) sugar

1 tablespoon freshly squeezed lemon or lime juice

BANANA SORBET

Makes about 1 quart (1l)

This sorbet should be frozen right after it's mixed to preserve the fresh flavor and color of the bananas. They should be very ripe. If you want to add a spoonful or more of dark rum to taste, feel free to do so. One of my recipe testers mentioned that this was the most budget-friendly dessert she'd ever made.

1. Cut the bananas into chunks and put them in a blender or food processor along with the water, sugar, and lime juice and puree until smooth. Freeze in your ice cream maker according to the manufacturer's instructions.

PERFECT PAIRINGS: Icy Espresso Granita (page 154) or Mocha Sherbet (page 126) is an excellent accompaniment, as is a garnish of Candied Pineapple (page 194).

4 medium ripe bananas, peeled

1 cup (250ml) water

¾ cup (150g) sugar

2 teaspoons freshly squeezed lime juice

PINEAPPLE SORBET

Makes about 3 cups (750ml)

Once upon a time, before the advent of mass transportation, only the rich were privileged enough to eat pineapples. The fruits became status symbols because only those with great wealth and much prosperity could afford them. Nowadays, fresh pineapples are available just about everywhere, and few of us have to deprive ourselves of enjoying a juicy, sweet pineapple whenever we want. Now that's my idea of progress.

To peel a fresh pineapple, use a knife to lop off the bottom and the top. Cut away the skin and pry out any "eyes" with the tip of a vegetable peeler. Then cut the pineapple flesh lengthwise into quarters and remove the tough inner core from each wedge.

½ fresh pineapple, peeled and cored

8 to 10 tablespoons (100 to 130g) sugar

½ cup (125ml) water

1. Cut the pineapple into chunks and puree in a blender with 8 tablespoons (100g) sugar and the water until smooth. Taste, then add up to another 2 tablespoons (30g) more sugar, if desired. You should have about 2 cups (500ml) puree.

2. Chill the mixture thoroughly in the refrigerator, then freeze it in your ice cream maker according to the manufacturer's instructions.

VARIATION: You can make Pineapple Popsicles by reducing the sugar to 2 tablespoons (30g), pouring the mixture into plastic Popsicle molds, and freezing until firm.

CAN I USE CANNED?

Although fresh pineapples are readily available, some people prefer the convenience of using canned pineapple. If you wish to do so, choose a brand that's unsweetened and packed in its own juice, not in heavy or light sugar syrup. Puree the fruit and the juice in a blender until smooth, then simply measure out the amount of pineapple puree called for in the recipe.

PINEAPPLE-CHAMPAGNE SORBET

Makes about 3 cups (750ml)

I'll bet Dom Pérignon, the monk who is often given credit for inventing champagne, would be turning over in his grave if he knew I had mixed his fizzy elixir with pineapple. But I'm sure I'd have his blessing if he tasted how good this combination is.

1. Cut the pineapple into chunks and puree in a blender with the sugar until smooth. Stir in the champagne. You should have about 2 cups (500ml) puree.

2. Chill the mixture thoroughly in the refrigerator, then freeze it in your ice cream maker according to the manufacturer's instructions.

PERFECT PAIRING: Serve in goblets, with a festive pour-over of champagne or sparkling wine.

½ fresh pineapple, peeled and cored

6 tablespoons (75g) sugar

½ cup (125ml) champagne or dry sparkling wine

PIÑA COLADA SHERBET

Makes about 1½ quarts (1½ l)

Should I ever find myself stranded on a deserted tropical island and could have only one dessert, this would be my choice. Admittedly, it would likely be my only choice, because all the ingredients are native to the tropics.

1. Cut the pineapple into chunks. Puree in a blender with the sugar, coconut milk, rum, and lime juice until smooth. You should have about 4 cups (1l) puree.

2. Chill the mixture thoroughly in the refrigerator, then freeze it in your ice cream maker according to the manufacturer's instructions.

NOTE: Thai coconut milk can be found in well-stocked supermarkets or Asian markets. Do not substitute Coco López, which is heavily sweetened.

1 fresh pineapple, peeled and cored

1 cup (200g) sugar

1 cup (250ml) Thai coconut milk (see Note)

1 tablespoon (15ml) dark rum

1 teaspoon freshly squeezed lime juice

TROPICAL FRUIT SORBET

Makes about 1 quart (1l)

If you don't have fresh passion fruit juice or pulp, make do by adding more tangerine juice. But I do advise looking around for it (see Resources, page 259) because its unmistakable flavor gives this sorbet a taste that will take you right to the tropics.

---

1. Cut the bananas and pineapples into small chunks. In a blender, puree the bananas, pineapple, tangerine juice, passion fruit juice, sugar, rum, and lime juice until very smooth.

2. Chill the mixture thoroughly in the refrigerator, then freeze it in your ice cream maker according to the manufacturer's instructions.

2 medium ripe bananas, peeled

½ fresh pineapple, peeled and cored

¾ cup (180ml) freshly squeezed tangerine or orange juice (from 4 to 6 tangerines or oranges)

¼ cup (60ml) passion fruit juice or pulp (or substitute tangerine juice)

1 cup (200g) sugar

4 teaspoons dark rum

1 teaspoon freshly squeezed lime juice

KIWIFRUIT SORBET

Makes about 1 quart (1l)

Kiwis are people from New Zealand. Kiwifruits are the emerald green fruits that we consume. The difference is important to New Zealanders, who are apt to look somewhat terrified if you present them with a bowl of sorbet and proudly tell them is made from fresh kiwis.

---

1. Peel the kiwifruits and, using the point of a paring knife, pluck out the woody nubbins within the stem ends. Cut the kiwifruits into chunks and puree them in a blender or food processor. You should have about 2 cups (500ml) puree.

2. Chill the mixture thoroughly in the refrigerator, then freeze it in your ice cream maker according to the manufacturer's instructions.

2 pounds (1kg) ripe green kiwifruits (10 to 15 kiwifruits)

¾ cup (150g) sugar

1⅓ cups (315ml) water

SPRITZ SORBET

Makes about 2½ cups (625ml)

One thing that surprises Americans when they travel to Europe is the dearth of ice in drinks. We're used to glasses filled to the brim with lots of frozen cubes clinking around in there. When presented at a café with a glass of tepid liquid with a lone cube of ice languishing on the surface, many get homesick for that feeling of being instantly refreshed by a very cold drink.

So I was surprised when I went to Trieste, an Italian city near Venice where the Spritz cocktail was invented, and saw lots of people at tables drinking bright orange drinks served in oversize goblets. Each contained more ice than I'd seen in the entire previous decade of living in Europe. And I've been enjoying my share of Spritzes ever since.

The classic Spritz is made with Prosecco, an Italian sparkling wine, and Aperol, which is sweeter than Campari, although my preference leans toward the more edgy Campari. You can use either. This sorbet freezes on the soft side and should be spooned into chilled glasses. You won't need any additional ice as the sorbet is cold enough. But don't worry—your guests won't miss it.

1. Warm ½ cup (125ml) of the Prosecco with the sugar in a medium saucepan, stirring until the sugar is dissolved. Remove from the heat and let cool to room temperature.

2. Add the remaining 1 cup (250ml) Prosecco, the grapefruit juice, and the Campari or Aperol. (If using Aperol, taste, and add another tablespoon if you want more of the flavor.)

3. Chill the mixture thoroughly in the refrigerator, then freeze it in your ice cream maker according to the manufacturer's instructions.

1½ cups (375ml) Prosecco, another dry sparkling wine, or champagne

6 tablespoons (75g) sugar

¾ cup (180ml) freshly squeezed pink grapefruit juice

3 tablespoons (45ml) Campari or Aperol

LECHE MERENGADA

Makes about 1 quart (1l)

Should you ever find yourself in Spain withering away in the fierce heat of summer, rejuvenate as the locals do at one of the many *heladerías* that make the country a top destination for any ice cream aficionado. I always order *leche merengada*, a cinnamon-and-lemon-flavored frozen meringue. To make it more invigorating, I sometimes ask for a shot of high-strength *café exprés* poured over.

---

1. Heat the milk in a medium, nonreactive saucepan with 6 tablespoons (75g) of the sugar, the salt, and the cinnamon. Zest the lemon directly into the saucepan. Once the mixture is warm and the sugar is dissolved, transfer it to a bowl and chill thoroughly in the refrigerator.

2. In a large metal or glass bowl, beat the egg whites with an electric mixer or by hand until they form soft peaks. Whip in the remaining 2 tablespoons (25g) sugar and continue to beat until the whites are stiff and glossy. Remove the cinnamon sticks, if using, from the chilled milk mixture. With a flexible rubber spatula, fold the mixture into the meringue.

3. Freeze in your ice cream maker according to the manufacturer's instructions. Leche Merengada will take longer to freeze than a traditional ice cream or sorbet. You can also freeze it right in the mixing bowl, checking it after an hour and occasionally beating it with a flexible rubber spatula while it's freezing.

2 cups (500ml) whole milk

½ cup (100g) sugar

Pinch of kosher or sea salt

Two 3-inch (8cm) cinnamon sticks or ⅛ teaspoon ground cinnamon

1 lemon, preferably unsprayed

2 large egg whites, at room temperature (see Note)

NOTE: This recipe calls for uncooked egg whites. Most supermarkets now carry pasteurized egg whites, which you may wish to use if you have concerns about consuming raw egg whites. Be sure to read the label, because some pasteurized egg whites aren't suitable for whipping.

PERFECT PAIRINGS: Pour a shot of very strong espresso over a scoop of Leche Merengada or serve it with shaved Espresso Granita (page 154) piled on top.

FLEUR DE LAIT

Makes about 1 quart (1l)

My lifelong dream has always been to own an ice cream shop. But rather than start from scratch, there's one in Paris that I dreamed of taking over: Raimo. The interior was a perfectly preserved mid-century ice cream parlor, with curved, undulating ceilings, shiny leather-and-chrome swivel chairs, and a truly contemporary touch for a city as old as Paris—a machine dispensing ice water. *Très moderne.*

Despite an unfortunate remodel a few years ago, Raimo still serves an unusual frozen *glace* called *fleur de lait*, which means "flower of milk." Although they once invited me into their workshop for a tasting, I was too intimidated to ask for the recipe. So I played around in my kitchen and got it just right by using cornstarch instead of eggs, which not only preserves the milky whiteness of the cream and milk but also adds a pleasing richness that's not overwhelming. If you ever come to Paris, stop in at Raimo. And if you see me behind the counter churning away, you'll know I'm no longer just a contented customer but an even happier *glacier.*

1. Warm the milk with the sugar and salt in a medium saucepan. In a small bowl, whisk the cornstarch and cream until combined, then stir the mixture into the milk. Heat the mixture, stirring constantly, until it begins to boil and bubble up. Lower the heat and simmer for 2 minutes, continuing to stir, then scrape it into a bowl. Chill thoroughly in the refrigerator, stirring the mixture occasionally as it cools.

2. Once the mixture is well chilled, whisk to remove any lumps, then freeze it in your ice cream maker according to the manufacturer's instructions.

PERFECT PAIRING: Try sandwiching Fleur de Lait between Oatmeal Ice Cream Sandwich Cookies (page 244).

2 cups (500ml) whole milk

¾ cup (150g) sugar

Pinch of kosher or sea salt

3 tablespoons cornstarch

1 cup (250ml) cold heavy cream

CHAPTER 4

Granitas

Italians just never seem to get enough granita. In fact, they're so fanatical about it that Sicilians are known to split open yeasted rolls during their sweltering summers and pile the frozen confection inside . . . for breakfast! But if you want to see Italians really in a granita frenzy, whatever the season (and at all hours), head to Tazza d'Oro in Rome, just across from the Pantheon. The long, curving counter is constantly abuzz with activity. Muscle your way to the front as baristas pack take-away cups full of industrial-strength espresso granita made from slick, dark espresso beans roasted in the rear of the shop, often moments before brewing. It's obligatory to top if off with a big, sweet dollop of whipped cream, or *panna*, a necessary foil to the hair-raisingly strong caffeinated crystals.

Just a few blocks away is Giolitti, where locals and tourists press their noses against the overloaded freezer displaying rows and rows of stainless-steel tubs filled with granitas in a hodgepodge of hues and colors. There's *fragole*, blended up from lush, ripe strawberries, and *arancia*, made of astonishingly red blood orange pulp. Although both are tempting, there's also *frutti di bosco*, a mixture of red berries to consider, and exotic *fichi d'India*, made from prickly pear cactus fruits. Once you elbow your way through the mob swarming the counter (a necessary skill if you expect to get served in any popular Roman *gelateria*), you can watch as they heap the icy crystals into a cup, top it off with an equivalent-size drift of *panna* (whipped cream), and send you back out into the fray of Rome.

Granita is simply a shaved ice, made from a lightly sweetened fruit puree or another liquid. Of all the frozen desserts, granita is the simplest to make, requiring nothing more than a dish, a freezer, and a fork. Forming fine-grained icy crystals is the goal.

I find that flat plastic containers are the easiest to use for making granita, because they're lightweight and unbreakable, although you can use containers made of earthenware, porcelain, or stainless steel, as long as they're 8 to 12 inches (20 to 30cm) across, with a 2-quart (2l) capacity. I recommend a dish with sides that are about 2 inches (5cm) high, to contain all the crystals.

Once frozen, the icy crystals are delightfully good spooned over any kind of ice cream or sorbet that you find makes an appealing combination. Or simply pile crystals of granita into a cup, top it off with sweetened whipped cream (as much as you dare), and dig in.

Most of the recipes in this chapter make about 1 quart (1l) of granita. But unlike ice creams or sorbets, which tend to be more compact and richer, a quart of granita will serve only four people for dessert. Feel free to increase the recipes if you're expecting more guests.

TO FREEZE GRANITA

To make granita, pour the mixture into the dish and place it in the freezer. Begin checking it after about 1 hour. Once it begins to freeze around the edges, take a fork and stir the mixture, breaking up the frozen parts near the edges into smaller chunks and raking them toward the center.

Return the dish to the freezer, then check the mixture every 30 minutes, stirring each time and breaking up any large chunks into small pieces with a fork, until you have beautiful, fine crystals of homemade granita. If at any time the granita freezes too hard, simply leave it out at room temperature for a few minutes until it softens enough to be stirred again with a fork and rake it back into crystals. Then return it to the freezer. If you want a slushier (and finer) granita, give it a final once-over and vigorously chop the crystals in the container with a flat metal pastry scraper to break them into tinier pieces.

ESPRESSO GRANITA

Makes about 2½ cups (0.6l)

This granita is a favorite in Italy, where it's topped with what seems like an unspeakable amount of whipped cream, which I see many Americans scraping off just after they walk out the door—to the shock of passing Italians. You don't need to heap it on quite as high, but a dollop of Whipped Cream (page 184) is always a welcome, and sometimes necessary, counterpoint to the strong coffee.

1. Mix the warm espresso with the sugar until the sugar is dissolved.

2. Freeze according to the instructions for freezing granita on page 152.

2 cups (500ml) warm espresso or very strongly brewed, top-quality coffee

¾ cup (150g) sugar

CHOCOLATE GRANITA

Makes about 1 quart (1l)

If you're looking for a chocolate dessert that's fudgy and festive without being fussy and filling, here it is. Using top-quality cocoa powder and just the right amount of dark chocolate ensures that this granita will satisfy any and all chocolate lovers.

1. In a large saucepan, whisk together the water, sugar, salt, and cocoa powder. Bring to a full boil and continue to boil, stirring occasionally, for 15 seconds.

2. Remove from the heat and add the chocolate. Stir the mixture until the chocolate is completely melted, then add the vanilla. Taste, and if you can feel any bits of cocoa powder in your mouth, puree the mixture in a blender for 15 seconds, or until smooth. Freeze according to the instructions for freezing granita on page 152.

PERFECT PAIRINGS: Spoon crystals of Chocolate Granita over White Chocolate Ice Cream (page 37) or in contrast to a dish of Tangerine Sorbet (page 124).

4 cups (1l) water

1 cup (200g) sugar

Pinch of kosher or sea salt

⅔ cup (70g) unsweetened Dutch-process cocoa powder

4 ounces (115g) bittersweet or semisweet chocolate, chopped

1 teaspoon pure vanilla extract

PLUM GRANITA

Makes about 1 quart (1l)

One of the best-tasting plums for cooking and eating are Santa Rosa plums. Their meaty, succulent yellow flesh contrasts in color and flavor with the tangy purple skin. When cooked, the sweet-tart flavors meld perfectly to make a heavenly granita. I like to keep it on the less-sweet side, but if you find this granita a bit too tart, serve it with a dollop of Whipped Cream (page 184).

1. Slice the plums in half and remove the pits. Cut each plum into eight pieces and put them in a medium, nonreactive saucepan with the water. Cover and cook over medium heat, stirring occasionally, for about 8 minutes, or until tender. Remove from the heat and stir in the sugar until dissolved. Let cool to room temperature.

2. Once the mixture is cool, puree it in a blender or food processor until smooth. Freeze according to the instructions for freezing granita on page 152.

1½ pounds (675g) plums (about 12 plums)

1¾ cups (430ml) water

½ cup (100g) sugar

NECTARINE GRANITA

Makes about 1 quart (1l)

Nectarines make a particularly enticing summertime granita that definitely merits precious freezer space as the temperature climbs. I patiently wait and wait for the first of the sweetest-smelling nectarines to appear, and then—bang!—I hit the markets, buying as many as I can. Try serving this granita surrounded by a jumble of raspberries, blueberries, and sliced strawberries sweetened with a touch of honey.

1. Slice the unpeeled nectarines in half and remove the pits. Cut the nectarines into small chunks and add them along with 1 cup (250ml) of the water to a medium, nonreactive saucepan. Cover and cook over medium heat, stirring occasionally, until the nectarines are soft and cooked through, about 10 minutes.

2. Remove from the heat and stir in the sugar. Let cool to room temperature. When cool, puree the mixture in a blender or food processor with the remaining ⅓ cup (80ml) water until smooth. Freeze according to the instructions for freezing granita on page 152.

6 ripe nectarines (about 2 pounds, 1kg)

1⅓ cups (330ml) water

½ cup (100g) sugar

VARIATION: To make Peach Granita, substitute 6 large peaches for the nectarines. Peel the peaches (see page 96) before cooking.

KIR GRANITA

Makes about 1 quart (1l)

Inspired by the classic Kir Royale, this granita makes a similarly elegant after-dinner dessert. Because of the quantity of champagne in this recipe, it takes a bit longer to freeze than other granitas.

1. In a medium, nonreactive saucepan, heat the sugar and water until the sugar is completely dissolved. Remove from the heat and add the champagne. Stir in the crème de cassis.

2. Freeze according to the instructions for freezing granita on page 152.

NOTE: Because this granita may melt rapidly, I suggest spooning it into chilled goblets and letting them rest in the freezer until you're ready to serve.

PERFECT PAIRING: Although Kir Granita is delicious just as it is, a scoop of Raspberry-Champagne Sorbet (page 138) at the bottom of the glass is an elegant touch.

½ cup (100g) sugar

1½ cups (375ml) water

2 cups (500ml) champagne or dry sparkling wine

⅓ cup (80ml) crème de cassis (black currant liqueur)

STRAWBERRY GRANITA

Makes about 1 quart (1l)

Serve the delicate, rosy crystals of this granita with a pour-over of sparkling wine, to make a rather sophisticated slushie. Or perfume it with a few drops of fragrant rose water, to transform it into something curiously exotic and beguiling.

1. Slice the strawberries and toss them in a large bowl with the sugar, stirring until the sugar begins to dissolve. Cover and let stand at room temperature for 1 hour, stirring every so often.

2. Combine the strawberries and their liquid with the water and lemon juice in a blender or food processor and puree until smooth. Press the mixture through a mesh strainer to remove any seeds. Freeze according to the instructions for freezing granita on page 152.

2 pounds (1kg) fresh strawberries, rinsed and hulled

6 tablespoons (75g) sugar

1 cup (250ml) water

A few drops freshly squeezed lemon juice

PEAR GRANITA

Makes about 1 quart (1l)

Few people think of pairing pears with chocolate, but it's a surprisingly good combination, and once you taste it, you'll wish you'd known about it sooner. Don't hesitate to use one of my Perfect Pairings that follow the recipe to make up for lost time.

1. Quarter the pears, peel them, and remove the cores. Dice the pears into 1-inch (3cm) pieces. Put them in a medium, nonreactive saucepan with the water and sugar and cook over medium heat, covered, stirring occasionally, until completely soft, about 8 minutes. A knife inserted into a pear chunk should meet no resistance. Let cool to room temperature.

2. Puree the pears and their liquid in a blender or food processor until smooth. Freeze according to the instructions for freezing granita on page 152.

PERFECT PAIRINGS: Serve Pear Granita with Chocolate Sorbet (page 126) or Chocolate Ice Cream, Philadelphia Style (page 32).

6 ripe pears (about 3 pounds, 1.5kg), such as Comice, Barlett, or French butter

1 cup (250ml) water

6 tablespoons (75g) sugar

CRANBERRY GRANITA

Makes about 1 quart (1l)

The arrival of cranberries in the fall magically coincides with the holiday food shopping frenzy. A wonder of nature? Or just good timing? Regardless, I'm happy whenever I find cranberries in abundance. Their flavor is invigorating and restorative, which is probably why they're so popular around the time of year when many of us could use help after overindulging in copious holiday feasts.

1. Put the cranberries, water, sugar, and orange juice in a medium, nonreactive saucepan and bring to a boil. Cover, remove from the heat, and let stand for 30 minutes.

2. Puree the mixture in a blender or food processor until smooth, then press through a mesh strainer to remove the bits of cranberry skin. Freeze according to the instructions for freezing granita on page 152.

PERFECT PAIRINGS: Serve with Tangerine Sorbet (page 124) or spicy Cinnamon Ice Cream (page 45).

3 cups (340g) cranberries, fresh or frozen

1 cup (250ml) water

1 cup (200g) sugar

½ cup (125ml) freshly squeezed orange juice (from about 2 oranges)

GRAPE GRANITA

Makes about 1 quart (1l)

The best grapes to use for making this granita are bold-tasting varieties. Full-flavored dark Muscat grapes are perfect, as are Concord grapes, which winemakers sometimes describe as tasting "foxy." Speaking of winemakers, just about any grapes used for winemaking make excellent granita. Don't use the common seedless grapes found in supermarkets, though, because they don't have much flavor once cooked.

The amount of water to add to the grape mixture will depend on the type of grapes you use. Before adding the water, taste the mixture. Begin with the smaller amount of water, and then taste it again to see whether it needs more.

1. Rinse the grapes and remove them from the stems (see No Separation Anxiety, below). Cut them in half if the skins are thick and tough. Cook the grapes with the sugar and ½ cup (125ml) water in a medium, nonreactive saucepan over medium heat, covered, stirring occasionally, until the skins have burst and the grapes are soft and cooked through.

2. Pass the grapes through a food mill or press them through a mesh strainer to separate the skins from the pulp. Add the lemon juice and taste, adding some or all of the remaining 1 cup (250ml) water, if you want a lighter flavor and icier texture. Freeze according to the instructions for freezing granita on page 152.

PERFECT PAIRINGS: This lively, colorful Grape Granita pairs nicely with Mascarpone Ice Cream (variation, page 72) or Pear Sorbet (page 116).

2 pounds (1kg) fresh grapes, preferably Concord or Muscat

⅔ cup (130g) sugar

½ to 1 cup (125 to 250ml) water

A few drops freshly squeezed lemon juice

NO SEPARATION ANXIETY

To quickly separate grapes from their stems, put bunches of grapes in the bowl of an electric stand mixer. Fit the mixer with the dough hook and turn it on at the lowest speed. The hook will easily separate the stems from the grapes.

MOJITO GRANITA

Makes about 1 quart (1l)

There's a good reason mojitos have become all the rage. Made with rum, a few handfuls of fresh mint, and just-squeezed lime juice, this lively Cuban cocktail practically begs to be made into a terrific granita. To make it more adult, drizzle a bit of extra rum over each serving and garnish with fresh mint sprigs.

1. Add the water and sugar to a small, nonreactive saucepan, then grate the zest of the 2 limes directly into the saucepan. Bring the mixture to a boil and cook, stirring occasionally, until the sugar is dissolved. Reserve 5 of the mint leaves, add the remaining mint to the saucepan, and remove from the heat. Cover and let stand for 8 minutes, then remove the cover and let cool to room temperature.

2. Once cool, strain the mixture into the container you plan to freeze the granita in, pressing firmly on the leaves to extract all the flavorful liquid. Discard the mint leaves. Stir in the lime juice and rum, then finely chop the reserved mint leaves and add them as well. Freeze according to the instructions for freezing granita on page 152.

PERFECT PAIRING: If you love the refreshing taste of mint as much as I do, pair this with a scoop of Fresh Mint Ice Cream (page 106).

2½ cups (625ml) water

½ cup (100g) sugar

2 limes, preferably unsprayed

1 cup (40g) lightly packed fresh mint leaves

½ cup (125ml) freshly squeezed lime juice (from about 6 limes)

3 tablespoons white or light rum

BLOOD ORANGE GRANITA

Makes about 1 quart (1l)

I love the word *spremuta*, which means "freshly pressed orange juice" in Italian. At any *caffè*, if you order one, you'll be brought a tall, vivid red glass of juice served with a few packets of sugar with a long, slender spoon alongside. Although years ago, Americans were astonished when first confronted with blood orange juice, this colorful citrus fruit has become common Stateside and can be found in supermarkets and at farmers' markets. When sliced open, they reveal a brilliantly colored interior, and, like snowflakes, each one intrigues me, because no two seem to be colored alike. The Moro variety of blood oranges is the most intensely colored, but other varieties, like Sanguinelli and Tarocco, make a remarkably colorful granita as well.

---

1. Warm the sugar with 1 cup (250ml) of the orange juice in a medium, nonreactive saucepan. Stir until the sugar is dissolved. Remove from the heat and add the remaining 3 cups (750ml) orange juice and the Grand Marnier.

2. Freeze according to the instructions for freezing granita on page 152.

PERFECT PAIRINGS: Think Italian and pair this with Anise Ice Cream (page 44), a flavor that goes very well with this deeply flavored Blood Orange Granita.

¾ cup plus 2 tablespoons (180g) sugar

4 cups (1l) freshly squeezed blood orange juice (from 14 to 16 blood oranges)

4 teaspoons Grand Marnier or Triple Sec

PINK GRAPEFRUIT GRANITA

Makes about 1 quart (1l)

I know people who are grapefruit dependent. They're addicted to starting their day with half a pink grapefruit. They absolutely have to have one, and frankly, that's a little odd to me. It's not that I don't like grapefruits—in fact, I often buy them with the intention of following in the healthy footsteps of my grapefruit-dependent friends. But the next morning I wake up and honestly can't seem to face anything but a much-needed cup of coffee and a couple of nonconfrontational slices of buttered toast.

Later in the day, those pink grapefruits become more and more appealing though, and I'll slice one in half and greedily attack the sections, slurping up the plentiful juice while leaning over the sink to contain the mess from my assault. So perhaps I do have some grapefruit issues of my own, but I wait until later in the day before I succumb and take my tumble off the citrus wagon.

1. In a small, nonreactive saucepan, warm ½ cup (125ml) of the grapefruit juice with the sugar, stirring until the sugar is dissolved. Add the remaining 3½ cups (775ml) grapefruit juice.

2. Freeze according to the instructions for freezing granita on page 152.

PERFECT PAIRING: Serve Pink Grapefruit Granita in tall champagne flutes with a rather dry champagne or sparkling wine poured over the top, along with a few fresh raspberries or wild strawberries.

4 cups (1l) freshly squeezed pink grapefruit juice (from 4 or 5 grapefruits)

¾ cup plus 2 tablespoons (180g) sugar

LEMON GRANITA

Makes about 1 quart (1l)

A few years back, while I was making a chocolate dessert during a cooking demonstration, I noticed a woman sitting in the third row watching me with what looked like disdain. Attempting to win her over, while everyone ate their samples, I asked what she thought and she responded matter-of-factly, "I don't really like chocolate." So smart-aleck me shot back, "You're probably one of those lemon people!" To which she sheepishly nodded yes.

I kept on baking and finished the class. But my accusatory words "one of those lemon people" stuck in my mind ever since, and I worried for a long time that she might have been affronted by my comment.

Years later, there she was again in my audience! I was happy to see her, because experts advocate finding resolution to traumatic events in your life (such as meeting someone who doesn't like chocolate). Attempting reparation, I asked whether I had offended her several years back. She was surprised that I even remembered and said that no, she wasn't offended in the least. In fact, she even brought me a tasty gift (not chocolate . . . but I'm letting *that* go) and then slipped off into the night. So this is my gift back to her, the mysterious lemon lover, whoever and wherever you are.

---

1. In a medium, nonreactive saucepan, mix ½ cup (125ml) of the water with the sugar. Grate the zest of the lemons directly into the saucepan. Heat, stirring frequently, until the sugar is completely dissolved. Remove from the heat, add the remaining 2 cups (500ml) water, and then chill in the refrigerator.

2. Stir the lemon juice into the sugar syrup, then freeze according to the instructions for freezing granita on page 152.

PERFECT PAIRING: Smooth and silky White Chocolate Ice Cream (page 37) makes a great counterpoint to tangy Lemon Granita.

2½ cups (625ml) water

1 cup (200g) sugar

2 lemons, preferably unsprayed

1 cup (250ml) freshly squeezed lemon juice (from about 6 lemons)

POP GOES THE GRANITA

Most of the granita recipes make excellent Popsicles too (except the Kir Granita, page 156; Negroni Slush, page 171; and Frozen Gimlets, page 169; which don't freeze quite so firmly). Simply pour the mixture into plastic Popsicle molds and freeze until very firm.

LIME GRANITA

Makes about 1 quart (1l)

Try this granita drizzled with a shot of tequila and sprinkled with a pinch of flaky sea salt for a "margranita."

1. In a medium, nonreactive saucepan, mix ½ cup (125ml) of the water with the sugar. Grate the zest of the limes into the saucepan. Heat, stirring frequently, until the sugar is completely dissolved. Remove from the heat, add the remaining 2½ cups (625ml) water, and then chill in the refrigerator.

2. Stir the lime juice into the sugar syrup, then freeze according to the instructions for freezing granita on page 152.

PERFECT PAIRINGS: Lime Granita is a tropical treat with Mango Sorbet (page 112) or Avocado Ice Cream (page 103).

3 cups (750ml) water

1 cup (200g) sugar

2 limes, preferably unsprayed

1 cup (250ml) freshly squeezed lime juice (from about 12 limes)

PINEAPPLE GRANITA

Makes about 1¼ quarts (1¼l)

Curiously, this granita really comes alive when a few grains of flaky sea salt are flecked over each serving. When I had friends over for a taste, they were surprised to see me salting their granita, but they quickly changed their minds when they tasted it. Try fleur de sel, hand-harvested salt crystals from France, or translucent squares of Maldon salt, from England. To make it south-of-the-border rather than across-the-Atlantic, sprinkle the top with Mexican chile powder or a drizzle of *chamoy*, a sweet-sour (and a bit spicy) sauce made of pickled fruits, which you can find in Latin markets.

1. Cut the pineapple into small chunks and puree them in a blender or food processor with the water, sugar, lime juice, and salt until completely smooth. You should have about 4 cups (1l) puree. If you wish, press the mixture through a mesh strainer for a more fine-textured granita.

2. Freeze according to the instructions for freezing granita on page 152.

PERFECT PAIRINGS: Serve this with Toasted Coconut Ice Cream (page 105) or another tropical flavor, such as Roasted Banana Ice Cream (page 82).

1 fresh pineapple, peeled and cored

1 cup (250ml) water

½ cup (100g) sugar

2 teaspoons freshly squeezed lime juice

Pinch of kosher or sea salt

MELON GRANITA

Makes about 3 cups (750ml)

Either cantaloupe or honeydew melon makes a wonderful granita. To find the best one, heft a few at the market or in the grocery store and let your nose guide you to the sweetest specimen. (Pictured opposite, right.)

1. Peel the melon, split it in half, and scoop out the seeds. Cut the melon into chunks and add them to a blender or food processor along with the sugar, lemon juice, water, and salt. Puree until completely smooth.

2. Freeze according to the instructions for freezing granita on page 152.

PERFECT PAIRINGS: Raspberry Ice Cream (page 101) and Raspberry Sherbet (page 138) make nice counterpoints to Melon Granita.

One 2-pound (1kg) ripe melon

⅔ cup (130g) sugar

1 teaspoon freshly squeezed lemon or lime juice

¼ cup (60ml) water

Pinch of kosher or sea salt

KIWIFRUIT GRANITA

Makes about 1 quart (1l)

To make the tastiest and most colorful granita, be sure to use kiwifruits that are tender and soft to the touch. They'll have the most vibrant green flesh and the fullest flavor. (Pictured opposite, middle.)

1. Peel the kiwifruits and, using the point of a paring knife, remove the tough nubbins just inside the stem ends. Cut the kiwifruits into small pieces, add them to a blender or food processor with the water and sugar, and puree until smooth.

2. Freeze according to the instructions for freezing granita on page 152.

PERFECT PAIRING: Serve Kiwifruit Granita with Tangerine Sorbet (page 124) or Strawberry Sorbet (page 134).

2 pounds (1kg) ripe kiwifruits (10 to 15 kiwifruits)

1⅓ cups (330ml) water

¾ cup (150g) sugar

RASPBERRY GRANITA

Makes about 2 cups (500ml)

Perhaps the most eye-popping of all the granitas, this one has a color that
perfectly matches the dazzling flavor of the raspberries. If using frozen
raspberries, let them thaw before you puree them. (Pictured on page 166, left.)

1. Pass the raspberries through a food mill, or puree in a food processor and press
through a sieve to remove the seeds. Add the water and sugar, stirring until the
sugar is dissolved.

2. Freeze according to the instructions for freezing granita on page 152.

PERFECT PAIRINGS: Super Lemon Ice Cream (page 93) and Lemon-Buttermilk
Sherbet (page 122) are two of my favorite pairings with Raspberry Granita.

4 cups (480g) raspberries,
fresh or frozen

1 cup (250ml) water

¼ cup (50g) sugar

FROZEN GIMLETS

Makes about 2½ cups (625ml)

Where have gimlets been all my life? For years I was a martini drinker (gin only, thank you very much), but once I discovered gimlets, my allegiances shifted. With a dose of fresh lime juice tempered with a little sugar syrup, it has become one of my favorite cocktails. Here, those flavors come together in bold, tangy scoops.

I like this on the gin-forward side, but depending on what kind of gin you use—some are heavy on botanicals, others are lighter—you may want to start with ½ cup (125ml) of gin and add a little more to taste. Be sure to zest the lime right into the gimlet mixture; you don't want to lose any of their flavorful oils.

1. In a medium saucepan, heat the sugar with ½ cup (125ml) of the water, stirring, until the sugar is dissolved. Remove from the heat and add the remaining 1 cup (250ml) water, the gin, and the lime juice. Grate the zest of the lime directly into the saucepan and stir to combine.

2. Chill thoroughly, then freeze according to the instructions for freezing granita on page 152.

PERFECT PAIRING: Gin has a great affinity for rosemary. To make rosemary syrup for drizzling over scoops of frozen gimlets, in a small saucepan, bring ½ cup (125ml) water and ½ cup (100g) sugar to a boil. Remove from the heat and add 2 tablespoons coarsely chopped fresh rosemary leaves. Let cool completely, then strain out the rosemary. Chill until ready to use.

6 tablespoons (75g) sugar

1½ cups (375ml) water

½ cup plus 2 tablespoons (155ml) gin

⅓ cup (80ml) freshly squeezed lime juice

1 lime, preferably unsprayed

EVERYTHING IN ITS PLACE—AND MODERATION

I may have had too many Frozen Gimlets when I placed this recipe in the book, and grouped it in with the granitas due to its icy-cold texture and flavor. But when I looked at the recipe again with a clearer head, I realized that I usually freeze it in my ice cream machine. So while I prefer to churn it, if you don't have an ice cream machine, or prefer an icier texture, you can stir it up as you would a granita and enjoy it that way—in moderation, of course.

NEGRONI SLUSH

Makes about 3 cups (750ml)

The Negroni has become one of the most popular cocktails at bars around the world. One reason for its success is the foolproof recipe: one part vermouth, one part Campari, and one part gin. When mixed together, these three ingredients make a dynamic, high-strength cocktail that demands to be served with a giant ice cube languishing in the glass, to keep the drink cold.

I upended the classic Negroni proportions and enlisted the help of a few supporting ingredients to create this adults-only slush. It's less boozy than the cocktail, so you can indulge in a second helping, but like a true Negroni, it's decidedly on the bitter side thanks to the Campari and grapefruit juice. If you want to make it less tangy, use orange juice in place of the more robust grapefruit juice. Or ramp up the color and use the juice of blood oranges, when they're in season.

1. Heat the water and sugar in a medium saucepan, stirring constantly, just until the sugar is dissolved. Remove from the heat and let cool to room temperature. Add the grapefruit juice, Campari, vermouth, and gin. Pour the mixture into a shallow container and freeze for 24 hours. Unlike granita, the slush doesn't need to be stirred while freezing.

2. Serve the Negroni Slush piled into well-chilled cocktail glasses or short tumblers. Just before serving, briskly stir the mixture with a soup spoon to break it up into slushy crystals.

PERFECT PAIRINGS: Garnish the slush with Candied Citrus Peel (page 193). To turn it into a fruit-forward dessert, spoon the slush over grapefruit, orange, and tangerine segments arranged in chilled soup bowls.

½ cup (125ml) water

¼ cup (60g) sugar

1 cup (250ml) freshly squeezed grapefruit juice

½ cup (125ml) Campari or another bitter red apéritif

½ cup (125ml) sweet (red) vermouth

2 tablespoons (30ml) gin

CHAPTER 5

Sauces and Toppings

What would a book on ice cream be without lots of recipes for sauces and toppings of all kinds? A perfect scoop of ice cream is great on its own, but add a ladle of sauce and you've got a full-fledged dessert. Whether you'll be serving crunchy granola over tangy frozen yogurt or a scoop of fresh fruit sorbet resting on a pool of brightly colored berry coulis, the recipes in this chapter are designed to give you lots of options for customizing any ice cream or sorbet as you wish.

One of life's great pleasures is spooning a homemade topping over scoops of ice cream and watching it ooze down the sides before digging in. Is there anything better than scraping warm, rich Classic Hot Fudge (page 178) off your spoon as it mingles with cool, creamy ice cream? Is there anyone out there who doesn't like a good hot fudge sundae? But in case you're not in the mood for a full-blown sundae extravaganza, you'll also find plenty of other chocolate sauces to choose from, including a Lean Chocolate Sauce (page 179) that's so chocolaty you won't feel deprived of anything. And if you're looking for a chocolate topping with kick, espresso-fueled Mocha Sauce (page 179) will turbocharge any dish of ice cream into something stratospherically good.

Anyone who knows me is aware that I, as a pastry chef, hold a singular, puffy marshmallow in the same high esteem that a savory cook reserves for a rare, pricey truffle. There's nothing I enjoy more than anything made with marshmallows, and in my headstrong youth I insisted that ice cream parlors replace the whipped cream they normally served on ice cream sundaes with sticky marshmallow sauce on mine. (Unfortunately, I could never convince them to give me both.) I'm sorry, but there's no substitute for the sweet sensation of diving into billowy Marshmallow Sauce (page 182).

We americans are famous for our love of butterscotch and gooey caramel, so there's a Pecan-Praline Sauce (page 195) loaded with toasted nuts and a Creamy Caramel Sauce (page 186) here as well. As a nod to ice cream lovers around the world, I've also gone global, with recipes such as Candied Red Beans (page 200), Cajeta (page 188), and Dulce de Leche (page 185). I think you'll enjoy making and eating them all, no matter where you call home.

SEMISWEET HOT FUDGE

Makes 3 cups (750ml)

This sauce is very rich and very thick. If you prefer your hot fudge on the sweeter side, this is the one for you.

1. Heat the cream, butter, corn syrup, and sugar in a large saucepan until the mixture begins to boil. Boil for 3 minutes, stirring occasionally, making sure it doesn't boil over.

2. Remove from the heat and add the chopped chocolate, stirring until melted and smooth. Stir in the vanilla. Serve warm.

STORAGE: This sauce can be stored in the refrigerator for up to 2 weeks. Rewarm it gently in a microwave or by stirring in a saucepan over very low heat.

1 cup (250ml) heavy cream

6 tablespoons (85g) unsalted butter, cut into pieces

2 tablespoons light corn syrup

⅔ cup (130g) sugar

8 ounces (230g) bittersweet or semisweet chocolate, chopped

1 teaspoon pure vanilla extract

CLASSIC HOT FUDGE

Makes 2 cups (500ml)

A chef once asked me if all pastry chefs were crazy. For better or worse, we do have that reputation, because many of us are obsessed perfectionists. If we get something in our minds, we're not satisfied until it's just right. When I imagined the perfect hot fudge sauce, I envisioned it being gooey, shiny, silky smooth, and full of deep, dark chocolate flavor. So I tinkered around until I came up with the perfect version. Call me what you want, but you'll find this sauce is crazy-good.

1. Mix the cream, brown sugar, cocoa powder, and corn syrup in a large saucepan. Bring to a boil and cook, stirring frequently, for 30 seconds.

2. Remove from the heat and add the chocolate and butter, stirring until melted and smooth. Stir in the vanilla. Serve warm.

STORAGE: This sauce can be stored in the refrigerator for up to 2 weeks. Rewarm it gently in a microwave or by stirring in a saucepan over very low heat.

¾ cup (180ml) heavy cream

¼ cup (45g) packed dark brown sugar

¼ cup (25g) unsweetened Dutch-process cocoa powder

½ cup (125ml) light corn syrup

6 ounces (170g) bittersweet or semisweet chocolate, chopped

1 tablespoon salted butter

½ teaspoon pure vanilla extract

LEAN CHOCOLATE SAUCE

Makes 3 cups (750ml)

This is my go-to chocolate sauce. Although the name says "lean," it tastes anything but. It's a wonderful alternative to richer chocolate sauces spiked with cream or butter, and gets its flavor from lots of chocolate and cocoa powder. This sauce gets gloriously thicker the longer it sits, which I find is a perfectly reasonable excuse for keeping a batch on hand in the refrigerator at all times.

1. In a saucepan, whisk together the water, cocoa powder, and corn syrup and bring to a boil. Turn the heat to very low and simmer for 3 minutes, stirring frequently.

2. Remove from the heat and add the chocolate, stirring until melted and smooth. Serve warm.

STORAGE: This sauce can be stored in the refrigerator for up to 2 weeks. Rewarm it gently in a microwave or by stirring in a saucepan over very low heat.

2 cups (500ml) water

1 cup (100g) unsweetened Dutch-process cocoa powder

1 cup (250ml) light corn syrup

4 ounces (115g) bittersweet or semisweet chocolate, chopped

MOCHA SAUCE

Makes 2 cups (500ml)

The coffee craze shows no sign of slowing down. And fueled by all that caffeine, it probably never will. This sauce combines coffee and chocolate to make mocha, which was named after an Arabian port famous for its coffee. Somewhere along the line, chocolate was added to coffee, and "mocha" nowadays means coffee fortified with a good dose of chocolate.

1. Whisk the espresso, sugar, and cocoa powder together in a medium saucepan and bring to a boil. Let the mixture cook at a low boil for 30 seconds without stirring.

2. Remove from the heat and whisk in the chocolate and butter, stirring until melted and smooth. Let the sauce stand for 1 hour before serving.

STORAGE: This sauce can be stored in the refrigerator for up to 2 weeks. Rewarm it gently in a microwave or by stirring in a saucepan over very low heat.

1 cup (250ml) espresso or strongly brewed coffee

¾ cup (150g) sugar

½ cup (50g) unsweetened Dutch-process cocoa powder

2 ounces (60g) bittersweet or semisweet chocolate, chopped

4 tablespoons (60g) butter, salted or unsalted, cut into pieces

CHOCOLATE SHELL

Makes ⅔ cup (160ml)

If you're looking for a "snappy" chocolate coating for drizzling or dipping, this is your recipe. Spooned over a bowl of ice cream or over scoops in a cone, it magically turns into a hard shell. The secret ingredient is coconut oil, which can be found in well-stocked supermarkets. I prefer refined coconut oil, which doesn't have the strong flavor of virgin coconut oil, which can overwhelm the chocolate, but you can use either.

Speaking of chocolate (one of my favorite subjects!), this is the place to use a high-percentage bittersweet chocolate, if you can. One that's at least 70 percent cocoa solids will provide the darkest, snappiest, crispiest chocolate coating.

1. Melt the chocolate and coconut oil together in a medium bowl set over a saucepan of barely simmering water, stirring until the chocolate is almost melted.

2. Remove from the heat and continue to gently stir until the chocolate is melted.

STORAGE: The chocolate shell can be stored for up to 2 weeks in the refrigerator or at room temperature. Rewarm it gently over a saucepan of simmering water.

7 ounces (200g) bittersweet chocolate, preferably 70 percent cocoa solids, coarsely chopped

2 tablespoons (30ml) refined coconut oil

MARSHMALLOW SAUCE

Makes 2 cups (500ml)

I love sticky marshmallows, perhaps more than anything else on the planet. When this sauce is spooned over a hot fudge sundae, the combination is pure bliss. Make it for yourself and see what all the fuss is about.

1. Pour ½ cup (120ml) of the water into a small bowl and sprinkle the gelatin over the top; set aside. In a small, heavy-bottomed saucepan fitted with a candy thermometer, mix the remaining ¼ cup (60ml) water with the sugar and the corn syrup. Put the egg white in the bowl of an electric stand mixer fitted with the whip attachment.

2. Bring the sugar mixture to a boil. When the syrup reaches about 225°F (110°C), begin beating the egg white with the salt on medium-high speed. Once the syrup reaches 240°F (116°C) and the egg white is stiff, while beating on high speed, pour the hot syrup into the mixer bowl in a slow stream. (Aim the syrup between the whip and the side of the bowl to keep the syrup from sticking to the side or clinging to the whip.)

3. Once you've added all the syrup, stop the mixer and scrape down the sides of the mixer bowl. Pour the softened gelatin into the still-warm saucepan and stir, allowing the heat of the pan to melt the gelatin. While beating on high speed, pour the melted gelatin into the egg white mixture as you did the sugar syrup. Continue to beat until the mixture thickens and cools to room temperature, then whip in the vanilla.

STORAGE: This sauce can be served right after it's made. It can be kept at room temperature for up to 8 hours, or refrigerated for up to 1 week. Either way, it will thicken upon standing. To make it smooth and spoonable again, if refrigerated, let it come to room temperature, then beat it briskly with a spatula or whisk.

NOTE: This sauce can be marbled (see Marbling, page 93) into ice cream, if you'd like ripples of marshmallow in it.

¾ cup (185ml) cold water

1 envelope (¼ ounce, 7g) unflavored powdered gelatin

¼ cup (50g) sugar

½ cup (125ml) light corn syrup

1 large egg white

Big pinch of kosher or sea salt

1 teaspoon pure vanilla extract

MARSHMALLOW–HOT FUDGE SAUCE

Makes 2 cups (500ml)

This decadently thick sauce is perfect if you're as nostalgic as I am for the incredibly thick hot fudge sauce served in old-fashioned ice cream parlors, many of which have disappeared. This sauce isn't going anywhere, thankfully, but it will likely disappear before you know it. It's that good.

Warning: This sauce is very, very thick!

1. Warm the milk and butter in a medium saucepan. Add the marshmallows and cook over low heat, stirring constantly, until they've melted.

2. Remove from the heat and add the chocolate. Let stand for 30 seconds, then stir until the sauce is smooth. Stir in the vanilla. Serve warm.

STORAGE: This sauce can be stored in the refrigerator for up to 2 weeks. Rewarm it gently in a microwave or by stirring in a saucepan over very low heat. If the sauce becomes too thick, stir in a few spoonfuls of milk.

⅔ cup (160ml) milk
(whole or low-fat)

2 tablespoons salted butter

30 large marshmallows
(page 232)

8 ounces (230g) bittersweet
or semisweet chocolate,
finely chopped

¼ teaspoon pure vanilla
extract

WHITE CHOCOLATE SAUCE

Makes 2 cups (500ml)

This sauce is easy to put together and lovely served with any of the dark chocolate ice creams or sorbets in this book, and it works equally well with any frozen dessert made with berries. I appreciate it for its creamy sweetness, and it rarely fails to impress. Be sure to use top-quality, real white chocolate, which is actually ivory colored due to an abundance of pure cocoa butter.

1. Warm the cream in a small saucepan.

2. Once it's hot but not boiling, remove it from the heat and stir in the white chocolate until it is completely melted and the sauce is smooth. Serve warm or at room temperature.

STORAGE: This sauce can be stored in the refrigerator for up to 5 days. Rewarm it gently in a double boiler or in a microwave oven. If the sauce gets too thick, thin it out with a tablespoon or two of whole milk.

VARIATIONS: For White Chocolate and Vanilla Bean Sauce, stir in ¾ teaspoon ground vanilla beans or 1 teaspoon vanilla bean paste. To make White Chocolate–Chartreuse Sauce, add 1 tablespoon (15ml) green Chartreuse liqueur.

1¼ cups (310ml) heavy cream

10 ounces (280g) white chocolate, finely chopped

WHIPPED CREAM

Makes 2 cups (500ml)

Successful whipped cream means starting with the best-tasting, freshest cream you can find. Buy heavy or whipping cream that hasn't been ultra-pasteurized, if you can. Farmers' markets and natural food stores often sell cream from local producers.

Before you start whipping, make sure your cream is very cold. If you chill the bowl and whisk beforehand, the cream will whip much faster, which is especially important in warmer weather.

1. With an electric mixer, or by hand with a whisk and stainless-steel bowl, whip the cream until it begins to mound and hold its shape.

2. Whisk in 1 tablespoon of the sugar and the vanilla. Taste, then add the remaining 1 tablespoon sugar, if you wish. Whip until the cream forms soft, droopy peaks.

NOTE: You can rescue overwhipped cream by gently folding in additional liquid cream with a rubber spatula until smooth.

1 cup (250ml) heavy cream

1 to 2 tablespoons sugar

½ teaspoon pure vanilla extract

DULCE DE LECHE

Makes 1 cup (250ml)

This is an oven-baked version of Cajeta (page 188). Slightly warmed, it's a superb sauce for ice cream, and is excellent layered or swirled into ice cream. Baking it in the oven means you don't need to watch it carefully while it cooks, but do make sure there's sufficient water in the outer pan while it's cooking. You can also add a vanilla bean at the beginning or stir in 1 tablespoon of sherry at the end.

1. Preheat the oven to 425°F (220°C).

2. Pour the condensed milk into an 8- or 9-inch (20 or 23cm) nonreactive metal pan or glass baking dish and sprinkle with the salt. Cover snugly with foil and set the baking dish within a larger pan, such as a roasting pan. Add hot water to the roasting pan until it reaches halfway up the outside of the baking dish.

3. Bake for 1 to 1¼ hours, checking a few times during baking and adding warm water to the roasting pan if it needs more. Once the milk is the color of dark butterscotch, remove it from the oven. Remove the foil and let cool to room temperature. If necessary, stir to smooth out the consistency.

STORAGE: This sauce can be stored in the refrigerator for up to 2 months. Rewarm it gently in a microwave or by stirring in a saucepan over very low heat. If it seems too thick, you can thin it with a small amount of milk.

One 14-ounce (397g) can sweetened condensed milk

Pinch of kosher or sea salt

CREAMY CARAMEL SAUCE

Makes 1½ cups (375ml)

There's nothing that beats the taste of darkly caramelized sugar transformed by a pour of cream into a suave, velvety caramel sauce. If you've never made caramel before, it's simple, but do take care, because the sugar gets very hot as it liquefies. Wear an oven mitt when stirring in the cream, and resist the temptation to peer too closely into the pot while it's bubbling and boiling away.

1. Warm the cream in a small saucepan. Remove from the heat and set aside.

2. Spread the sugar in an even layer on the bottom of a large, heavy-bottomed saucepan or Dutch oven. Cook the sugar over low to medium heat, watching it carefully. When it begins to liquefy and darken at the edges, use a heatproof spatula to very gently stir it to encourage even cooking.

3. Tilt the pan and stir gently until all of the sugar is melted and the caramel begins to smoke and turns a deep amber color. Immediately remove from the heat and gradually whisk in half of the warm cream, which may steam and bubble up furiously. Carefully stir until the sugar is dissolved, then gradually whisk in the remaining cream, the salt, and the vanilla. If there are any bits of hardened sugar, whisk the sauce over low heat until smooth. Serve warm.

STORAGE: This sauce can be stored in the refrigerator for up to 2 weeks. Rewarm it gently in a microwave or by stirring in a saucepan over very low heat. If the sauce is too thick, you can thin it by adding a small amount of milk or additional cream.

1¼ cups (310ml) heavy cream

1 cup (200g) sugar

¼ teaspoon kosher or sea salt

½ teaspoon pure vanilla extract

CAJETA

Makes 1¼ cups (310ml)

I think of cajeta as the risotto of dessert sauces because it's made on the stove top and requires vigilant attention while it simmers. With cooking, cajeta's ordinary ingredients (milk and sugar) are transformed into a deeply browned, sticky-sweet paste. The first cajeta I tasted was made from goat's milk, and it was absolutely the best thing I'd ever had. If you are not able to find goat's milk, or if it's not to your taste, cow's milk makes yummy cajeta as well.

Begin your cajeta in a very large pot, one with a capacity of at least 8 quarts (8l), because the mixture can bubble up unexpectedly. It should be a heavy-duty pot with a thick bottom. Be sure to pay attention while you're cooking, especially during the last 20 minutes, when it's vital to keep watch. If you don't stir constantly during that final stage of cooking, the mixture is likely to scorch on the bottom. If it does, strain it to remove any browned bits.

1. In a large, heavy-bottomed Dutch oven or soup pot, heat the milk, sugar, corn syrup, baking soda, cinnamon stick or vanilla bean, and salt until the mixture comes to a boil. As the milk begins to foam up, begin stirring it with a heatproof spatula or wooden spoon.

2. Lower the heat so the milk is at a low, rolling boil and continue to cook, stirring frequently and scraping the bottom, allowing the mixture to reduce.

3. After about 20 minutes, the milk will begin to thicken and turn a light beige color. At this point, lower the heat as much as possible (if you have a flame tamer, you may wish to use it), and be vigilant, scraping the bottom constantly as it cooks.

4. Continue to cook for about 15 minutes more, stirring vigilantly, until the milk is the color of coffee with a touch of cream. Remove from the heat and let cool to room temperature. Once cool, remove the cinnamon stick or vanilla bean.

4 cups (1l) whole milk (cow's milk or goat's milk)

1 cup (200g) sugar

2 tablespoons light corn syrup

¼ teaspoon baking soda

1 cinnamon stick or ½ vanilla bean

Big pinch of kosher or sea salt

STORAGE: Cajeta can be stored in the refrigerator for up to 2 months. Rewarm it gently in a microwave or by stirring it in a saucepan over very low heat to serve as an accompaniment to ice cream. If it's too thick, you can thin it with a little milk.

NOTE: Cajeta can be layered into ice cream, in generous spoonfuls as you remove the just-churned ice cream from the machine; see Mixing It In, page 231. This is easiest to do when the cajeta is at room temperature and not chilled.

SALTED BUTTER CARAMEL SAUCE

Makes 1½ cups (375ml)

We all need heroes in life. Someone to look up to, whom you idolize, and who does something that changes your life forever.

For me, that person is Henri Le Roux, maker of caramel-butter-salt caramels (nicknamed CBS) in the seaside town of Quiberon, on the Atlantic coast of France. The residents of Brittany are famous for consuming ridiculous amounts of butter, most of it heavily flecked with sea salt to preserve and complement its buttery goodness. When Monsieur Le Roux unwrapped one of his meltingly tender salted caramels and popped it in my mouth, I knew I'd found my hero.

To get the same flavor in this sauce, be sure to use a good-quality kosher or sea salt, such as fleur de sel (see Resources, page 259), recognizable by its delicate, shimmering crystals. It makes a difference.

1. Warm the cream in a small saucepan. Remove from the heat and set aside.

2. Melt the butter in a large, deep, heavy-bottomed saucepan or Dutch oven. Add the sugar and cook, stirring frequently, until the sugar is a deep golden brown and starts to smoke.

3. Remove from the heat and immediately whisk in half of the cream until smooth (wear an oven mitt, because the mixture will steam and splatter and may bubble up furiously). Stir in the rest of the cream, then the vanilla and salt. If there are any lumps of caramel, whisk the sauce gently over low heat until smooth. Serve warm.

STORAGE: This sauce can be stored in the refrigerator for up to 2 weeks. Rewarm it gently in a microwave or by stirring in a saucepan over very low heat.

1 cup (250ml) heavy cream

6 tablespoons (85g) butter, salted or unsalted

¾ cup (150g) sugar

½ teaspoon pure vanilla extract

1¼ teaspoons kosher or flaky sea salt

LEMON CARAMEL SAUCE

Makes 1 cup (250ml)

Do you have OSD? When you see something in a saucepan, do you find that you can't stop yourself from giving it a stir? If so, you've probably got Obsessive Stirring Disorder, and you need to curb that kind of behavior if you want to caramelize sugar properly.

When making caramel, mix the sugar as little as possible, just enough to keep it from burning. Stirring encourages the jagged little crystals to join together and crystallize, which you want to avoid, and it's best to tilt the pan to incorporate the sugar and water. Your vigilance will pay off in lemony sauce that's superb drizzled over any lemon-flavored ice cream served in Profiteroles (page 255) or offered alongside ice cream–filled Crêpes (page 253).

1 cup (200g) sugar

1 cup (250ml) water

2 to 3 tablespoons freshly squeezed lemon juice

1. In a large, heavy-bottomed saucepan or skillet, spread the sugar in an even layer. Pour ½ cup (125ml) of the water over it and add a few drops of the lemon juice. Cook the sugar, without stirring, over medium heat until the mixture begins to bubble and the sugar starts to dissolve. Tilt the pan gently if the sugar is cooking unevenly, or use a heatproof utensil to ever so gently stir the mixture.

2. Once the sugar begins to smoke and becomes a deep amber color, remove it from the heat and add the remaining ½ cup (125ml) water. Let the steam subside, then whisk the caramel until smooth (wear an oven mitt, as the hot caramel can splatter).

3. Stir in 2 tablespoons lemon juice and let the mixture cool to room temperature. Strain it if there are any bits of undissolved sugar. Once the caramel cools, taste it and add the remaining lemon juice if you wish. Serve at room temperature or warm.

STORAGE: This sauce can be stored in the refrigerator for up to 1 month. Rewarm it gently in a microwave or by stirring in a saucepan over very low heat.

VARIATION: To make Whiskey (or Rum) Caramel Sauce, replace the lemon juice with 1 tablespoon whiskey (or rum). Once the mixture cools to room temperature, taste and add more liquor if desired.

SOUR CHERRIES IN SYRUP

Makes 2 cups (600g)

If you're as wild about sour cherries as I am, you'll be as happy as I was to discover that big jars of them are available in Eastern European markets and specialty grocers (see Resources, page 259). They come packed in light syrup and are a fraction of the cost of their pricey Italian counterparts, and they're simple to candy yourself.

Once the cherries are cooked and cooled, if you wish to mix them into ice cream, drain them of their syrup completely (until they feel dry and sticky), and then fold them into your favorite flavor. I recommend White Chocolate Ice Cream (page 37), or try the Toasted Almond and Candied Cherry Ice Cream (page 70). Or simply use one to top off an ice cream sundae. (Save any leftover syrup to mix with sparkling water to make homemade sour cherry soda.) This recipe calls for 3 cups of cherries, which includes their syrup.

---

1. Mix the cherries with their syrup and the sugar in a large, nonreactive saucepan. Fit the pan with a candy thermometer and cook over medium heat, stirring infrequently, until the syrup reaches 230°F (110°C).

2. Remove from the heat and let cool to room temperature. Serve a few cherries with their thick, ruby-colored syrup over ice cream.

STORAGE: These cherries can be kept in the refrigerator for up to 1 month. Allow them to come to room temperature before serving.

3 cups sour cherries from a jar, with their light syrup (about 1½ pounds, 675g)

1 cup (200g) sugar

CANDIED CITRUS PEEL

Makes about 1 cup (200g), drained

Not only does this candied peel make a tasty tangle atop a scoop of citrus-flavored sorbet or ice cream, it's also terrific drained, finely chopped, and folded into just-churned Super Lemon Ice Cream (page 93), Fresh Ginger Ice Cream (page 43), or Cheesecake Ice Cream (page 75).

If you don't have a candy thermometer, simply cook the peel until the liquid resembles heavy syrup and the fine threads of peel are shiny and translucent.

4 large lemons or oranges, preferably unsprayed

2 cups (500ml) water

1 cup (200g) sugar

1 tablespoon light corn syrup

Pinch of kosher or sea salt

1. With a vegetable peeler, remove strips of peel 1 inch (3cm) wide from the lemons or oranges, cutting lengthwise down the fruit. Remove just the colorful outer peel, leaving behind the bitter white pith. Using a very sharp chef's knife, slice the peel lengthwise into thin strips no wider than a matchstick.

2. Put the strips of peel in a small, nonreactive saucepan, add enough water to cover them by a few inches, and bring to a boil. Lower the heat to a gentle boil and cook until the peel is tender, 5 to 8 minutes. Drain the peel in a mesh strainer and rinse with fresh water.

3. Combine the 2 cups (500ml) water, sugar, corn syrup, and salt in the same saucepan. Fit the pan with a candy thermometer and bring to a boil. Add the blanched peel, lower the heat, and cook at a very low boil for about 25 minutes, until the syrup is reduced and the thermometer reads 210°F (99°C). Turn off the heat and let the peel cool to room temperature in the syrup.

4. Once cool, lift the peel out of the syrup with a fork, letting the syrup drain away, and serve atop ice cream or sorbet.

STORAGE: Candied Citrus Peel can be stored in its syrup in the refrigerator for up to 2 months. If the syrup gets too thick during storage or if the peel crystallizes, rewarm the candied peel and syrup with a small amount of water, to loosen them up.

CANDIED PINEAPPLE

Makes about 2 cups (600g)

The sweet-tart taste of candied pineapple spiked with fragrant vanilla makes a tasty accompaniment to any tropical fruit–flavored ice cream or sorbet. Be sure to cook the pineapple long enough so the juices and sugar mingle together and caramelize to a dark amber color for maximum flavor.

1. Dice the pineapple into ½-inch (2cm) pieces. Add the pineapple along with the sugar and vanilla bean to a large, nonstick saucepan or skillet. Cook over medium heat until the sugar is dissolved and the pineapple becomes very juicy and shiny.

2. Continue cooking the pineapple until most of the liquid is gone; about 20 minutes.

3. Continue to cook, stirring constantly at this point, until the pineapple becomes sticky and the syrup thickens. Remove from the heat and let the pineapple cool in the pan. (Remove the vanilla bean before serving; it can be rinsed and saved for another use.) Serve warm or at room temperature.

STORAGE: Candied Pineapple can be stored in the refrigerator for up to 1 week. Let it come to room temperature before serving, or rewarm it in a microwave or a saucepan over very low heat.

NOTE: If you wish to use canned pineapple, use 4 cups (600g), drained, unsweetened diced pineapple packed in its own juice.

1 large pineapple, peeled, cored, and eyes removed

¾ cup (150g) sugar

1 vanilla bean, split in half lengthwise

PECAN-PRALINE SAUCE

Makes 2 cups (500ml)

Although I like to make this chunky sauce all year-round and use it to top everything from Super Lemon Ice Cream (page 93) in the fall to Fresh Apricot Ice Cream (page 81) in the summer, you can make it winter holiday–friendly by adding a handful of dried cranberries in place of some of the pecans (see the variation at the end of the recipe). Then try it ladled over Cinnamon Ice Cream (page 45) for a real treat, or spooned over pumpkin or apple pie topped with a scoop of Vanilla Ice Cream (page 28). Make the sauce in advance, if possible, and let it sit for a few hours so all the ingredients can mingle and meld together deliciously.

1. In a medium, heavy-duty saucepan, melt the butter. Stir in the sugar and corn syrup and cook, stirring frequently, until the mixture becomes deep amber, the color of coffee with a touch of cream.

2. Remove from the heat and whisk in the water. Because the mixture can splatter, you may wish to wear an oven mitt. (The sugar might seize when you add the water, but it will smooth out as you stir.) Bring to a low boil, whisking, until the sugar is dissolved and the sauce is smooth.

3. Remove from the heat and stir in the cream, pecans, salt, whiskey, and vanilla. Serve warm.

STORAGE: This sauce can be stored in the refrigerator for up to 2 weeks. Rewarm it gently in a microwave or by stirring in a saucepan over very low heat.

VARIATION: To make Pecan, Cranberry, and Praline Sauce, substitute ¼ cup (30g) of chopped dried cranberries for ¼ cup (30g) of the pecans.

4 tablespoons (60g) butter, salted or unsalted, cut into pieces

¾ cup (150g) sugar

2 tablespoons light corn syrup

½ cup (125ml) water

¼ cup (60ml) heavy cream

1¼ cups (125g) pecans, toasted (see page 16) and coarsely chopped

⅛ teaspoon kosher or sea salt

3 tablespoons whiskey

½ teaspoon pure vanilla extract

STRAWBERRY SAUCE

Makes 2 cups (500ml)

When I see the first gorgeous baskets of strawberries at the markets, I perk up, knowing that spring has truly arrived. Strawberry season lasts throughout the summer, so you'll find that this sauce goes perfectly well with any of the summer fruit ice creams, sorbets, or frozen yogurts in this book.

1. Puree the strawberries with the sugar and lemon juice in a blender or food processor, until smooth.

2. Press the puree through a mesh strainer to remove the seeds. Serve chilled or at room temperature.

STORAGE: This sauce can be stored in the refrigerator for up to 3 days.

1½ pounds (675g) fresh strawberries, rinsed and hulled

¼ cup (50g) sugar

1 teaspoon freshly squeezed lemon juice

SMOOTH RASPBERRY SAUCE

Makes 1 cup (250ml)

This sauce is so intensely flavored that just a minimal amount is needed for maximum impact. It goes particularly well with anything sharp and lemony, such as Super Lemon Ice Cream (page 93) or Lemon Sherbet (page 122).

1. Puree the raspberries in a blender or food processor with the sugar and water until smooth.

2. Press the mixture through a mesh strainer to remove the seeds. Mix in the lemon juice. Serve chilled or at room temperature.

STORAGE: This sauce can be stored in the refrigerator for up to 3 days.

2 cups (225g) raspberries, fresh or frozen

2 tablespoons sugar

¼ cup (60ml) water

A few drops freshly squeezed lemon juice

CHUNKY RASPBERRY SAUCE

Makes 1 cup (250ml)

All raspberry sauces need not be created equal. Unlike the previous sauce, this one is loaded with big, chunky raspberries. It was inspired by a sauce that baking guru Nick Malgieri whizzed up during a cooking demonstration, and I've been making it ever since.

1. Puree 1 cup (115g) of the raspberries with 3 tablespoons of the sugar in a blender or food processor until smooth.

2. Put the remaining 1 cup (115g) raspberries in a bowl. Set a mesh strainer over the bowl and press the puree through the strainer, over the whole raspberries. Stir the puree into the raspberries, mashing the berries just a bit as you stir. Add the lemon juice. Taste, then add the remaining 1 tablespoon sugar, if you wish. Serve chilled or at room temperature.

STORAGE: This sauce can be stored in the refrigerator for up to 3 days.

2 cups (230g) raspberries, fresh or frozen

3 to 4 tablespoons sugar

A few drops freshly squeezed lemon juice

MIXED BERRY COULIS

Makes 2 cups (500ml)

Coulis is a fancy word that simply means a sauce made with fresh, uncooked ingredients. Feel free to change the mix of berries as you wish, depending on what's available. If you find fresh red currants at your market, toss in a handful; the tangy little berries are a wonderful addition to this sauce.

1. Slice the strawberries and toss them in a bowl with half of the raspberries and half of the blackberries. Puree the remaining berries in a blender or food processor with 3 tablespoons (45g) of the sugar. Mix the berry puree into the sliced berries. Taste, then add the remaining 1 tablespoon (15g) sugar, if you wish. Serve chilled or at room temperature.

STORAGE: This sauce can be stored in the refrigerator for up to 3 days.

VARIATION: Add a splash of liqueur, such as Grand Marnier, Cognac, or kirsch to the sauce.

8 ounces (230g) fresh strawberries, rinsed and hulled

1 cup (115g) raspberries, fresh or frozen

1 cup (115g) blackberries, fresh or frozen

3 to 4 tablespoons sugar

BLUEBERRY SAUCE

Makes 1 cup (250ml)

I'm a big fan of the all-American blueberry, and why not? They're so easy to transform into a versatile sauce that's equally at ease atop Philly-friendly Cheesecake Ice Cream (page 75) or alongside Hollywood-healthy Vanilla Frozen Yogurt (page 55). Or go Franco-American by adding crème de cassis, the deep, dark black currant liqueur from Dijon (see the variation at the end of the recipe).

1. In a medium, nonreactive saucepan, heat the blueberries and sugar until the blueberries begin to release their juices. In a small bowl, mix the cornstarch with the water and lemon juice until lump free, then stir the slurry into the blueberries.

2. Bring to a boil, then lower the heat to a simmer and cook for 1 minute. Remove from the heat, stir in the kirsch, and let cool to room temperature. Serve chilled or at room temperature.

STORAGE: This sauce can be stored in the refrigerator for up to 3 days.

VARIATION: To make Blueberry-Cassis Sauce, increase the amount of cornstarch to 2 teaspoons. After you mix the cornstarch slurry into the cooked blueberries, stir in ¼ cup (60ml) crème de cassis, then simmer as directed in the recipe.

2 cups (225g) blueberries, fresh or frozen

¼ cup (50g) sugar

1½ teaspoons cornstarch

1 tablespoon cold water

1 tablespoon freshly squeezed lemon juice

2 teaspoons kirsch or gin

CANDIED RED BEANS

Makes 1½ cups (550g)

One of my great pleasures in life is stopping at the "shave ice" stands (as the locals call them, inexplicably dropping the *d*) in Hawaii. I watch as they tuck sweetened red beans in the bottom of a paper cone and then pile shaved ice on top. I always choose *lilikoi*, or passion fruit syrup, to be drizzled over the ice. It has remarkable complexity and tastes as if every possible tropical flavor has been packed together into one single fruit. To finish it up, a shot of sweetened condensed milk is poured over it all. I slurp the whole thing down, then I'm ready to tackle the surf again. Or, more likely, just take a snooze under the shade of a palm tree.

The inspiration likely came from Japan, where sweetened red beans are spooned over ice cream or pureed for beautifully intricate pastries called *wagashi*. You can make them at home from adzuki beans, available in well-stocked supermarkets and natural food stores. Their sweet-starchy flavor is especially good paired with Asian-inspired ice creams, such as Green Tea Ice Cream (page 40) and Toasted Coconut Ice Cream (page 105). I find chewing on these sticky little beans positively addictive.

1. Sort the beans and discard any foreign matter, then rinse them in a colander. Put them in a large saucepan and cover with plenty of water. Soak for at least 4 hours, or up to overnight.

2. Drain the beans in the colander, then return them to the saucepan and add the 4 cups (1l) water and the baking soda. Bring to a boil, then lower the heat and simmer for 1 hour. (If the water boils away too quickly, add another ½ cup, 125ml, to keep the beans submerged.)

3. When the beans are tender, add the sugar and corn syrup. Continue to cook the beans, stirring constantly, for 10 minutes, until the liquid is thick and syrupy. Serve warm or at room temperature.

STORAGE: Stored in their syrup, these beans will keep in the refrigerator for up to 1 week.

½ cup (100g) dried adzuki beans, rinsed

4 cups (1l) water

Pinch of baking soda

½ cup (100g) sugar

½ cup (125ml) light corn syrup

HONEYED CASHEWS

Makes 1 cup (200g)

These cashews are simple to make and can be sprinkled over ice cream sundaes. Be sure to store them in an airtight container at room temperature, to keep them as crisp as possible.

1. Very lightly grease a rimmed baking sheet with vegetable oil or line it with a silicone baking mat.

2. Heat the honey and salt in a 10-inch (25cm) skillet, preferably nonstick. Once the honey starts to bubble, mix in the cashews. Cook over medium heat, stirring frequently, for 3 to 3½ minutes, until the cashews are thickly glazed.

3. Tip the cashews onto the prepared baking sheet and gently stir the nuts as they cool, scraping up the honey and basting the cashews with it for about 30 seconds. Let cool completely.

4. Break up the clumps of cashews.

STORAGE: Store in an airtight container at room temperature. Serve the same day.

2½ tablespoons honey

Big pinch of kosher or sea salt

1 cup (150g) whole cashews, lightly toasted (see page 16)

HOT HONEY

Make 1 cup (250ml)

I first had Hot Honey—where else?—in hip Brooklyn, where anything locally made is celebrated. The idea is said to have originated in Brazil, although I don't know anyone who takes honey more seriously than the French, who preceded the hipsters by buying honey according to where the bees live and what plants the bees collect from. Hot Honey, though, didn't catch on in Paris due to their aversion to spicy foods. (Although every pizza place in Paris offers a bottle of chile-infused oil on the table. So maybe they're holding out on us?)

Chiles vary in heat. I use fresh Thai or bird's eye chiles, but if you have another favorite, use those, or support local producers and play around with favorite chiles from your farmers' market. The Hot Honey may taste quite spicy on its own, but when drizzled over a dish of Chocolate Ice Cream (page 30), Chocolate Sorbet (page 126), or Panforte Ice Cream (page 79), the flavor is tamed a bit by the cold scoop. If you like things extra-spicy, feel free to add more chiles right from the start.

1. Warm the honey in a small saucepan with the chiles. Remove from the heat and let infuse for 1 hour, or until the flavor is to your liking.

2. Rewarm the honey to liquefy it, then pour it through a fine-mesh strainer into a jar.

NOTE: Hot Honey is excellent drizzled on goat cheese–topped crostini, baked squash, or pepperoni pizza.

1 cup (250ml) honey

4 fresh Thai or bird's eye chiles, cut into 4 pieces

HONEY CRUNCH GRANOLA

Makes 5 cups (600g)

I can't say I make a habit of, or admit to, meeting women online. But I got lucky. I fell for Heidi Swanson, who entices men (and women) with her gorgeous website, www.101cookbooks.com. An accomplished photographer and cookbook author, she presents tried-and-true recipes that are always accompanied by stunning photos.

When we finally met in person, she was just as charming as online—which I hear makes me luckier than most of the other fellows out there. Here's a recipe I've adapted from her site. It makes a healthy, delightfully crunchy topping for ice cream or frozen yogurt for dessert, and because the recipe makes a bit more than you might need, you can keep some on hand for a great breakfast treat as well. If you want to give it a little kick, make it with Hot Honey (page 202).

1. Preheat the oven to 300°F (150°C).

2. In a large bowl, mix together the oats, sunflower seeds, almonds, coconut, sesame seeds, and salt.

3. In a small saucepan, warm the honey and vegetable oil. Pour the warm honey mixture over the dry ingredients and stir until they're well coated. Spread evenly on a rimmed baking sheet and bake, stirring occasionally, for 30 minutes, or until golden brown.

4. Remove from the oven and let cool to room temperature.

5. Once the granola is completely cool, stir in the dried fruit.

STORAGE: Store in an airtight container at room temperature for up to 2 months.

NOTE: Use any combination of raisins, date pieces, apricots, cherries, cranberries, pineapple, and papaya; cut larger fruits into ½-inch (2cm) dice.

3 cups (300g) old-fashioned rolled oats (not instant)

½ cup (70g) raw shelled sunflower seeds

½ cup (40g) sliced almonds

½ cup (40g) dried shredded coconut, unsweetened or sweetened

2 tablespoons sesame seeds

Big pinch of kosher or sea salt

6 tablespoons (90ml) strongly flavored honey

2 tablespoons vegetable oil

½ cup (80g) diced dried fruit (see Note)

FRENCH ALMONDS

Makes 2 cups (200g)

After dinner one night at a cozy restaurant in Paris, I finished up with a dessert of housemade ice cream topped with the most perfect, crispy caramelized almonds I'd ever imagined. As we were leaving, I passed the kitchen window, and got up the nerve to ask the chef how he made those fabulous almonds. He hefted a pitcher of liquid and told me they were simply coated with equal parts water and sugar. The next morning, I got to work on my own version, coming up with just the right proportions for making these incredibly addictive crispy almond flakes.

1. Preheat the oven to 350°F (175°C).

2. In a small skillet, heat the water and sugar, stirring a bit, just until it begins to boil. Remove from the heat and stir in the almonds to coat them with the syrup.

3. Spread the almonds on a nonstick rimmed baking sheet, or a rimmed baking sheet lined with a silicone baking mat. Bake for 20 minutes, stirring twice during baking and separating any clumps. Remove from the oven when the almonds are a medium golden brown. Let cool to room temperature.

STORAGE: Store in an airtight container for up to 1 week.

VARIATION: For Candied Oats, toast 1 cup (100g) old-fashioned rolled oats on a rimmed baking sheet in a 350°F (175°C) oven for 7 minutes. Transfer the oats to a bowl. If the baking sheet is not nonstick, line it with a silicone baking mat. In a small saucepan, heat 1½ tablespoons water, 1½ tablespoons sugar, and a big pinch of cinnamon. Mix the oats into the syrup, spread the mixture on the baking sheet, and stir a few times during baking.

2 tablespoons water

2 tablespoons sugar

2 cups (160g) sliced almonds, blanched or unblanched

SALT-ROASTED PEANUTS

Makes 2 cups (400g)

Salted peanuts are incredibly simple to make and will have you feeling like an accomplished candy maker with minimal effort. The only problem you'll have is not eating them all before you scatter them over a towering hot fudge sundae.

I use raw peanuts, not ones that have been previously salted and roasted. If you wish, you can use unsalted roasted peanuts (sometimes called "cocktail peanuts") and shorten the baking time to 15 minutes.

1. Preheat the oven to 350°F (175°C). Very lightly oil a rimmed baking sheet with peanut or vegetable oil, or line it with a silicone baking mat.

2. In a bowl, mix together the peanuts, corn syrup, and brown sugar until the peanuts are sticky and evenly coated. Sprinkle the salt over the peanuts and stir a few times.

3. Spread the nuts evenly on the baking sheet and bake for 25 to 30 minutes, stirring three times during baking, until the nuts are deep golden brown and glazed. Let cool completely to room temperature.

STORAGE: Store in an airtight container, to preserve their crispness, at room temperature for up to 1 week.

2 cups (300g) raw (unroasted) peanuts

¼ cup (60ml) light corn syrup

2 tablespoons packed light or dark brown sugar

1½ teaspoons kosher or sea salt

CHAPTER 6

Mix-Ins

There's something quintessentially American about mixing things into ice cream. Perhaps it's because we like to have our cake . . . and cookies and brownies and candies . . . and eat them, too—especially when they're smashed into ice cream! Like the American Revolution a few centuries back, the rising up of the ice cream mix-ins revolution took hold in Boston, when an ice cream shop came up with the idea of offering a panoply of popular candies, toasted nuts, nuggets of cake, and hunks of cookies—just about anything you could think of—and patrons were faced with that all-important decision of how to customize their scoops.

Once customers decided (for some reason, I always seemed to be stuck behind the ones who couldn't), the young clerks behind the counter would slap a mound of ice cream onto a thick slab of cold marble and layer on whatever treats had been chosen. With brute force, they'd go to work, smashing and mashing the jumble of ingredients until everything came together into a chaotic, wildly cohesive mass. Then they'd heap the impossibly large mound into a cone and off you'd go.

The great thing about homemade ice cream is that it gives you the freedom to mix in whatever you want, in any quantity you want. You may not have slabs of marble in your kitchen, nor biceps like those ice cream smashers, but you can still load it up by adding chunks of Dark Chocolate Truffles (page 230) to White Chocolate Ice Cream (page 37), folding Candied Cherries (page 214) into Toasted Almond and Candied Cherry Ice Cream (page 70), or using melted chocolate to turn any ice cream or gelato into Stracciatella (page 230).

So here's your chance to unleash your creativity and customize your ice cream as you like. I've given guidelines throughout the book, called Perfect Pairings, that are meant to plant the seeds of possibility. I find that 1½ to 2 cups (200 to 400g) of goodies makes a good mix-in for 1 quart (1l) of ice cream. But this is just a suggestion; some people prefer less stuff added to their ice cream, while others like the extravagance of lots (and lots) of it, so by all means take some personal liberties here. All of the mix-in recipes can easily be doubled and any leftovers can be stored in the freezer in a zip-top bag and used for the next batch. And remember, if you're adding mix-ins to your ice cream, you'll want to have a big enough container, larger than 1 quart (1l), to hold the finished ice cream along with the mix-ins.

When adding mix-ins, speed is vital because you don't want your just-churned ice cream to melt. While your ice cream is churning, it helps to scatter a few handfuls of mix-ins into the bottom of your storage container, then put it in the freezer, so they're cold and don't melt the ice cream. As soon as your ice cream is churned, add the rest of the mix-ins, stirring quickly to disperse them evenly, then transfer the ice cream to the storage container. Put a lid on it, then get the container right into the freezer without delay.

If the mix-ins are in small pieces, I add them directly into the machine during the last minute of churning so they get distributed evenly. Larger mix-ins are best folded in after you're done churning, because they can get stuck in the dasher and cause the motor to rebel. A good rule is that anything larger than a chocolate chip is probably best folded in after the ice cream has been churned.

As for ripples and swirls, resist the temptation to overmix them into the just-frozen ice cream. You don't want a muddy mess; you want to end up with distinct layers. The best way to get those is to begin with a big spoonful of the swirl mixture at the bottom of the storage container, because there's nothing worse than getting to the bottom and finding only plain ice cream. Continue to layer the mixture, alternating ice cream, swirl mixture, more ice cream, and then more swirl. If you're a lily gilder, add chunks of nuts or any of the other mix-ins as you go.

One final word: If a mix-in doesn't come out as you think it should or if you mess something up, go ahead and use it; it will likely taste delicious in the ice cream. And feel free to crumble any cookies or bits of cake you may have left over into freshly churned ice cream. Many of the things that have gotten mixed into ice cream in the past were probably mistakes or leftovers that someone was trying to use up. And why am I so sure? I've done it myself, and no one was the wiser.

CONTINUED

MIXING IN MIX-INS

No one loves mix-ins in their ice cream more than I do, which you probably can tell by how many suggestions for them I have in this book. Some ice cream makers do their best to help people like me by creating openings in the lids of their machines so fans of mix-ins can add them during the last few minutes of churning. The ice cream attachments for stand mixers have made it even easier, leaving things wide open, so you can easily add nuts, brittles, and even a swirl of Stracciatella (page 230) without having to aim so carefully.

Still, there are other machines that don't offer an easy way to add mix-ins, so they'll need to be added once the ice cream is churned. Most times you can simply pull out the dasher, scrape any ice cream off it (and don't tell, but I'm known to lick it clean, just to make sure), and add the mix-ins with a spatula.

CANDIED LEMON SLICES

Makes enough for 1 quart (1l) of ice cream

When I was at culinary school in France, my instructor advised adding a bit of salt when candying citrus peel. When I asked why, he said that it made the peel soften, but he couldn't explain why. So although it may be just a culinary superstition, I've added salt ever since. If you aren't superstitious, simply toss the salt over your shoulder and candy the lemons without it.

Although it's not required equipment, a candy thermometer fitted to the side of the saucepan will help you know when the lemon slices are done. When the peel is candied, it should read 225°F (107°C).

1. Cut the lemons crosswise into very thin slices. Pick out and discard any seeds.

2. Put the lemon slices in a heavy-duty, nonreactive saucepan and add enough water to cover them by a few inches. Bring to a boil, turn down the heat to a low boil, and cook for 15 minutes, turning the slices occasionally with a spoon.

3. Drain the lemon slices, return them to the saucepan, add more water, and blanch them again for 15 minutes.

4. Drain the lemon slices again. Return them to the saucepan and add the 1 cup (250ml) water, sugar, and salt. Bring to a boil, then turn down the heat to a very low boil and cook for 20 minutes, or until the liquid is reduced to a thick, shiny syrup and the lemon slices are translucent. If the syrup is too frothy to gauge whether the slices are done, remove the pan from the heat and let it cool for a moment.

5. Remove from the heat and let the lemon slices cool in their syrup.

MIXING THEM IN: Place the Candied Lemon Slices in a strainer and drain off as much of the syrup as possible. Chop the lemon slices into small pieces, then fold them into 1 quart (1l) of ice cream as you remove it from the machine.

STORAGE: Store in an airtight container in the refrigerator for up to 3 weeks.

VARIATION: To make Candied Orange Slices, substitute 2 oranges for the lemons.

3 lemons, preferably unsprayed

1 cup (250ml) water

1½ cups (300g) sugar

Big pinch of kosher or sea salt

CANDIED CHERRIES

Makes 2 cups (650g)

This is my favorite way to preserve fresh cherries during their relatively short season. As they cook, their ruby red juices gush out and continue to deepen in color until they thicken to a flavorful syrup. Before folding them into ice cream, you'll want to make sure they're dry, because excess syrup will muddy the ice cream. First drain the cherries in a strainer for 1 hour, until they are sticky and dry (save the syrup for drizzling over ice cream). Then coarsely chop the cherries, or fold them into the ice cream whole as you remove it from the machine. Candied Cherries are excellent on top of Lemon Sherbet (page 122) and Olive Oil Ice Cream (page 90), and, of course, they're the perfect finish atop homemade ice cream sundaes.

1. Remove the stems and pit the cherries. Heat the cherries, water, sugar, and lemon juice in a large, nonreactive saucepan or skillet until the liquid starts to boil.

2. Turn down the heat to a low boil and cook the cherries for 25 minutes, stirring frequently during the last 10 minutes of cooking to make sure they are cooking evenly and not sticking.

3. Once the syrup is reduced to the consistency of maple syrup, remove the pan from the heat, add the almond extract, and let the cherries cool in their syrup.

MIXING THEM IN: Drain the cherries in a mesh strainer for about 1 hour (reserve the syrup for another use), then coarsely chop the drained cherries and fold them into 1 quart (1l) of ice cream as you remove it from the machine.

STORAGE: Candied Cherries can be kept in the refrigerator for up to 2 weeks.

1 pound (450g) cherries, fresh or frozen

1½ cups (375ml) water

1 cup (200g) sugar

1 tablespoon freshly squeezed lemon juice

1 drop pure almond extract

BUTTERED PECANS

Makes 1½ cups (175g)

I used to cringe every time a grumpy relative would start a sentence with, "When I was your age...," knowing that I was in for a lecture heavy with nostalgia for days gone by. But nowadays, I find myself saying it to young whippersnappers.

But it's true, when I was younger (perhaps when I was your age?), my local ice cream parlor would serve, alongside their lofty ice cream sundaes, little paper cups filled way up to the brim with buttered pecans roasted in real, honest-to-goodness butter, for just five cents. Five cents!

Times may have changed but you can still have this treat at home for whatever you have to spend on the butter and pecans at today's prices, but I guarantee you won't be doing any complaining.

---

1. Preheat the oven to 350°F (175°C).

2. Melt the butter in a skillet. Remove from the heat and toss the pecans with the melted butter until well coated, then sprinkle with the salt. Spread evenly on a baking sheet and toast in the oven for 10 to 12 minutes, stirring once during baking.

3. Remove from the oven and let cool completely.

MIXING THEM IN: Chop the Buttered Pecans coarsely, then add them to 1 quart (1l) of Butterscotch Ice Cream (see page 46) during the last minute of churning, or sprinkle them over when serving the ice cream.

STORAGE: Store in an airtight container at room temperature for up to 2 days.

1½ tablespoons butter, salted or unsalted

1½ cups (150g) pecan halves

¼ teaspoon kosher or sea salt

IN A HURRY? CHEAT.

If you don't have time to make your own ice cream, take a pint of your favorite store-bought premium vanilla ice cream and soften it in an electric stand mixer using the paddle attachment.

Once it's softened slightly, add whatever flavorings you want. You can add mint or citrus oil (start with ⅛ teaspoon per pint, then taste and add more if desired), a favorite liqueur (up to 4 tablespoons, 60ml, per pint), or any of the crunchy mix-ins in this chapter. Return the ice cream to the freezer and chill firmly before you serve it.

Another cheater's tip: To make instant crème anglaise, melt some premium vanilla ice cream. *Voilà!*

PRALINED ALMONDS

Makes 1½ cups (250g)

This is one of my all-time favorite and most requested recipes. These nuts are lots of fun to make, and you'll feel like a real candymaker as you triumphantly tilt your first batch out of the pan. Whole almonds get cooked in a syrup, simmering until the sugar crystallizes and clings to them, creating a crackly caramelized coating. This recipe can easily be doubled, which I often do.

¼ cup (60ml) water

½ cup (100g) sugar

1 cup (135g) whole almonds, unblanched and untoasted

⅛ teaspoon fleur de sel or kosher or sea salt

1. Combine the water, sugar, and almonds in a large, heavy-duty skillet over medium-high heat and cook, stirring constantly with a wooden spoon, until the sugar dissolves and the liquid boils.

2. Lower the heat to medium and continue cooking and stirring for just a few minutes, until the liquid crystallizes and becomes sandy. Very soon the crystals of sugar on the bottom of the pan will begin to liquefy. Stir the amber-colored syrup at the bottom of the pan over the nuts to coat them. Continue to stir the nuts and scrape the syrup over them until the almonds are glazed and become a bit glossy and shiny. (Sometimes I remove the pan from the heat a few times while they're cooking to moderate the temperature and better control the glazing, so they cook evenly and none get burned.)

3. Remove the pan from the heat and sprinkle the almonds with the salt. Tip them onto an ungreased baking sheet and let cool completely. As they cool, break up any clusters that are stuck together.

MIXING THEM IN: Chop the Pralined Almonds coarsely, then add them to 1 quart (1l) of ice cream during the last minute of churning.

STORAGE: Store in an airtight container at room temperature for up to 1 week.

VARIATION: Substitute 1 cup (150g) roasted or raw shelled peanuts for the almonds to make Pralined Peanuts.

SPICED PECANS

Makes 2 cups (300g)

They say that when you sell your house, you should bake something aromatic and spicy to entrance potential buyers with a homey scent wafting from the kitchen.

These pecans are simple enough to make in the mad scramble before opening your home to strangers, and there's no better way to fill your home with a heady mix of spices. I recommend folding them into bourbon ice cream (see variation, page 49), which you can happily eat to toast the closing of the deal.

---

1. Preheat the oven to 300°F (150°C). Coat a rimmed baking sheet with nonstick cooking spray.

2. Whisk the egg white in a medium bowl for about 15 seconds, until loose and foamy. Stir in the brown sugar, spices, vanilla, and pecans. Spread the coated nuts evenly on the prepared baking sheet.

3. Bake for 30 minutes, stirring twice during baking, until the coating has hardened onto the pecans and they're nice and dry. Remove from the oven and let cool completely.

MIXING THEM IN: Chop the Spiced Pecans coarsely, then add them to 1 quart (1l) of ice cream during the last minute of churning. They can also be sprinkled over ice cream when serving.

STORAGE: Store in an airtight container at room temperature for up to 2 weeks.

VARIATION: Make Spiced Walnuts by substituting untoasted walnut halves for the pecans.

1 large egg white

¼ cup (45g) packed light brown sugar

2 teaspoons ground cinnamon

½ teaspoon ground ginger

¼ teaspoon ground cloves

A few grinds of black pepper

½ teaspoon kosher or sea salt

¼ teaspoon ground chile powder or cayenne pepper

1 teaspoon pure vanilla extract

2 cups (200g) pecan halves

WET WALNUTS

Makes 1½ cups (290g)

I was going to call these "Walnuts Gone Wild" but took a less steamy-sounding route and decided on simply Wet Walnuts. You can draw your own conclusions. But there's nothing indecent about these maple-glazed walnuts, except how good they taste.

1. Heat the maple syrup in a small skillet or saucepan until it just begins to come to a full boil. Stir in the walnuts, then cook until the liquid comes to a full boil once again. Stir the nuts for 10 seconds, then remove them from the heat.

2. Sprinkle the nuts with the salt and let cool completely. The nuts will still be wet and sticky when cooled.

MIXING THEM IN: Chop Wet Walnuts coarsely and add them to 1 quart (1l) of ice cream during the last minute of churning.

STORAGE: Store in an airtight container at room temperature for up to 1 day, but the nuts will lose a bit of their crispness overnight, so it's best to prepare them shortly before using them.

VARIATION: To make Wet Pecans, substitute toasted pecans for the walnuts.

½ cup plus 1 tablespoon (140ml) dark amber maple syrup

1½ cups (150g) walnuts, toasted (see page 16) and very coarsely chopped

Big pinch of kosher or sea salt

CHOCOLATE-COVERED PEANUTS

Makes 1½ cups (265g)

These easy-to-make peanuts will make you feel like a chocolatier assembling a world-class candy bar. If you're anything like me, you can't keep chocolate bars around the house without breaking off a hunk every time you pass by, so by all means double (or triple!) the recipe if you want, just to make sure there's enough for folding into the ice cream later on.

1. Stretch a piece of plastic wrap over a dinner plate. Put the chocolate in a clean, dry bowl. Set the bowl over a saucepan of barely simmering water and melt the chocolate, stirring until smooth.

2. Once the chocolate is melted, remove it from the heat and stir in the peanuts, coating them with the chocolate. Spread the mixture on the prepared plate and chill.

MIXING THEM IN: Use a chef's knife to chop the chocolate-covered block of peanuts into bite-size pieces, then mix them into 1 quart (1l) of ice cream as you remove it from the machine.

STORAGE: Store in an airtight container in the refrigerator or at room temperature for several months.

VARIATION: You can substitute Salt-Roasted Peanuts (page 207) or Pralined Peanuts (variation, page 217) for the roasted peanuts in this recipe.

4 ounces (115g) semisweet or bittersweet chocolate, chopped

1 cup (150g) roasted, unsalted peanuts

PEANUT BRITTLE

Makes 2 cups (500g)

In spite of what you might see on television or read in cooking magazines, restaurant cooking is demanding, hectic work. Luckily, I baked professionally at Chez Panisse in Berkeley, California, with Mary Jo Thoresen for many years. Although we worked really hard, we managed by finding humor in the craziest things, things that made no sense to anyone but us. We did everything from making up movie titles by substituting with the word *quince* (*Rebel Without a Quince, Quince on a Hot Tin Roof*, etc.) to writing a rap song about baking. At perhaps the depths of our silliness, we became obsessed with all things Scoopy, the clown on the box of ice cream cones you buy at the supermarket. Soon I started finding little pictures of him stuck in the oddest places in the pastry area where we worked. (I even discovered one on the windshield of my car one night after my shift ended.) Naturally, my nickname became Scoopy.

Now that we've both become grown-ups, Mary Jo (aka Scary Jo) is back in the kitchen at Chez Panisse. Here's her recipe for Peanut Brittle, which she crushes into brickly bits and adds to Vanilla Ice Cream (page 28), dousing it with warm chocolate sauce for a wonderfully over-the-top peanut brittle sundae that should make sense to anyone. If you want to get creative, try mixing Peanut Brittle bits into Fresh Ginger Ice Cream (page 43) or Peanut Butter Ice Cream (page 59), and top it off with chocolate sauce as well. Whatever you mix it into, I'm sure you'll find the result absolutely scoop-endous.

½ teaspoon baking soda

½ cup (125ml) light corn syrup

½ cup (100g) sugar

2 tablespoons water

1½ cups (225g) salted roasted peanuts or Salt-Roasted Peanuts (page 207)

1. Line a baking sheet with a silicone baking mat, or grease it lightly with vegetable oil. Have the baking soda measured and ready.

2. In a medium, heavy-bottomed saucepan fitted with a candy thermometer, mix together the corn syrup, sugar, and water. Bring the syrup to a full boil, then add the peanuts. Cook, stirring frequently with a heatproof spatula, making sure the peanuts aren't burning as the syrup cooks (some like to hide behind the thermometer, so keep an eye out for them). When the temperature reaches between 300°F and 305°F (149°C and 151°C), remove the pan from the heat and immediately stir in the baking soda.

3. Working quickly, pour the mixture onto the prepared baking sheet and spread it as thinly as possible with the spatula. Let cool completely. Once cool, break the brittle into bite-size pieces.

MIXING IT IN: Fold the crumbled Peanut Brittle into 1 quart (1l) of ice cream as you remove it from the machine; reserve a few extra pieces for scattering over the top.

STORAGE: Store in an airtight container at room temperature for up to 2 weeks.

BUTTERCRUNCH TOFFEE

Makes 2 cups (400g)

When I put this recipe on my blog, I wasn't prepared for the onslaught of accolades. It seems I'm not the only one out there who craves toffee—especially this buttery-crisp candy enrobed in dark chocolate and showered with lots of toasted almonds. It's very good folded into ice cream, and although the recipe makes a bit more than you'll need, I don't think you'll have any problem figuring out what to do with the rest.

1. Using half of the chopped almonds, form an 8-inch (20cm) circle in an even layer on an ungreased baking sheet.

2. Fit a small, heavy-duty saucepan with a candy thermometer, then add the water, butter, granulated sugar, and brown sugar, mixing them together. Have the baking soda and vanilla measured and ready.

3. Cook the mixture over medium heat, stirring as little as possible. When the mixture reaches 300°F (150°C), remove the pan from the heat and immediately stir in the baking soda and vanilla. Mix just until combined; don't overstir. Right away, pour the hot toffee mixture over the circle of almonds on the baking sheet. Using as little movement as possible, spread the toffee to cover the circle.

4. Scatter the chocolate pieces over the toffee and wait for 2 minutes to allow them to melt. Use a spatula to spread the chocolate into an even layer, then scatter the remaining chopped almonds on top, pressing them into the chocolate. Let cool completely, until the chocolate is firm. Depending on the temperature of your kitchen, you may need to chill the toffee in the refrigerator. Remove it once the chocolate has hardened.

MIXING IT IN: Chop the Buttercrunch Toffee into coarse chunks, then fold the pieces into 1 quart (1l) of ice cream as you remove it from the machine.

STORAGE: Store in an airtight container in the freezer or at room temperature for up to 2 weeks.

VARIATIONS: Feel free to substitute toasted hazelnuts or pecans for the almonds. I also like to fleck a few grains of flaky sea salt over the chocolate before adding the nuts. You can substitute milk chocolate for the dark chocolate, if you wish.

1 cup (135g) whole almonds, toasted (see page 16) and finely chopped

1 tablespoon water

4 tablespoons (60g) butter, salted or unsalted, cut into pieces

½ cup (100g) granulated sugar

2 tablespoons packed light or dark brown sugar

⅛ teaspoon baking soda

½ teaspoon pure vanilla extract

½ cup (80g) chocolate chips or 3 ounces (85g) bittersweet or semisweet chocolate, chopped

CROQUANT

Makes 2 cups (350g)

Croquant is French for "crunchy," and this version certainly lives up to its name and reputation. This simple mix-in of toasted nuts enrobed in glossy caramel is wonderful when crushed and added to ice cream. You can crack it as fine or as coarse as you want. One tip: Adding the just-toasted nuts to the caramel while they're still warm will make them easier to mix.

1. Line a baking sheet with aluminum foil, shiny-side down.

2. Spread the sugar in a heavy-bottomed skillet and cook over medium heat, watching it carefully. When it begins to liquefy and darken at the edges, use a heatproof spatula to stir it very gently, encouraging the heat of the liquefied sugar around the edges to moisten and melt the sugar crystals in the center.

3. Add the nuts and stir gently but quickly, coating them with the caramel. Scrape the nuts onto the prepared baking sheet and spread as evenly as possible. Let cool completely. Once cool, break the Croquant up in a food processor, or place it in a zip-top freezer bag and use a mallet or rolling pin to crush it.

MIXING IT IN: Add 1 to 2 cups (175 to 350g) of crushed Croquant to 1 quart (1l) of ice cream during the last minute of churning.

STORAGE: Store in an airtight container in the freezer or at room temperature for up to 1 week.

1 cup (200g) sugar

1½ cups (150g) whole almonds, pecans, walnuts, hazelnuts, or peanuts, toasted (see page 16)

HONEY-SESAME BRITTLE

Makes 1 cup (270g)

This delicate but highly flavored brittle may lose its appealing crispness after it cools, so I recommend baking it just an hour or so before adding it to just-churned ice cream. I like it mixed into ice creams that are exotically flavored, such as Anise Ice Cream (page 44) or Lavender-Honey Ice Cream (page 76). Sesame seeds are very flavorful, so you'll find that a small amount of this brittle will provide lots of flavor to any ice cream you choose to mix it into.

1. Preheat the oven to 350°F (175°C). Line a baking sheet with a silicone baking mat or grease it lightly with vegetable oil.

2. In a skillet, warm the honey. Remove from the heat and stir in the sesame seeds, coating them with the honey until they're evenly moisted. Spread the mixture into an even layer on the prepared baking sheet and bake for 25 minutes. Remove from the oven and let cool completely.

MIXING IT IN: Break the Honey-Sesame Brittle into little pieces, then add them to 1 quart (1l) of ice cream in the machine during the last minute of churning.

3 tablespoons (45ml) good-flavored honey

1½ cups (210g) sesame seeds

OATMEAL PRALINE

Makes 1 cup (175g)

If you take a bite of the finished Oatmeal Praline (which I don't recommend, however tempting), you'll find that it's stubbornly hard. But don't worry. After you've smashed it into bits, folded it into your favorite ice cream, and left it in the freezer a bit, the pieces will soften up perfectly and become toothsome nuggets.

1. Preheat the oven to 350°F (175°C). Line a rimmed baking sheet with aluminum foil, shiny-side down.

2. Spread the oats evenly on the prepared baking sheet and bake for 10 minutes, stirring once or twice, until fragrant and nicely toasted. Remove from the oven.

3. Spread the sugar in a medium, heavy-bottomed skillet and cook over medium heat, watching it carefully. When the sugar begins to liquefy and darken at the edges, use a heatproof spatula to stir it very gently, encouraging the heat of the liquefied sugar around the edges to moisten and melt the sugar crystals in the center.

4. Tilt the pan and stir gently until all the sugar is melted and the caramel begins to smoke. Once the mixture is deep golden, remove it from the heat and immediately add the oats to the skillet, using the foil to guide them in quickly, then return the foil to the baking sheet. Stir the oats gently but quickly, coating them with the caramel.

5. Scrape the oats onto the foil-lined baking sheet and spread them as thinly as possible. Sprinkle with the salt and let cool completely.

¾ cup (75g) old-fashioned rolled oats (not instant)

½ cup (100g) sugar

Pinch of kosher or sea salt

MIXING IT IN: Break the pralined oats into small pieces by pulsing them in a food processor or placing the pieces in a heavy-duty plastic bag and smacking them with a mallet or rolling pin. Fold the Oatmeal Praline pieces into 1 quart (1l) of ice cream as you remove it from the machine.

STORAGE: Store in an airtight container in the freezer or at room temperature for up to 1 week.

PEPPERMINT PATTIES

Makes 2 cups (450g)

These mint disks are adapted from Elizabeth Falkner, a friend and pastry chef, who challenges other chefs on television in culinary competitions. Fortunately, I didn't have to go to battle with her for this recipe, which is simple to put together, and you can adjust the mint flavor to your liking. Taste a bit and add more if you wish, as mint extracts and oils vary. I make my Peppermint Patties very minty, which hold their own when crumbled into deep, dark chocolate ice cream, so both sides win.

---

1. Line a rimmed baking sheet with plastic wrap or parchment paper and dust it with about 1 tablespoon of the powdered sugar. Line a dinner plate with plastic wrap.

2. In a bowl, combine the corn syrup, water, and mint extract. Gradually stir in the remaining powdered sugar. As the mixture thickens, knead it with your hands until it forms a smooth ball (it will seem dry at first, but it will come together).

3. Pat the dough out onto the sugar-dusted baking sheet into a disk about 1/3 inch (1cm) thick and let it dry, uncovered, for at least 8 hours or up to overnight.

4. Melt the chocolate in a clean, absolutely dry bowl set over barely simmering water, stirring until smooth. Remove from the heat. Cut the mint disk into six triangular wedges, as if cutting a pie, and brush off any excess powdered sugar. Using two forks, dip each wedge in the chocolate, turning it over to coat both sides, then transfer to the prepared dinner plate. (The patties are going to be chopped up, so don't worry if they're not museum quality.)

5. Chill in the refrigerator or freezer until the chocolate has firmed up.

MIXING THEM IN: Chop the Peppermint Patties into bite-size pieces, then fold them into 1 quart (1l) of ice cream as you remove it from the machine.

STORAGE: Store in the refrigerator or freezer, well wrapped, for up to 1 month.

2 cups (225g) powdered sugar

3 tablespoons light corn syrup

2 teaspoons water

Scant 1/8 teaspoon pure peppermint extract or oil

6 ounces (170g) bittersweet or semisweet chocolate, chopped

PEANUT BUTTER PATTIES

Makes 16 mini patties

You don't need me to tell you that anything made with peanut butter is best when embedded in chocolate ice cream, and these homemade patties are much better than anything you can buy. To make them, use your favorite crunchy or smooth peanut butter, or natural-style, as long as it's well-stirred and not too oily. You don't have to dip the patties in chocolate; although if you'd like to go the extra distance and do so, ones made with natural peanut butter are easier to dip if they're well-chilled.

1. Mix together the peanut butter and powdered sugar in a small bowl until smooth. Line a dinner plate with plastic wrap.

2. Pinch off small pieces of the peanut butter mixture and roll them into balls. Flatten each ball into a disk about 1-inch (3cm) in diameter and place on the plastic-lined plate. (If you're using natural-style peanut butter, chill the disks in the refrigerator if you plan to dip them in chocolate.)

3. To dip the patties in chocolate, stretch a piece of plastic wrap over another dinner plate and put the chocolate in a clean, dry bowl. Set the bowl over a saucepan of barely simmering water and melt the chocolate, stirring until smooth.

4. Remove the chocolate from the heat. Using two forks, dip the peanut butter patties into the chocolate, one at a time, using one fork to dip and turn each patty in the chocolate and the second fork to help slide the patty off the fork onto the prepared plate. (Don't worry if they're not picture-perfect; once buried in ice cream, the patties' appearance won't matter.)

5. Refrigerate or freeze the chocolate-dipped patties until firm. Chop the patties into bite-size pieces, then chill again until ready to use.

MIXING THEM IN: Fold the chopped Peanut Butter Patties into 1 quart (1l) of ice cream as you remove it from the machine.

STORAGE: Store in the refrigerator or freezer for up to 1 month.

9 tablespoons (135g) peanut butter

3 tablespoons powdered sugar

6 ounces (170g) bittersweet or semisweet chocolate, chopped (optional)

SPECULOOS

Makes 1½ cups (200g)

These cookie chunks are inspired by the famous spiced cookies from Belgium. Zippier than American gingersnaps, Speculoos have become popular worldwide thanks to a (very) hard-to-resist spread made with them. Soft-baked Speculoos meld wonderfully when folded into ice cream, but if you'd like to make them crunchier, break the cookies into little bite-size nuggets and toast them in a 325°F (165°C) oven for about 10 minutes, until dry and crispy. Let cool completely, then fold the crunchy bits into your ice cream.

1. Preheat the oven to 350°F (175°C) and line a baking sheet with parchment paper or a silicone baking mat.

2. Beat together the butter and brown sugar in a medium bowl until smooth. Stir in the molasses and egg yolk.

3. In a small bowl, stir together the flour, baking soda, and spices. Stir the dry ingredients into the butter mixture and mix until smooth. Transfer the dough to the prepared baking sheet, and, using your hands, pat it into a circle about 5 inches (12cm) in diameter. Bake for 18 minutes. Remove from the oven and let cool completely.

MIXING THEM IN: Break the Speculoos into bite-size chunks and fold them into 1 quart (1l) of ice cream as you remove it from the machine.

STORAGE: The unbaked dough can also be wrapped well and stored in the freezer for up to 1 month. Once baked, Speculoos can be stored at room temperature for up to 3 days or in the freezer for up to 1 month.

2 tablespoons salted butter, at room temperature

3 tablespoons packed light or dark brown sugar

1 tablespoon molasses

1 large egg yolk

½ cup (70g) flour

¼ teaspoon baking soda

2 teaspoons ground cinnamon

1 teaspoon ground ginger

1 teaspoon ground allspice

STRACCIATELLA

Makes enough for 1 quart (1l) of ice cream

Just about every *gelateria* in Italy features stracciatella, or vanilla ice cream riddled with lots of little chocolate "chips." It results from a technique that clever Italians devised for pouring warm, melted chocolate into cold ice cream. The flow of chocolate immediately hardens into streaks, which get shredded (*stracciato*) into "chips" as the ice cream is stirred.

The trick to stracciatella is to pour it into your ice cream maker in a very thin stream during the last moment of churning. If your aim isn't very good, or your ice cream machine has a small opening, transfer the melted chocolate to a measuring cup with a pouring spout. You can also drizzle it over the ice cream as you layer it into the storage container, stirring it very slightly while you're pouring.

1. In a clean, absolutely dry bowl set over a saucepan of barely simmering water, melt the chocolate, stirring until it's completely smooth.

MIXING IT IN: Drizzle the warm chocolate in a very thin stream into 1 quart (1l) of ice cream during the final moment of churning.

5 ounces (140g) bittersweet or semisweet chocolate, finely chopped (do not use chocolate chips)

DARK CHOCOLATE TRUFFLES

Makes about forty ½-inch (12mm) truffles

These truffles will stay slightly soft in frozen ice cream. You can make them smaller or larger than indicated.

1. Heat the cream with the corn syrup in a small saucepan until the mixture just begins to boil. Remove from the heat and add the chocolate, stirring gently until it's melted and the mixture is smooth. Mix in the Cognac. Scrape the mixture into a small bowl and freeze until firm, about 1 hour.

2. Line a dinner plate with plastic wrap. To form ½-inch (12mm) truffles, scoop up a heaping teaspoonful of truffle mixture, then scrape it off with another spoon onto the prepared dinner plate (if you want knobbly truffles), or roll it into a round with your hands. Repeat, using all the truffle mix. Freeze the truffles until ready to mix in.

MIXING THEM IN: If you wish, break or chop the chilled Dark Chocolate Truffles into smaller pieces, then fold them into 1 quart (1l) of ice cream as you remove it from the machine.

½ cup plus 1 tablespoon (140ml) heavy cream

3 tablespoons light corn syrup

6 ounces (170g) bittersweet or semisweet chocolate, chopped

2 teaspoons Cognac, rum, or other liquor or liqueur

FUDGE RIPPLE

Makes 1 cup (250ml)

This has the authentic taste and glossy sheen of old-fashioned fudge ripple. You can swirl it through any ice cream you like. Try it in Fresh Mint Ice Cream (page 106) or as a contrasting swirl through White Chocolate Ice Cream (page 37).

1. Whisk together the sugar, corn syrup, water, and cocoa powder in a medium saucepan. Cook over medium heat, whisking constantly, until the mixture comes to a low boil. Continue to cook for 1 minute, whisking frequently.

2. Remove from the heat, stir in the vanilla, and let cool completely. Chill thoroughly in the refrigerator.

MIXING IT IN: The Fudge Ripple should be thoroughly chilled, as it's easiest to use when very cold. Just before you remove the ice cream from the machine, spoon some of the Fudge Ripple onto the bottom of the storage container. As you remove the ice cream from the machine, layer generous spoonfuls of the sauce between the layers of ice cream. Avoid stirring the layers, as it will make the ice cream muddy looking.

STORAGE: Store in an airtight container in the refrigerator for up to 2 weeks.

VARIATION: To make Mocha Ripple, substitute strongly brewed espresso for the water in the recipe, or stir in 1 tablespoon of best-quality instant or espresso coffee granules along with the vanilla.

½ cup (100g) sugar

⅓ cup (80ml) light corn syrup

½ cup (125ml) water

6 tablespoons (50g) unsweetened Dutch-process cocoa powder

½ teaspoon pure vanilla extract

MARSHMALLOWS

Makes 30 to 50 marshmallows, depending on size

These marshmallows are chewy and compact, designed to be folded into ice cream. They are indispensable in Rocky Road Ice Cream (variation, page 30) but can be deliciously added to lots of other flavors as well. To measure powdered gelatin, open the envelopes and measure the granules with a tablespoon. You'll want to get out your sturdy stand mixer for making this recipe.

1. Pour ¼ cup (60ml) of the water into the bowl of an electric stand mixer and sprinkle the gelatin over the top to soften. Fit the mixer with the whip attachment.

2. In a small, heavy-duty saucepan fitted with a candy thermometer, combine the remaining 2 tablespoons (30ml) water with the sugar, corn syrup, and salt.

3. Cook the mixture over medium-high heat until it reaches 250°F (121°C), tilting the saucepan to make sure the tip of the thermometer is submerged in the syrup to get an accurate reading.

4. When the syrup is ready, turn the mixer to medium-high speed and slowly begin pouring the hot syrup into the mixer bowl in a thin stream, aiming the syrup near the side of the mixer bowl (if you pour it over the beaters, the syrup will get splattered onto the sides of the bowl rather than mixed into the gelatin). Continue to pour the syrup into the gelatin in a steady, threadlike stream. Once you've added all the syrup, turn the mixer to high speed and whip for 8 minutes, until the mixture is a stiff foam. Whip in the vanilla.

5. Sift ½ cup (60g) of the powdered sugar onto a rimmed baking sheet, in an area roughly 8 by 10 inches (20 by 25cm). Scrape the marshmallow mixture from the mixer bowl and the beaters and spread it over the sugar-dusted area of the baking sheet so that it is about ½ inch (12mm) thick. Very lightly dampening the spatula with water will make spreading easier. Let stand, uncovered, for about 2 hours.

6. Put some of the remaining 1 cup (120g) powdered sugar into a large bowl and dust a pair of kitchen shears with the sugar. Working in batches, snip the marshmallow into strips, then dust the strips with powdered sugar. Cut the strips into little pieces, dropping them directly into the powdered sugar as you cut. Once you're halfway through, toss the marshmallows with the powdered sugar to coat, then place in a mesh strainer and shake off the excess sugar. Set the marshmallows to dry in an even layer on a second baking sheet. Continue until all the marshmallows are cut, adding more powdered sugar as needed.

MIXING THEM IN: Fold the marshmallows into 1 quart (1l) of ice cream as you remove it from the machine.

¼ cup plus 2 tablespoons (90ml) cold water

1 tablespoon unflavored gelatin powder

⅔ cup (130g) sugar

¼ cup (60ml) light corn syrup

Pinch of kosher or sea salt

½ teaspoon pure vanilla extract

About 1½ cups (180g) powdered sugar, plus more for tossing with the marshmallows

WHITE CHOCOLATE TRUFFLES

Makes about forty ½-inch (12mm) truffles

White truffles are especially fun to fold into chocolate ice cream (see pages 30 and 32) for the contrast of color and taste.

---

1. In a small saucepan, heat the cream until it begins to boil. Remove from the heat and stir in the white chocolate until it's melted and the mixture is smooth. Scrape the truffle mixture into a small bowl and freeze until firm, about 1 hour.

2. Line a dinner plate with plastic wrap. To form ½-inch (12mm) truffles, scoop up a teaspoonful of the chilled chocolate mixture and scrape it off with another spoon onto the dinner plate. Repeat, using all of the truffle mix. Freeze the truffles until ready to use.

MIXING THEM IN: Fold the White Chocolate Truffles into 1 quart (1l) of ice cream as you remove it from the machine.

STORAGE: Store wrapped well in the refrigerator or freezer for up to 2 weeks.

½ cup plus 1 tablespoon (140ml) heavy cream

9 ounces (255g) white chocolate, finely chopped

CHOCOLATE CHIP COOKIE DOUGH

Makes 2 cups (300g)

I was an early trendsetter and was snitching bites of raw cookie dough in the '60s, long before anyone else was eating it, so I would like to take credit for starting the craze.

Okay, maybe I wasn't the first kid to snitch a few bites of raw cookie dough. But whoever came up with the idea for adding cookie dough to ice cream rightly deserves the accolades from ice cream lovers across America.

This soft, egg-free brown sugar dough is packed with crunchy nuts and lots of chocolate chips. I debated whether this recipe makes too much cookie dough for the average person to add to ice cream. Then, after much nibbling (while thinking about it), I decided that it was just not possible to have too much cookie dough!

1. In a medium mixing bowl, stir together the butter and brown sugar until smooth. Stir in the flour, then the vanilla, nuts, and chocolate chips.

2. Form the dough into a disk about ½ inch (12mm) thick, wrap it in plastic wrap, and refrigerate until firm.

3. Once chilled, unwrap the disk and chop the dough into bite-size pieces, then store the pieces in the freezer until ready to mix in.

MIXING IT IN: Fold pieces of Chocolate Chip Cookie Dough into 1 quart (1l) of ice cream as you remove it from the machine.

STORAGE: Store wrapped well in the refrigerator for up to 5 days or in the freezer for up to 2 months.

5 tablespoons (70g) salted butter, melted

⅓ cup (60g) packed light brown sugar

¼ cup (35g) flour

½ teaspoon pure vanilla extract

½ cup (50g) walnuts, pecans, or hazelnuts, toasted (see page 16) and coarsely chopped

¾ cup (120g) semisweet or bittersweet chocolate chips, or coarsely chopped chocolate

CHAPTER 7

Vessels

Everything in the world deserves a proper final nesting place, and you won't find any better ways to present your homemade ice creams and sorbets than perched atop, or tucked within, the array of vessels in this chapter.

The most famous, and surely most popular, way to eat ice cream is undoubtedly via the ice cream cone. Its origins are rife with controversy. One story goes that a Middle Eastern man at the St. Louis World's Fair in 1904 invented the cone when he ran out of dishes for serving ice cream and rolled up one of the Persian wafers he was baking. A conflicting account gives credit to an Italian who evidently patented a mold for creating cones a decade before. Whoever came up with the idea, there's no denying that cones have become the global go-to way to enjoy ice cream.

If you've never made your own cones, it's really quite simple and well worth trying. Although you can bake them on cookie sheets, electric waffle cone makers are affordable fun, and I can't think of anything more enjoyable than peeling a freshly baked, buttery cone off the griddle, rolling it up, and, once cool and crisp, piling a few scoops of homemade ice cream inside.

Cakelike Brownies (page 240) and Blondies (page 241) have also become the rage for accompanying ice cream. And why not? Top a chocolate brownie with a fun-packed scoop of Butterscotch Ice Cream with Peanut Butter, Chocolate, and Pretzel Brittle (page 46), spoon lots of Whiskey Caramel Sauce (variation, page 190) over it, and add a handful of Spiced Pecans (page 218) to top it all off. What's not to like? Should you have leftovers, chocolate brownies are wonderful when crumbled into little fudgy bits and folded into ice cream.

Speaking of leftovers, a wonderful use for an overabundance of egg whites is Meringue Nests (page 256), or *vacherins*, as the French call them. These sweetly simple dessert shells can be used to cradle any ice cream or sorbet in a flavorful foil that's shatteringly crisp. These feather-light nests turn any frozen dessert into an elegant event, making them suitable for a simple dinner party or a swanky soirée. We also have the French to thank for giving us Profiteroles (page 255). Americans have happily adopted these eggy little cream puffs, filling them with ice creams of all kinds, and you'll find they're just as good when doused with slick Mocha Sauce (page 179) as they are when floating in a pool of summer-fresh Mixed Berry Coulis (page 198).

But I don't know of any country other than America that can take credit for the ice cream sandwich: two oversized soft cookies encasing a big scoop of ice cream and then mellowed in the freezer. It's a perfect partnership, undoubtedly the result of good old American ingenuity. But there's more to cookies and ice cream than ice cream sandwiches. Cookie cups can be downright upscale, like lacy and delicate Lemon–Poppy Seed Cookie Cups (page 249) with crackly poppy seeds and lemon zest, or Almond Butterscotch Cookie Cups (page 248) that are rich with brown sugar and crackly almonds.

CAKELIKE BROWNIES

Makes 12 brownies

If you like your brownies not too dense, these are the ones for you.

---

1. Preheat the oven to 350°F (175°C). Line an 8-inch (20cm) square pan with a long sheet of aluminum foil or parchment paper that covers the bottom and reaches up two sides. If it's not large or wide enough, cross another sheet of foil over it, making a large cross with edges that overhang the other two sides. Grease the bottom and sides of the foil with butter or nonstick spray.

2. Melt the butter in a medium saucepan. Add the chocolate and stir constantly over very low heat until the chocolate is melted. Remove from the heat and whisk in the cocoa powder until smooth. Mix in the sugar, then whisk in the eggs one at a time, followed by the vanilla. Stir in the flour, salt, and nuts, if using.

3. Scrape the batter into the prepared pan and smooth the top. Bake for 35 to 40 minutes, until the center feels just slightly firm. Remove from the oven and let cool completely. Serve topped with ice cream and sauce.

STORAGE: Wrap the pan of brownies with foil and store at room temperature. These brownies are actually better the second day and will keep well for up to 3 days.

VARIATIONS: To make Chocolate–Dulce de Leche Brownies, use 1 cup (250ml) Dulce de Leche (page 185) or Cajeta (page 188). Spread half of the brownie batter in the pan. Take ⅓ cup (80ml) of the Dulce de Leche and drop 5 spoonfuls of it, evenly spaced, over the brownie batter. Cover with the remaining brownie batter, then drop tablespoonfuls of the remaining Dulce de Leche in dollops over the top of the brownie batter. Drag a knife through the batter three or four times to slightly swirl the layers. Be careful not to overswirl; you want distinct puddles of dulce de leche in the finished brownies. Bake for 45 to 50 minutes, or until the brownies feel slightly firm in the center.

To make Peppermint Brownies, scatter 1½ cups (350g) crumbled Peppermint Patties (page 226) or store-bought Thin Mint pieces into the batter and substitute ¾ teaspoon mint extract for the vanilla extract.

½ cup (115g) unsalted butter, cut into pieces

6 ounces (170g) bittersweet or semisweet chocolate, finely chopped

¼ cup (25g) unsweetened Dutch-process cocoa powder

1 cup (200g) sugar

3 large eggs, at room temperature

1 teaspoon pure vanilla extract

1 cup (140g) flour

⅛ teaspoon kosher or sea salt

1 cup (100g) pecans or walnuts, toasted (see page 16) and coarsely chopped (optional)

BLONDIES

Makes 12 blondies

When I was looking for the perfect blondie, I went to the source on all things chocolate-chipified: my friend and fellow baker Dede Wilson, author of *A Baker's Field Guide to Chocolate Chip Cookies*. I knew she'd come through with a killer recipe, and boy, did she.

1. Preheat the oven to 350°F (175°C). Line an 8-inch (20cm) square pan with two sheets of aluminum foil or parchment that criscross and cover all four sides.

2. In a large mixing bowl, whisk together the flour, baking powder, baking soda, and salt.

3. Melt the butter in a saucepan, then let it cool to room temperature. Stir the brown sugar and vanilla into the melted butter, then stir in the egg. Add the melted butter mixture to the dry ingredients and stir until combined. Fold in the chocolate chips and nuts.

4. Transfer the batter into the prepared pan and smooth the top. Bake for 30 minutes, until slightly puffed in the center. Remove from the oven and let cool completely. Serve topped with ice cream and sauce.

STORAGE: Wrap the pan with aluminum foil and store at room temperature for up to 3 days.

1 cup (140g) flour

½ teaspoon baking powder, preferably aluminum-free

⅛ teaspoon baking soda

⅛ teaspoon kosher or sea salt

½ cup (4 ounces, 115g) unsalted butter

1 cup (180g) packed light brown sugar

1 teaspoon pure vanilla extract

1 large egg

⅔ cup (115g) semisweet chocolate chips

⅔ cup (65g) pecans or walnuts, toasted (see page 16) and coarsely chopped

CHEWY-DENSE BROWNIES

Makes 12 brownies

These are the best brownies for crumbling into ice cream. They'll stay nice and chewy, even after they're frozen.

---

1. Preheat the oven to 350°F (175°C). Line an 8-inch (20cm) square pan with a long sheet of aluminum foil that covers the bottom and reaches up two sides. If it's not large or wide enough, cross another sheet of foil over it, making a large cross with edges that overhang the other two sides. Grease the bottom and sides of the foil with butter or nonstick spray.

2. Melt the butter in a medium saucepan. Add the chocolate and whisk constantly over very low heat until the chocolate is melted. Remove from the heat and stir in the sugar, then the eggs one at a time, followed by the vanilla. Stir in the flour and salt. Beat the batter vigorously for 30 seconds, until it begins to form a smooth ball. Stir in the chocolate chips and nuts, if using.

3. Scrape the batter into the prepared pan and smooth the top. Bake for 30 minutes, until the center feels almost set. Remove from the oven and let cool completely. Serve topped with ice cream and sauce.

STORAGE: Wrap the pan of brownies with foil and store at room temperature for up to 3 days.

½ cup (4 ounces, 115g) unsalted butter, cut into pieces

4 ounces (115g) unsweetened chocolate, chopped

1¼ cups (250g) sugar

2 large eggs, at room temperature

1 teaspoon pure vanilla extract

½ cup (70g) flour

⅛ teaspoon kosher or sea salt

½ cup (80g) semisweet or bittersweet chocolate chips

¾ cup (75g) hazelnuts, pecans, almonds, or walnuts, toasted (see page 16) and chopped (optional)

THE BATTLE OF THE BROWNIES

It seems that the entire world—well, my world—is divided into two camps. On one side are the folks who like cakelike brownies and on the other side are those who like chewy-dense brownies. To keep the peace, I'm giving you both recipes. Because both types of brownies can be somewhat sticky once baked, it's best to line the pan with a crisscross of two sheets of aluminum foil that goes up and overhangs all four sides of the pan. (Extra-wide foil is available, too, and worth keeping a roll on hand if you make a lot of brownies.) After baking, you'll be able to lift the brownies right out of the pan with the greatest of ease.

OATMEAL ICE CREAM SANDWICH COOKIES

Makes 16 cookies, for 8 ice cream sandwiches

This recipe makes jumbo-size, chewy oatmeal cookies ideal for sandwiching ice cream. They are especially good (in my humble opinion) filled with Plum Ice Cream (page 85). Let them cool completely before trying to lift them off the baking sheet. They'll be somewhat soft because they're designed to retain their tenderness even after they're frozen.

These cookies are larger than normal, so I find that I can get only six onto a standard baking sheet (11 by 17 inches, or 28 by 43cm), so that even when they spread, they don't touch. If you have several baking sheets, this is a great time to put them into service. If not, let your baking sheet cool completely before baking the next batch of cookies.

1. Preheat the oven to 350°F (175°C). Line several baking sheets with parchment paper or silicone baking mats.

2. Whisk together the flour, granulated and brown sugars, baking soda, cinnamon, and salt in a large mixing bowl, breaking up any lumps of brown sugar. Stir in the oats and raisins.

3. Make a well in the center, then pour in the oil and milk. Add the egg and stir until the batter is well combined.

4. Drop six heaping tablespoons, evenly spaced apart, on each baking sheet. With the back of the spoon, spread each mound of batter into a circle 3 inches (8cm) in diameter.

5. Bake the cookies for 20 minutes, rotating the baking sheets midway during baking. Remove from the oven and let cool completely.

6. Once cooled, sandwich ice cream between 2 cookies, then wrap each ice cream sandwich in plastic wrap and store in the freezer.

⅔ cup (90g) flour

¼ cup (50g) granulated sugar

6 tablespoons (90g) packed light brown sugar

½ teaspoon baking soda

¾ teaspoon ground cinnamon

¼ teaspoon kosher or sea salt

1½ cups (150g) old-fashioned rolled oats (not instant)

½ cup (80g) raisins

½ cup (125ml) vegetable oil

3 tablespoons whole milk

1 large egg, at room temperature

CHOCOLATE ICE CREAM SANDWICH COOKIES

Makes 16 cookies, for 8 ice cream sandwiches

These resemble classic ice cream sandwich cookies but taste much better, and are far fudgier, than those soggy, dark rectangles you'll soon forget about.

---

1. Preheat the oven to 350°F (175°C). Line two baking sheets with parchment paper or silicone baking mats.

2. Beat together the butter and sugar in the bowl of an electric stand mixer, or by hand, until smooth. Beat in the egg and vanilla.

3. In a separate bowl, whisk together the cocoa powder, flour, baking powder, and salt. Gradually stir the dry ingredients into the butter mixture until completely incorporated and there are no streaks of butter.

4. Form the dough into sixteen 1½-inch (4cm) balls. You should be able to fit eight cookies on a standard 11 by 17-inch (28 by 43cm) baking sheet, with three going lengthwise down the sides and two in the center, evenly spaced in between. Once placed on the baking sheets, flatten the rounds so they're 3 inches (8cm) across.

5. Bake the cookies for 20 minutes, rotating the baking sheets midway during baking. Remove from the oven and let cool completely.

6. Once cooled sandwich ice cream between 2 cookies, then wrap each ice cream sandwich in plastic wrap and store in the freezer.

½ cup (4 ounces, 115g) unsalted butter, at room temperature

1 cup (200g) sugar

1 large egg, at room temperature

1 teaspoon pure vanilla extract

6 tablespoons (50g) unsweetened Dutch-process cocoa powder

1½ cups (210g) flour

1 teaspoon baking powder, preferably aluminum-free

⅛ teaspoon kosher or sea salt

COOKIE SMACKDOWN!

Butter cookies tend to "dome," creating rounded tops, when they bake. The result may be cookies for ice cream sandwiches that are a little heftier than you want. If you want them flat and a little more dense, during the last minute of baking or right after you take the cookies out of the oven, rap them gently, but assuredly, on top with a spatula or pancake turner, to flatten and compress the cookies. Not only will that even out the tops, it'll also give the cookies a chewier texture.

CHOCOLATE CHIP ICE CREAM SANDWICH COOKIES

Makes 16 cookies, for 8 ice cream sandwiches

These oversized cookies are packed with nuts and chocolate chips, perfect for making the best ice cream sandwiches you've ever had. Feel free to pack as much ice cream between them as you like.

1. Beat the butter with the granulated and brown sugars in the bowl of an electric stand mixer, or by hand, until smooth. Beat in the egg and vanilla.

2. In a separate bowl, whisk together the flour, baking soda, and salt, making sure there are no lumps of baking soda. Stir the dry ingredients into the creamed butter mixture, then mix in the chocolate chips and nuts. Wrap the dough in plastic wrap, flatten it into a disk, and chill for 1 hour.

3. Preheat the oven to 350°F (175°C). Line two baking sheets with parchment paper or silicone baking mats.

4. Form the dough into sixteen 1½-inch (4cm) balls. Flatten the rounds of dough into 3-inch (8cm) disks, spaced evenly apart on the baking sheets. You should get eight on a standard 11 by 17-inch (28 by 43cm) baking sheet. Because they don't spread much, you can leave 1 inch (3cm) of space between them.

5. Bake the cookies for 15 minutes, rotating the baking sheets midway during baking. Remove from the oven.

6. Once cooled, sandwich ice cream between 2 cookies, then wrap each ice cream sandwich in plastic wrap and store in the freezer.

PERFECT PAIRING: To dial up the fun, add sprinkles to your sandwich. Spread a nice layer of sprinkles (or mini chocolate chips or chopped nuts) on a dinner plate and roll the sides of the ice cream sandwiches in the sprinkles, pressing gently as you roll, so they stick. Don't skimp!

½ cup (4 ounces, 115g) unsalted butter, at room temperature

¼ cup (50g) granulated sugar

⅓ cup (70g) packed light brown sugar

1 large egg, at room temperature

1 teaspoon pure vanilla extract

1 cup (140g) flour

Slightly rounded ¼ teaspoon baking soda

¼ teaspoon kosher or sea salt

¾ cup (120g) semisweet or bittersweet chocolate chips

½ cup (50g) walnuts or pecans, toasted (see page 16) and chopped

ALMOND BUTTERSCOTCH COOKIE CUPS

Makes 12 cookie cups

These edible cups are easiest to bake on baking sheets lined with parchment paper rather than thick silicone baking mats because the cups are whisper thin and somewhat fragile. Overturned teacups or an upside-down muffin tin, make great molds, although you can use anything that's relatively wide with a flat bottom, such as custard cups or ramekins.

After baking, if any cookies cool before you've had a chance to mold them into cookie cups, simply pop the baking sheet back in the oven for about 30 seconds to make them supple and try again.

1. Preheat the oven to 350°F (175°C). Line a baking sheet with parchment paper. Have ready four overturned teacups or an inverted muffin tin.

2. Melt the butter in a small saucepan with the corn syrup and brown sugar. Remove from the heat and stir in the almonds, flour, and almond extract.

3. Drop slightly rounded tablespoons of batter in four evenly spaced mounds on the prepared baking sheet. Use the back of the spoon to spread each mound into a circle 2 inches (5cm) in diameter.

4. Bake the cookies until they're deep golden brown, about 12 minutes. Let rest for 30 to 45 seconds, then lift each cookie off the baking sheet with a flexible metal spatula and flip it over onto an upended teacup or overturned muffin tin. (If the cookies get too firm to shape, return them to the oven for about 30 seconds to soften them.) Let the cookies cool on the cups or tin, then transfer them to a wire rack. Let the baking sheet cool, then repeat with the remaining batter.

STORAGE: The batter can be made and refrigerated for up to 1 week in advance, let it come to room temperature before baking. Once baked and cooled, the cookie cups can be stored in an airtight container, but are best eaten the day they're made.

4 tablespoons (60g) butter, salted or unsalted

¼ cup (60ml) light corn syrup

¼ cup (45g) packed light brown sugar

½ cup (40g) sliced almonds

6 tablespoons (60g) flour

⅛ teaspoon pure almond extract

LEMON-POPPY SEED COOKIE CUPS

Makes 12 cookie cups

The delightful crunch of poppy seeds in these very pretty, delicate cookie cups is the perfect foil for any homemade ice cream or fruity sorbet.

1. Melt the butter in a small saucepan. Remove from the heat and stir in the lemon juice, sugar, and flour. Mix in the almonds and poppy seeds and let the mixture rest for 1 hour at room temperature.

2. Preheat the oven to 350°F (175°C). Line a baking sheet with parchment paper. Have ready four overturned teacups or an inverted muffin tin.

3. Put level tablespoons of batter in four evenly spaced mounds on the prepared baking sheet. Use the back of the spoon to spread each mound into a circle 2 inches (5cm) in diameter.

4. Bake the cookies for 10 minutes, until they're deep golden brown. Let rest for 30 to 45 seconds, then lift each cookie off the baking sheet with a spatula and flip it over onto an upended teacup or overturned muffin tin. (If the cookies get too firm to shape, return them to the oven for 30 seconds to soften them.) Let the cookies cool on the cups or tin, then transfer them to a wire rack. Let the baking sheet cool, then repeat with the remaining batter.

STORAGE: The batter can be made and refrigerated for up to 1 week in advance, let it come to room temperature before baking. Once baked and cooled, the cookie cups can be stored in an airtight container, but are best eaten the day they're made.

3 tablespoons butter, salted or unsalted

2 tablespoons freshly squeezed lemon juice

7 tablespoons (85g) sugar

3 tablespoons flour

½ cup (40g) sliced almonds

2 tablespoons poppy seeds

ICE CREAM CONES

Makes 6 cones

Making ice cream cones at home is very easy. It's especially fun if you have an electric waffle-cone maker (see Resources, page 259), although you can also bake them in the oven with success.

The batter is simplicity itself: just a few ingredients mixed together, baked, and rolled up into cones . . . which is the fun part! You will need a conical cone-rolling form made of wood or plastic (see Resources). Most machines come with one.

A few tips for baking cones by hand: The batter recipe can easily be doubled to allow for a few practice cones, which may come in handy if it's your first time making them. If baking the cones in the oven, I prefer to use parchment paper to line the baking sheet rather than a silicone baking mat because they're easier to get off the parchment paper. Also, I let the baking sheet cool between batches, or have another baking sheet handy, as the batter is much easier to handle when the baking sheets are at room temperature, not warm or hot. To roll the cones, you may wish to wear clean rubber gloves or use a tea towel, because the just-baked cookies may be too warm for you to handle with bare hands.

If using an electric ice cream cone maker, some models require 3 tablespoons (45ml) of batter for each cone, so you may get only four cones from this recipe. Follow the instructions that come with your machine.

1. Preheat the oven to 350°F (175°C). Line a baking sheet with parchment paper.

2. In a small mixing bowl, stir together the egg whites, sugar, and vanilla. Stir in the salt and half of the flour, then mix in the melted butter. Beat in the rest of the flour until the batter is smooth.

3. On one half of the prepared baking sheet, use a small offset spatula or the back of the spoon to spread two level tablespoons of the batter into a circle 6 inches (15cm) in diameter, then repeat with additional batter on the other half of the baking sheet. Try to get the circles as even and smooth as possible.

4. Put the baking sheet in the oven and begin checking the cones after about 10 minutes. Depending on your oven, they'll take between 10 and 15 minutes to bake. The circles should be a deep golden brown throughout (some lighter and darker spots are inevitable, so don't worry).

CONTINUED

¼ cup (60ml) egg whites (about 2 large egg whites)

7 tablespoons (85g) sugar

½ teaspoon pure vanilla extract

⅛ teaspoon kosher or sea salt

⅔ cup (90g) flour

2 tablespoons unsalted butter, melted

5. Remove the baking sheet from the oven. Use a thin metal spatula to loosen the edge of one circle. Slide the spatula under the circle, quickly flip it over, and immediately roll it around the cone-rolling form, pressing the seam firmly on the counter to close the cone and pinching the point at the bottom securely closed. Let the cone cool slightly on the mold until it feels firm, then slide it off and stand it upright in a tall glass to cool. Roll the other cone the same way. (If it's too firm to roll, return the baking sheet to the oven for a minute or so until it's pliable again.)

6. Repeat the process using the remaining batter.

STORAGE: The batter can be made up to 4 days in advance and stored in the refrigerator. Let the batter come to room temperature before using. Once baked and cooled, store the cones in an airtight container until ready to serve. They're best eaten the same day they're baked.

VARIATIONS: For Sesame or Poppy Seed Ice Cream Cones, stir 3 tablespoons toasted sesame or poppy seeds and a few swipes of grated lemon zest into the batter.

For Chocolate Ice Cream Cones, increase the sugar to ½ cup (100g), decrease the flour to 6 tablespoons (60g), and add 3 tablespoons unsweetened Dutch-process cocoa powder along with the flour.

For Gingersnap Ice Cream Cones, increase the sugar to ½ cup (100g) and add 1 tablespoon mild molasses and ¼ teaspoon each ground cinnamon, ginger, and nutmeg to the batter.

For Honey-Cornmeal Ice Cream Cones, melt 2 teaspoons strongly flavored honey with the butter. Substitute 1 large egg plus 1 large egg white for the ¼ cup (60ml) egg whites, decrease the flour to ½ cup (70g), and add ¼ cup (35g) stone-ground cornmeal along with the flour.

For Rosemary Ice Cream Cones, add 2 teaspoons finely chopped fresh rosemary to the Honey-Cornmeal Ice Cream Cone batter.

CRÊPES

Makes 8 crêpes

If you've never made crêpes before, you'll find that it's one of life's most satisfying accomplishments. You spend a few minutes dipping, swirling, and flipping and end up with a neat stack of delicious crêpes. As with traditional pancakes, the first one is usually a dud, so don't be discouraged. Once you've slid a few out of the frying pan, you'll feel like a pro. This recipe can easily be doubled and the crêpes freeze beautifully, so there's no reason not to keep an extra stack in the freezer for a last-minute crêpe fix.

---

1. Pour the milk and melted butter into a blender. Add the eggs, sugar, and salt. Blend briefly. Add the flour and blend until smooth. Transfer to a bowl, cover and refrigerate for at least 1 hour or up to overnight.

2. When ready to fry the crêpes, let the batter come to room temperature, then whisk it to thin it out a bit.

3. Warm a 12-inch (30cm) nonstick skillet over medium-high heat. When a few drops of water sprinkled on the pan sizzle, use a paper towel to wipe the bottom of the pan with a small amount of vegetable oil or melted butter, and pour in ¼ cup (60ml) of batter. As you pour, quickly tilt the pan so the batter spreads across and covers the bottom.

4. Cook the crêpe for about 45 seconds, until the edges begin to darken. Use a flexible spatula to flip it over, then cook for another 45 seconds on the reverse side.

5. Slide the crêpe onto a dinner plate, then repeat with the remaining batter, wiping the pan with oil or butter before frying each crêpe, if necessary.

6. Preheat the oven to 300°F (150°C). Fold the crêpes in half and arrange them, overlapping slightly, in a buttered baking dish. Cover with aluminum foil and bake for 10 to 15 minutes, until hot. Serve the hot crêpes on individual plates topped with a scoop of ice cream and a drizzle of sauce.

STORAGE: Once cool, crêpes can be wrapped in plastic wrap and stored in the refrigerator for up to 2 days. Or, wrap them in plastic wrap and then in aluminum foil and freeze for up to 2 months.

¾ cup (180ml) whole milk

2 tablespoons butter, melted

3 large eggs

1 teaspoon sugar

¼ teaspoon kosher or sea salt

¾ cup (110g) flour

Vegetable oil or additional melted butter, for frying the crêpes

PROFITEROLES

Makes 30 cream puffs

Many people come to Paris with dreams of falling in love, and I know more than one person who's returned home starry-eyed after a steamy love affair—with profiteroles. Who can resist buttery cream puffs filled with vanilla ice cream, heaped on plates, served with a gleaming silver pitcher of warm chocolate sauce? It's a tableside ritual that takes place nightly in romantic restaurants and cozy cafés across the city: dashing waiters dousing profiteroles with warm sauce and the molten chocolate gushing over the golden puffs, filling every little nook and crevice possible. The profiteroles are served forth with a sly grin (and perhaps a bit of a wink), leaving you free to indulge.

Profiteroles are seductively simple to make at home, and you can't go wrong with any ice cream and sauce combination that sounds good to you. My personal favorite is profiteroles filled with Chartreuse Ice Cream (page 68), drizzled with Classic Hot Fudge (page 178), and scattered with lots and lots of crispy French Almonds (page 205). *J'adore!*

1. To make the cream puffs, preheat the oven to 425°F (220°C). Line a baking sheet with parchment paper or a silicone baking mat.

2. Warm the water, sugar, salt, and butter in a small saucepan over medium-high heat, stirring frequently, until the butter is melted. Add the flour all at once. Stir briskly until the mixture is smooth and pulls away from the sides of the pan.

3. Remove from the heat and allow the dough to cool for 2 minutes, then scrape the mixture into the bowl of a stand mixer fitted with the paddle attachment. Briskly beat in the eggs one at a time, until the dough is smooth and shiny. If you don't have a stand mixer, add the eggs one at a time directly to the saucepan, stirring vigorously and constantly to avoid scrambling the eggs.

4. Scoop up a mound of dough roughly the size of an unshelled walnut with one spoon and scrape it off with another spoon onto the prepared baking sheet (or you can use a pastry bag or spring-loaded ice cream scoop). Place the mounds, evenly spaced, on the baking sheet.

5. To make the glaze, in a small bowl, lightly beat together the egg yolk and milk and brush the top of each mound with some of the glaze. Avoid letting the glaze drip down the sides, which can hinder the cream puffs from rising.

6. Bake the cream puffs until puffed and well browned, 25 to 30 minutes. Turn off the heat and leave them in the oven with the door ajar for 5 minutes.

STORAGE: Cream puffs are best eaten the day they're made. Once cooled, they can be frozen in a zip-top freezer bag for up to 2 months. Defrost at room temperature, then warm briefly on a baking sheet in a 350°F (180°C) oven until crisp.

CREAM PUFFS

1 cup (250ml) water

2 teaspoons sugar

½ teaspoon kosher or sea salt

6 tablespoons (85g) unsalted butter, cut into small chunks

1 cup (140g) flour

4 large eggs, at room temperature

GLAZE

1 egg yolk

1 teaspoon milk

MERINGUE NESTS

Makes 8 meringue nests

Crispy nests of meringue—also known as *vacherins*—lend a certain savoir faire and offer a very dramatic presentation for any ice cream or sorbet, especially when you add a ladleful of sauce over the top. The combination of crackly meringue, scoops of frosty-cold ice cream, and warm sauce is justifiably known as one of the great French dessert classics. It is certain to become a well-loved part of your repertoire as well.

Use a light hand when folding in the powdered sugar. Aggressive overmixing can cause the meringue to start deflating.

1. Preheat the oven to 200°F (100°C). Line a baking sheet with parchment paper or a silicone baking mat.

2. In the bowl of an electric stand mixer, whip the egg whites with the salt at medium speed until frothy.

3. Increase the speed to medium-high and whip until the egg whites thicken and begin to hold their shape. Continue whipping the whites while adding the granulated sugar, 1 tablespoon at a time. Once the sugar has been added, add the vanilla and continue to whip for 2 minutes, until the egg whites are stiff and glossy.

4. Remove the bowl from the mixer and sift the powdered sugar over the meringue while simultaneously folding it in with a flexible silicone spatula.

5. Divide the meringue into eight equally sized and evenly spaced mounds on the baking sheet. (They'll all fit if you arrange three down each side lengthwise and two in the center.) Take a spoon, dip it in water, tap off the excess, and make a hollow in the center of each meringue, like mashed potatoes in preparation for gravy.

6. Bake the meringues for 1 hour. Turn the oven off and leave the meringues in the oven for 1 hour more. They are done when they feel dry and lift easily off the parchment paper or silicone baking mat.

STORAGE: Store the meringues in an absolutely airtight container for up to 1 week.

VARIATIONS: Meringue nests lend themselves to many variations. Here are some of my favorites. Simply fold the additional ingredients into the meringue after adding the powdered sugar.

Almond: Replace the vanilla with ¼ teaspoon almond extract and press 2 tablespoons sliced almonds into each meringue before baking.

4 large egg whites (about ½ cup, 125ml), at room temperature

Pinch of kosher or sea salt

½ cup (100g) granulated sugar

¼ teaspoon pure vanilla extract

¼ cup (35g) powdered sugar

Chocolate: 3 tablespoons unsweetened Dutch-process cocoa powder

Chocolate Chip: ½ cup (80g) semisweet or bittersweet chocolate chips (regular or mini)

Chocolate–Chocolate Chip: 3 tablespoons unsweetened Dutch-process cocoa powder and ⅓ cup (60g) semisweet or bittersweet chocolate chips (regular or mini)

Cinnamon: 1 tablespoon ground cinnamon

Cocoa Nib: 6 tablespoons (60g) cocoa nibs

Coconut: ½ cup (40g) dried shredded coconut, toasted

Coffee: 1 tablespoon best-quality instant coffee (crush the crystals into a fine powder with the back of a spoon first) or espresso powder

Green Tea and Black Sesame: 1½ teaspoons matcha (green tea powder) and 2 tablespoons black sesame seeds

TARTUFI

Makes 8 tartufi

Tartufo means "truffle" in Italian and refers to how ice cream mounds look when dipped in chocolate that forms a neat, crisp coating. You can make your *tartufi* any size you wish, but I usually make mine about golf ball size (about 2 ounces, 60g, each) and serve two per person.

The trick to making *tartufi* is to work rather quickly and neatly. Keep the ice cream mounds in the freezer until the absolute last moment prior to dipping.

1. Line two large dinner plates with plastic wrap or parchment paper and place them in the freezer. Once the plates are chilled, use an ice cream scoop to form eight balls of your favorite ice cream, setting them on one of the plates. Make sure that the scoops are solid and well formed, with no dangling bits of ice cream; if necessary, use your (clean) hands to smooth them. Freeze the ice cream scoops until thoroughly frozen.

2. Melt the chocolate, butter, and corn syrup in a medium bowl set over a pan of simmering water. Once the chocolate is melted and the mixture is smooth, remove the bowl of chocolate from the double boiler. Remove the ice cream balls from the freezer, and the second plate as well.

3. Here, the trick is going to be trying to get as thin a shell as possible around the ice cream. Using two soup spoons, drop a ball of ice cream into the chocolate mixture and toss it quickly until it's coated. Lift it out and transfer it onto the second dinner plate. Repeat with the remaining scoops of ice cream, then return the *tartufi* to the freezer until ready to serve.

2 cups (500ml) ice cream

6 ounces (170g) bittersweet or semisweet chocolate, chopped

6 tablespoons (85g) unsalted butter, cut into pieces

1½ tablespoons light corn syrup

RESOURCES

AMAZON
www.amazon.com
Ice cream equipment and ingredients, including ice cream machines, ice cream cone makers and molds, and storage containers.

BIALETTI
www.bialetti.com
Top-quality stove-top espresso makers.

BOYAJIAN
www.boyajianinc.com
Peppermint flavoring, as well as natural citrus oils.

BREVILLE
www.brevilleusa.com
Ice cream machines, mixers, and other kitchen appliances.

CHEF'S CHOICE
www.chefschoice.com
Ice cream cone–making machines, cone-rolling forms, and cone stands.

CHOCOSPHERE
www.chocosphere.com
High-quality chocolates from around the world, including chocolate in bulk. Cocoa powder and cocoa nibs are available as well.

CUISINART
www.cuisinart.com
Comprehensive line of ice cream machines, as well as blenders and food processors.

FRONTIER CO-OP
www.frontiercoop.com
Organic mint oils and extracts.

GUITTARD
www.guittard.com
American-made chocolate and chocolate chips.

KING ARTHUR FLOUR
www.kingarthurflour.com
Baking ingredients, including chocolate, extracts, and malt powder.

KITCHENAID
www.kitchenaid.com
Ice cream machines and freezing attachments for KitchenAid stand mixers, as well as other kitchen equipment.

LE CREUSET
www.lecreuset.com
Makers of my favorite flexible spatulas, called Spatula Spoons, that have a curved shape for reaching into corners of pots and a slight "bowl," ideal for custard making.

OXO
www.oxo.com
Makers of heatproof spatulas, as well as sturdy measuring cups and spoons, whisks, ice cream scoops, and strainers.

PENZEYS SPICES
www.penzeys.com
Best-quality spices, as well as vanilla and orange extracts.

THE PERFECT PURÉE
www.perfectpuree.com
Frozen passion fruit puree, as well as other fruit and berry purees.

SALTWORKS
www.seasalt.com
Large selection of sea salts, including French fleur de sel and Maldon salts from Great Britain.

STAR KAY WHITE
www.starkaywhite.com
Almond and mint extracts.

SUR LA TABLE
www.surlatable.com
Cookware, espresso makers, ice cream machines, ice cream cone forms, and thermometers.

TOVOLO
www.tovolo.com
Maker of various types of reusable ice cream storage containers, as well as ice-pop makers.

TRADER JOE'S
www.traderjoes.com
Nationwide grocery chain with a wide selection of dried fruits, nuts, sour cherries in light syrup, and unsweetened coconut. Also chocolate sold in bulk and baking ingredients.

THE VANILLA COMPANY
www.vanillaqueen.com
Excellent pure bourbon, Mexican, and Tahitian vanilla extracts; whole vanilla beans; and dried, ground beans. All vanilla is sustainably grown and growers are paid a fair price.

WHITE MOUNTAIN
www.whitemountainproducts.com
Old-fashioned wooden-bucket ice cream makers, motorized or hand-cranked.

WILLIAMS-SONOMA
www.williams-sonoma.com
Ice cream makers, espresso makers, scoops, and a variety of equipment for making ice cream.

ZEROLL
www.zeroll.com
Professional ice cream scoops.

ACKNOWLEDGMENTS

I was thrilled when my publisher, Ten Speed Press, let me write *The Perfect Scoop* several years ago, and just as excited when Aaron Wehner asked me if I'd like to update it. So thanks to him, as well as to Julie Bennett and Ashley Pierce, who took on the task of being my editors and shared my enthusiasm for this new edition. (And to Clancy Drake, for steering the original book toward fruition.) To Ashley Lima and Serena Sigona for making the book so beautiful.

Thank you to Ed Anderson, who perfectly captured my ice creams with his camera and shared my passion for food and drink. And to food stylist Lillian Kang for coaxing the ice cream into place.

Thanks to Juliet Pries of The Ice Cream Bar in San Francisco and Gia Giasullo from Brooklyn Farmacy & Soda Fountain who let us shoot photographs in their shops.

I'll always be grateful to Lindsey Shere at Chez Panisse for teaching me much of what I know about making ice cream and pursuing pure flavors, as well as to Mary Jo Thoresen and Diane Wegner, who also watched over me (and gave advice) as I learned to make ice cream. And to Alice Waters, for providing fertile, and organic, grounds at Chez Panisse for all of us to grow from.

Thank you to my agent, Bonnie Nadell, for rolling up her sleeves, again.

And to Romain Pellas, my Frenchman, who was astonished by his first egg-white omelet (made with whites left over from testing all the ice cream custards in this book), but ate through them all, followed by lots of ice cream afterward.

INDEX

All rights reserved.
Published in the United States by Ten Speed Press, an imprint of the Crown
Publishing Group, a division of Penguin Random House LLC, New York.
www.crownpublishing.com
www.tenspeed.com

Ten Speed Press and the Ten Speed Press colophon are registered trademarks
of Penguin Random House LLC.

Library of Congress Cataloging-in-Publication Data:
Names: Lebovitz, David, author.
Title: The perfect scoop : 200 recipes for ice creams, sorbets, gelatos, granitas,
and sweet accompaniments / David Lebovitz ; photography by Ed Anderson.
Description: Revised and updated. | [Berkeley] California : Ten Speed Press,
[2018] | Includes bibliographical references and index.
Identifiers: LCCN 2017030281 (print) | LCCN 2017032075 (ebook)
Subjects: LCSH: Ice cream, ices, etc. | LCGFT: Cookbooks.
Classification: LCC TX795 (ebook) | LCC TX795 .L45 2018 (print) | DDC
641.86/2—dc23
LC record available at https://lccn.loc.gov/2017030281

Hardcover ISBN: 978-0-399-58031-4
eBook ISBN: 978-0-399-58032-1

Printed in China

Design by Ashley Lima
Food Styling by Lilian Kang
Food Styling on pages 11, 203, 246, and 254 by Emily Caneer
Prop Styling by Ethel Brennan

10 9 8 7 6 5 4 3 2 1

First Edition